영어학 최고의 선택 명/쾌/한 설명으로 영어학이 쉬워진다!

INTERMEDIATE

최진호
영어학

NEW
중등교원 임용고시
시험대비

PREFACE

영어학 이론의 **알짜배기**

항상 그렇듯이, 중등영어 교원시험은 매년 영어학이 응시자의 합격 당락을 좌우하는 **변별 과목**이었습니다. 이 책은 그런 중요한 영어학에서 출제되는 내용만을 담은 군더더기 없는 교재입니다.

최진호 영어학 Intermediate는 다음과 같은 특징을 가진 교재로 만들었습니다.

1. 중급 수준의 기본서

1~2월 강의용 기본서는 너무 기본적인 내용만 담아서는 안 된다(수준이 낮아서는 안 된다)고 생각하기에 **중급 이상의 내용**도 넣었습니다. 기본서만으로도 **시험 준비에 큰 도움이 되어야** 한다고 생각합니다. 그렇게 내용을 구성하였고 그래서 책 제목에 Intermediate가 들어가 있습니다.

2. 기출년도 표시

각 개념에 기출년도를 표시하여 수험생이 일일이 기출여부를 조사해서 적어 넣어야 하는 번거로움을 없애고 편리함을 더했습니다.

3. Mind map

영어학 학습자는 현재 학습하는 내용이 전체적인 숲의 어느 부분인지 몰라서 '왜 이런 걸 배우나'라고 생각하기 십상입니다. **전체 숲을 보는 것**은 각 내용을 암기하는 데에도 큰 도움을 줍니다.

각 챕터의 시작 부분에 mind map이 있어서 숲을 볼 수 있게 해 줍니다. 복습할 때 mind map을 수시로 보고 정리를 하는 게 좋습니다. mind map은 일부러 자세하게는 만들지 않았습니다. 수험생 여러분이 복습하면서 mind map을 더 자세하게 그려서 보관해 두면 나중에 자신만의 큰 무기가 될 것입니다.

기출된 개념들은 mind map에 **파란 깃발**로 표시해서 무엇이 중요한지 한 눈에 파악할 수 있게 했습니다.

영어학은 이해하는 것도 암기하는 것도 어렵기에 여러 번 반복해서 책을 읽는 게 좋습니다. 이 책이 중등영어교사가 되기 위해 치르는 교원시험에 큰 도움이 되길 바랍니다.

2021년을 맞이하며
최진호

CONTENTS

1 Phonology

Table of Contents

1 Consonants ······ 27
   1. The Vocal Tract ······ 28
   2. Place of Articulation ······ 29
      (1) Bilabial ······ 29
      (2) Labiodental ······ 30
      (3) Interdental ······ 30
      (4) Alveolar ······ 30
      (5) Palatal ······ 31
      (6) Velar ······ 31
      (7) Glottal ······ 31
   3. Manner of Articulation ······ 32
      (1) Stops ······ 32
      (2) Fricatives ······ 33
      (3) Affricates ······ 33
      (4) Nasals ······ 33
      (5) Liquids ······ 33
      (6) Glides (= Semi-vowels) ······ 34

2 Vowels ······ 34
   1. Vowels ······ 34
      (1) Tongue Height ······ 34
      (2) Tongue Advancement ······ 35
      (3) Tenseness ······ 35
      (4) Lip Rounding ······ 35
   2. Diphthongs ······ 36

3 Distinctive Features ······ 39
   1. Distinctive Features (1) ······ 39
      (1) Syllabic (syl) ······ 39

- (2) Soronant (son) ·· 39
- (3) Consonantal (cons) ·· 39
- (4) Continuant (cont) ··· 39
- (5) Strident ·· 40
- (6) Delayed Release ·· 40
- (7) Nasal (nas) ··· 40
- (8) Lateral (lat) ·· 41
- (9) Anterior (ant) ·· 41
- (10) Coronal (cor) ·· 41
- (11) Dorsal ·· 41
- (12) [± voice] ··· 42
- (13) [± labial] ·· 42
- (14) [± sibilant] ·· 42
- (15) [± tense] ··· 42
- 2. Distinctive Features (2) ·· 46
  - (1) Distinctive Features: Major classes [Sonorant], [Continuant] and [Consonantal] ··············· 46

4 Phonemes vs. Allophones ·· 47
- 1. Finding phonemes and allophones [Distribution of Sounds] ··············· 50
  - (1) Minimal pairs and contrastive distribution ··························· 50
  - (2) Complementary Distribution ·· 52
  - (3) Free variation ··· 52
- 2. Diacritical Marks ·· 54

5 Consonant Allophones ·· 54
- 1. Aspiration ·· 54
- 2. Glottal Stop Replacement [Glottalization] ····························· 57
- 3. Velar Nasal /ŋ/ ··· 58
- 4. Clear l and Dark l ·· 59
  - (1) Velarized /l/ = dark [ɫ] ·· 60
- 5. Syllabic Consonants ··· 62
  - (1) Syllabic Nasals ··· 62
  - (2) Syllabic Liquids ·· 62

CONTENTS

6 Syllables ... 64
1. The Syllable Structure ... 64
2. Sonority Sequencing Principle (SSP) ... 64
3. Syllabification ... 67
4. Phonotactics ... 68
   (1) Onset constraints ... 68
5. Accidental and systematic gaps ... 70

7 Stress ... 71
1. Word Stress ... 71
2. Suffixes & Stress ... 72
   (1) Stress-bearing (attracting) suffixes ... 72
   (2) Stress-neutral suffixes ... 73
   (3) Stress-shifting (fixing) suffixes ... 74
3. Sentence Stress [Tonic Accent] ... 76
   (1) Content vs. Function Words ... 76
   (2) Placement of main stress in sentences ... 77
   (3) Contrastive stress ... 78
4. Emphatic Stress ... 78
5. Stress Shift ... 79
6. Foot ... 80
7. Full Forms and Reduced Forms ... 81

8 Intonation ... 83
1. What is intonation? ... 83
2. Final intonation ... 83
   (1) Rising-falling intonation ... 83
   (2) Rising intonation ... 84
3. Non-final intonation ... 85
   (1) Rising-falling intonation ... 85
   (2) Continuation rise ... 86
4. Tag questions ... 87

9 Phonological Processes ... 88

1. Assimilation ······ 88
   (1) Progressive assimilation ······ 88
   (2) Regressive assimilation ······ 89
   (3) Coalescent assimilation ······ 92
   (4) Total assimilation [Gemination] ······ 93
2. Dissimilation ······ 94
   (1) fricative dissimilation ······ 94
   (2) -al suffix ······ 94
3. Deletion ······ 95
   (1) Consonant Cluster Reduction (CCR) ······ 95
   (2) /t/-deletion in /nt/ sequence ······ 96
   (3) /g/-deletion ······ 96
   (4) /b/-deletion ······ 97
   (5) Schwa Deletion ······ 97
4. Insertion [Epenthesis] ······ 97
5. Metathesis ······ 98
6. Haplology ······ 98
7. Neutralization ······ 99
   (1) Vowel Reduction [Schwa Rule] ······ 99
   (2) Flapping ······ 100
   (3) Glottalization ······ 101

10 Phonological Rules ······ 102

1. Format & Notation ······ 102
   (1) Parenthesis Notation ······ 102
   (2) Brace Notation ······ 103
   (3) Alpha Notation ······ 103
2. Dentalization ······ 103
3. Labiodentalization ······ 104
4. Devoicing ······ 105
5. Velarization ······ 105
6. Vowel Lengthening ······ 107
7. Vowel Nasalization ······ 108

CONTENTS

2 Morphology

Table of Contents

1 Basic Concepts & Derivation 113
    1. Free and bound morphemes 113
        (1) derivational morphemes vs. inflectional morphemes 113
    2. Content Words and Function Words 114
    3. Roots and Stems 115
    4. Allomorphs 116
        (1) Plural Morpheme {-Z} 116
        (2) Past Tense {-D} 117
    5. The Hierarchical Structure of Derived Words 117

2 Constraints on Derivation 118
    1. Accidental Gaps vs. Systematic Gaps 118
    2. *-en* suffix 119
    3. *-al* suffix 120
    4. Class 1 vs. Class 2 Suffixes 121
    5. *un-* prefix (semantic constraint) 123

3 Word-Formation Processes 124
    1. Compounds 124
        (1) Ambiguity 125
        (2) Exocentric and Endocentric Compounds 126
        (3) Stress in Compounds vs. Phrases 126
    2. Blends 127
    3. Clipping 127
    4. Acronyms 128
    5. Initialisms [(Alphabetic) abbreviations] 128
    6. Conversion 129
    7. Back Formation 130
    8. Coinage 130
    9. Word from Names (Eponyms) 131

3 Syntax

Table of Contents

1 Predicates, Arguments and Thematic Roles ·· 135
   1. Predicates and arguments ·· 135
   2. Thematic Roles [θ-roles, Thematic Relations, Semantic Roles] ·· 135
      (1) Nonreferential *it* and *there* ·· 136
   3. Selectional Restrictions ·· 137

2 X-Bar Theory ·· 138
   1. Heads, Complements and Specifiers ·· 138
   2. Adjuncts ·· 139
      (1) Adjuncts can be optional ·· 139
      (2) Adjuncts can be stacked ·· 140
      (3) Complements, not adjuncts, are closer to the Head ·· 140
   3. Subcategorization ·· 143
   4. Complements and Adjuncts ·· 143
      (1) Complements and Adjuncts in NPs ·· 143
      (2) Complements and Adjuncts in VPs ·· 147
      (3) Clausal Complements vs. Clausal Adjuncts ·· 148

3 Clauses ·· 149
   1. Raising and Control Constructions ·· 149
   2. Differences between Raising and Control Verbs ·· 152
      (1) Subject Raising and Control ·· 152
      (2) Object Raising and Control ·· 155
   3. Infinitival Complementation ·· 156
      (1) *Believe* Verbs: Subject-to-Object Raising ·· 157
      (2) *Want* Verbs ·· 158
      (3) *Persuade* Verbs: Object Control ·· 159
   4. Complementizers *that, for, whether, if* ·· 161
   5. Complementizers *whether* vs. *if* ·· 162

CONTENTS

4 Ambiguity — 164
1. Syntactic Ambiguity — 164
2. Lexical Ambiguity — 165
3. Lexico-Syntactic Ambiguity — 166

5 Constituency Tests — 170
1. Movement — 170
   (1) Topicalization (= Preposing) — 170
   (2) VP-Preposing — 170
   (3) *Though*-Movement — 171
   (1) Heavy-NP-Shift — 171
   (2) Extraposition from NP — 172
2. Substitution — 172
   (1) Proform Substitution — 173
   (2) *One*-Substitution — 173
   (3) *Do so*-Substitution — 176
3. Coordination — 177
   (1) Ordinary Coordination — 177
   (2) Right Node Raising — 177
4. Cleft and Pseudocleft Sentences — 177
5. (Adverb) Insertion — 178
6. The Constituent Response Test — 178

6 Syntactic Argumentation — 179
1. Phrasal Verbs vs. Prepositional Verbs — 179
   (1) Movement — 179
   (2) Coordination — 179
   (3) Shared Constituent Coordination Test — 180
   (4) Sentence Fragment — 180
   (5) (VP-Adverb) Insertion — 180
   (6) Gapping [V-Deletion] — 181
   (7) Clefting — 181

  (8) Word Order ·· 181
  (9) Stress Pattern ··· 181
 2. Binding Theory ·· 182
  (1) Anaphors (Reflexives & Reciprocals) ·· 182
  (2) Pronominals [(Personal) Pronouns] ·· 183
 3. Case Theory ··· 185
  (1) Case Filter and Adjacency Requirement ·· 185
  (2) NOMINATIVE and ACCUSATIVE case ······································· 185
  (3) Adjectives and Nouns ·· 187

CONTENTS

4 Grammar

Table of Contents

1 Determiners ··· 200
   1. Determiners ··· 200
      (1) order restriction ·· 200
      (2) co-occurrence restriction ··· 200
   2. Genitives ·· 201
      (1) Meanings of Genitives ··· 201
      (2) Double Genitive ·· 201

2 Adjectives ·· 202
   1. Stative and Dynamic Adjectives ·· 202
   2. Relative Clauses ·· 203
      (1) Punctuation ·· 203
      (2) Modification of a proper nouns ··· 204
      (3) Modification of *any*, *every*, *no*, etc. ··· 204
      (4) *That* as relative pronoun ·· 204
      (5) Stacking ·· 204
      (6) Sentence modification ··· 205
   3. Verbal Participles vs. Adjectival Participles ·· 205
   4. Unmarked and Marked Adjectives ··· 206
   5. Attributive-Only Adjectives ··· 207
      (1) Adjectives of Degree ·· 208
      (2) Quantifying Adjectives ··· 208
      (3) Adjectives of Time and Location ·· 208
      (4) Associative Adjectives ·· 208
   6. Predicative-Only Adjectives ·· 209
      (1) Adjectives Beginning with the Prefix *A-* ·· 209
      (2) Adjective That Take Complements ··· 210
      (3) Adjectives Referring to Medical Conditions or Health ···························· 210

3 Adverbials ... 210

1. Subjuncts ... 210
   - (1) Viewpoint subjuncts ... 211
   - (2) Courtesy subjuncts ... 211
   - (3) Item subjuncts ... 211
2. Disjuncts ... 213
   - (1) Style disjuncts ... 213
   - (2) Content disjuncts ... 214

4 Pronouns ... 216

1. Reference ... 216

5 Verb Complementation ... 217

1. *That*-Complements ... 217
2. Infinitival Complements ... 217
   - (1) Type 1 Complements: *Persuade* verbs ... 217
   - (2) Type 2 Complements: *Want* verbs ... 218
   - (3) Type 3 Complements: *Believe* verbs ... 219

6 Tense and Aspect ... 221

1. Present Perfect vs. Simple Past ... 221
   - (1) Anteriority: definite or indefinite time ... 221
   - (2) Time Adjuncts and the Present Perfect Aspect ... 222
   - (3) Current Relevance ... 223
2. Will vs. Be going to ... 223
3. The present tense in adverbial clauses ... 225
   - (1) will + R → the present tense ... 225
   - (2 will have pp → have pp ... 225
4. Stative Progressives ... 226
   - (1) Giving statements more emotional strength and intensity ... 226
   - (2) Focusing on behavior as a change from the norm ... 226
   - (3) Focusing on evolving change ... 227
   - (4) Hedging or softening a definitive opinion ... 227

CONTENTS

5. Lexical Aspects of Verbs (1) ··· 228
   - (1) States ··· 228
   - (2) Activities ··· 228
   - (3) Accomplishments ··· 229
   - (4) Achievements ··· 229
6. Lexical Aspects of Verbs (2) ··· 234
   - (1) Aspectual Classes ··· 234
   - (2) Diagnostic Tests for Lexical Aspects ··· 235

7 Passive Voice ··· 238
1. Semantic Constraints on Using the Passive ··· 238
2. *Get* Passives ··· 239
3. Past Participles: Adjectives or Passive? ··· 240
4. Ergative Verbs [Unaccusative Verbs] ··· 241
5. Middle Verbs ··· 244

8 Negation ··· 246
1. Clausal Negation ··· 246
   - (1) Subject-Auxiliary Inversion ··· 246
2. Local Negation ··· 246
3. Syntactic features of clausal negation ··· 247
4. Nonassertive items [NPIs] ··· 248
5. Transferred Negation ··· 248
6. Scope of Negation ··· 249

9 Pro-forms and Ellipsis ··· 251
1. Pro-forms ··· 251
   - (1) *One* as pro-form ··· 251
   - (2) Do it, do that, do so ··· 252
   - (3) *So* and *not* as pro-forms for object *that*-clause ··· 252
2. Elliptical noun phrases ··· 253

10 Inversion ··· 254
1. Subject-Auxiliary Inversion ··· 254
   - (1) So+S+V vs. So+V+S ··· 254

  (2) Negative adverb +V+S ··· 254
 2. Subject-Verb Inversion ··· 255

11 Coordination ··· 256
 1. Combinatory and Segregatory Coordination of NPs ··· 256
 2. Indicators of segregatory meaning ··· 257

12 Multiword Verbs ··· 258
 1. The Distinction between Prepositional Verbs and Phrasal Verbs ··· 258
 2. Separable and Inseparable Phrasal Verbs ··· 259
  (1) Separable phrasal verbs ··· 259
  (2) Inseparable phrasal verbs ··· 260
  (3) Permanently separated phrasal verbs ··· 261

13 Dative Alternation ··· 261
 1. Subcategorization of English Verbs that Take Indirect Objects ··· 261
 2. Semantics Governing Postverbal Position for Indirect Objects ··· 262
 3. The Ambiguity of *For* Phrases ··· 263
 4. Conditions on Indirect Object Alternation ··· 264
  (1) End-focus principle ··· 264
  (2) End-weight principle ··· 265
  (3) Verbs that Are Restricted to One Pattern ··· 265

14 Constructions ··· 266
 1. Cleft and Pseudo-cleft Sentences ··· 266
  (1) Structure ··· 266
  (2) Clefting is a presupposition trigger ··· 267
  (3) Ambiguity ··· 267
 2. Existential Sentences ··· 268
  (1) Indefinite NPs: preference for the existential over the non-existential ··· 269
  (2) Displaced definite NPs ··· 269
 3. Tough Movement ··· 271
  (1) Object-to-Subject Raising (Tough Movement) ··· 271
  (2) Subject-to-Subject Raising ··· 272

5 Semantics & Pragmatics

Table of Contents

1 Referential Semantics ········· 278
- 1. Reference vs. Referent ········· 278
- 2. Anaphora vs. Cataphora ········· 278

2 Lexical Relations ········· 279
- 1. Synonymy ········· 279
- 2. Antonymy ········· 279
  - (1) Complementary [Binary] antonyms ········· 279
  - (2) Gradable antonyms ········· 279
  - (3) Reverses ········· 281
  - (4) Converses [Relational opposites] ········· 281
- 3. Hyponymy ········· 282
- 4. Different Meanings: Homonymy ········· 282
- 5. Related Meanings: Polysemy ········· 283

3 Sentential Relations ········· 283
- 1. Entailment ········· 283
- 2. Presupposition ········· 284
  - (1) "Constancy Under Negation" Test ········· 285
- 3. Presupposition Triggers ········· 286
  - (1) *Wh*-question ········· 286
  - (2) Factive predicates vs. Non-factive predicates ········· 287
- 4. Factive Predicates vs. Non-factive Predicates ········· 287
  - (1) Factive Predicates ········· 287
  - (2) Non-factive Predicates ········· 288
- 5. Implicative Verbs ········· 289

4 Deixis [Deictic Expressions] ········· 290
- 1. Deictic vs. Non-deictic expressions ········· 291
  - (1) Deixis vs. Anaphora ········· 291

5 Cooperative Principle & Conversational Maxims — 292
   1. Maxim of Quantity — 292
   2. Maxim of Quality — 293
   3. Maxim of Relation — 293
   4. Maxim of Manner — 293
   5. Conversational Implicature — 294
      (1) Scalar Implicature (SI) — 295
   6. Hedges — 297

6 Speech Acts — 302
   1. Performative Sentences — 302
   2. Three Facets of Speech Acts — 303
   3. Searle's Typology of Illocutionary Acts — 304
      (1) Representatives — 304
      (2) Directives — 305
      (3) Commissives — 305
      (4) Expressives — 305
      (5) Declarations — 306
   4. Direct and Indirect Speech Acts — 306

최 진 호
영 어 학

INTERMEDIATE

Chapter 01 **Phonology**

Chapter 02 **Morphology**

Chapter 03 **Syntax**

Chapter 04 **Grammar**

Chapter 05 **Semantics & Pragmatics**

Phonology 01-03 mind map

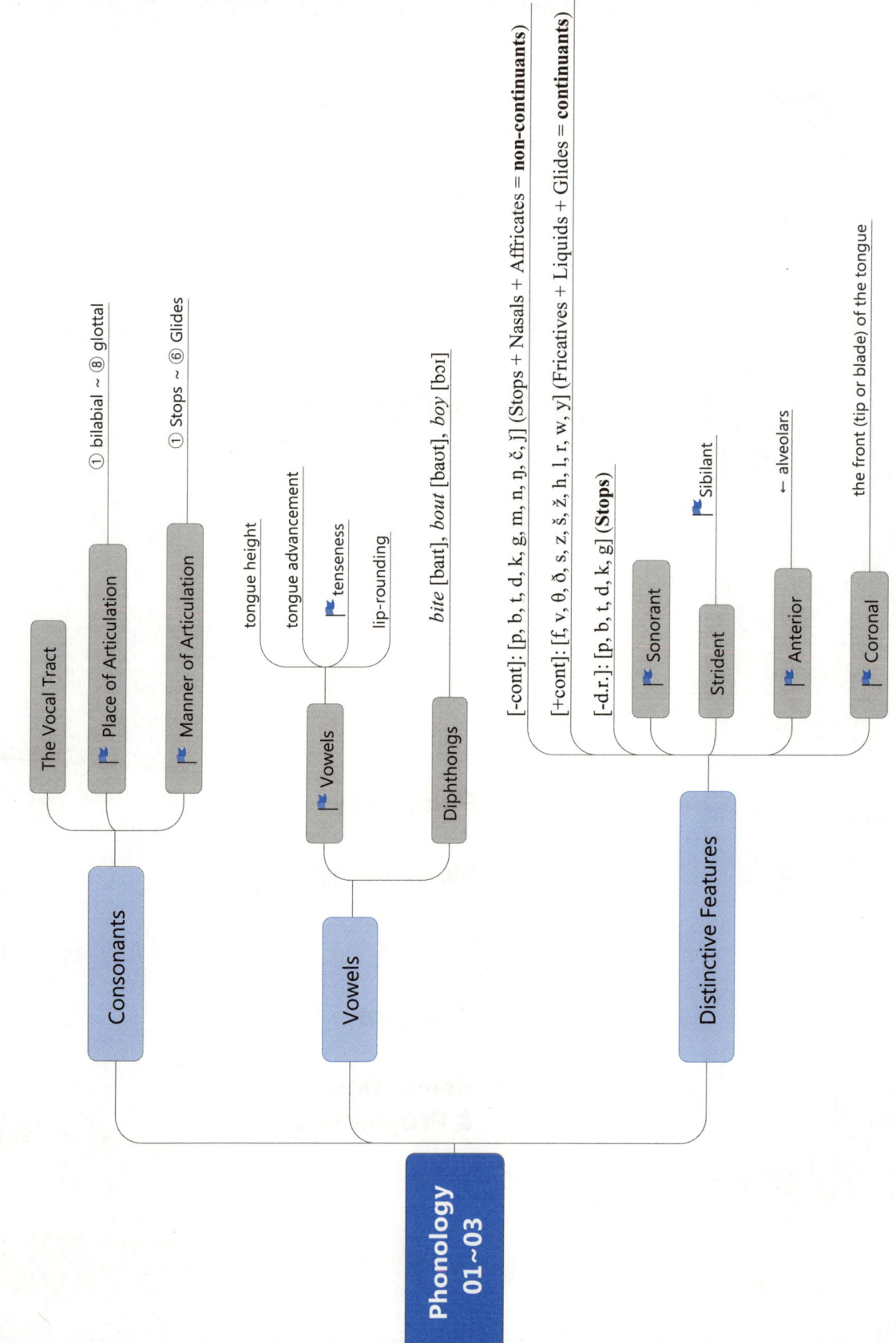

Phonology 04-06 mind map

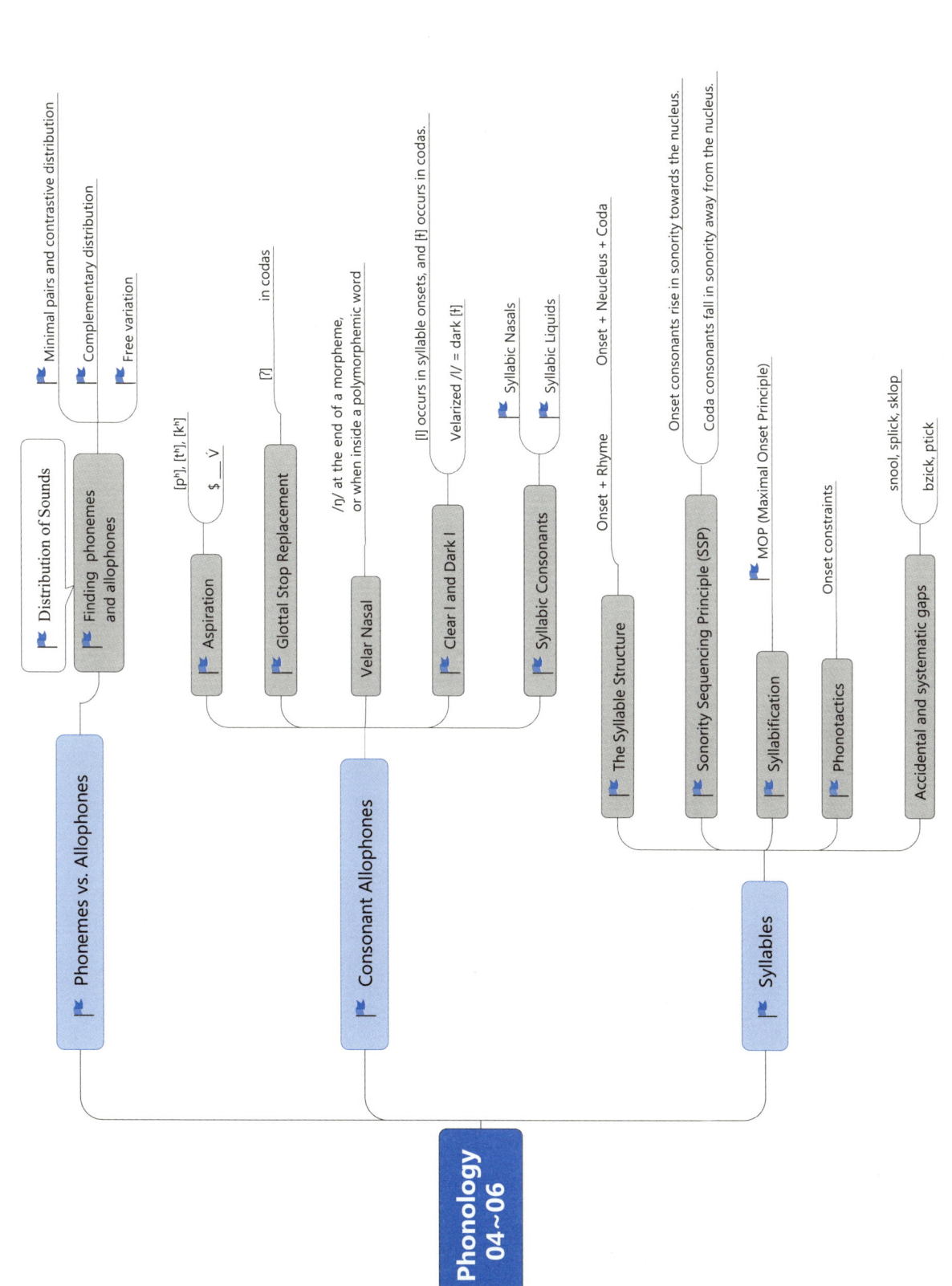

Phonology 07 mind map

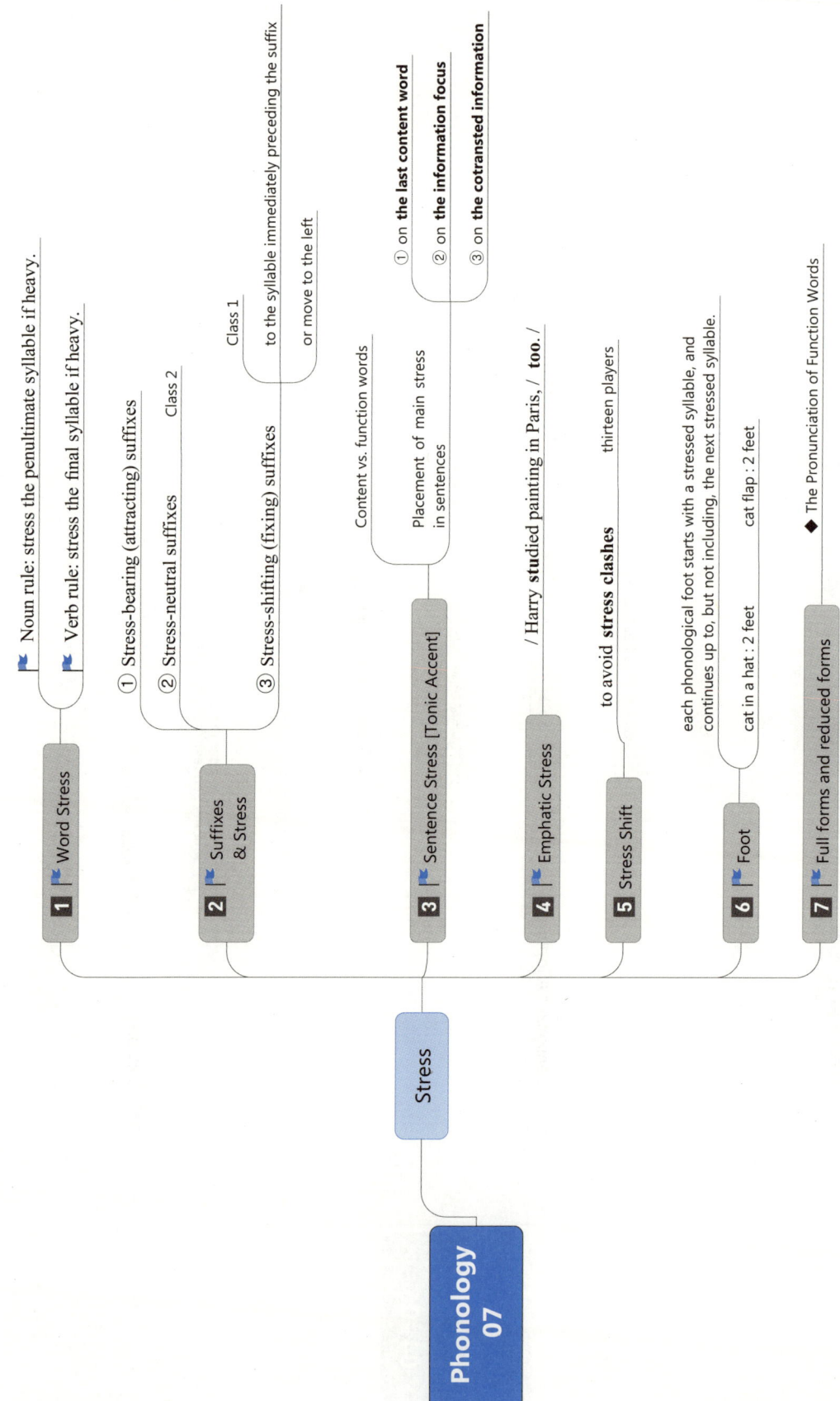

Phonology 08 mind map

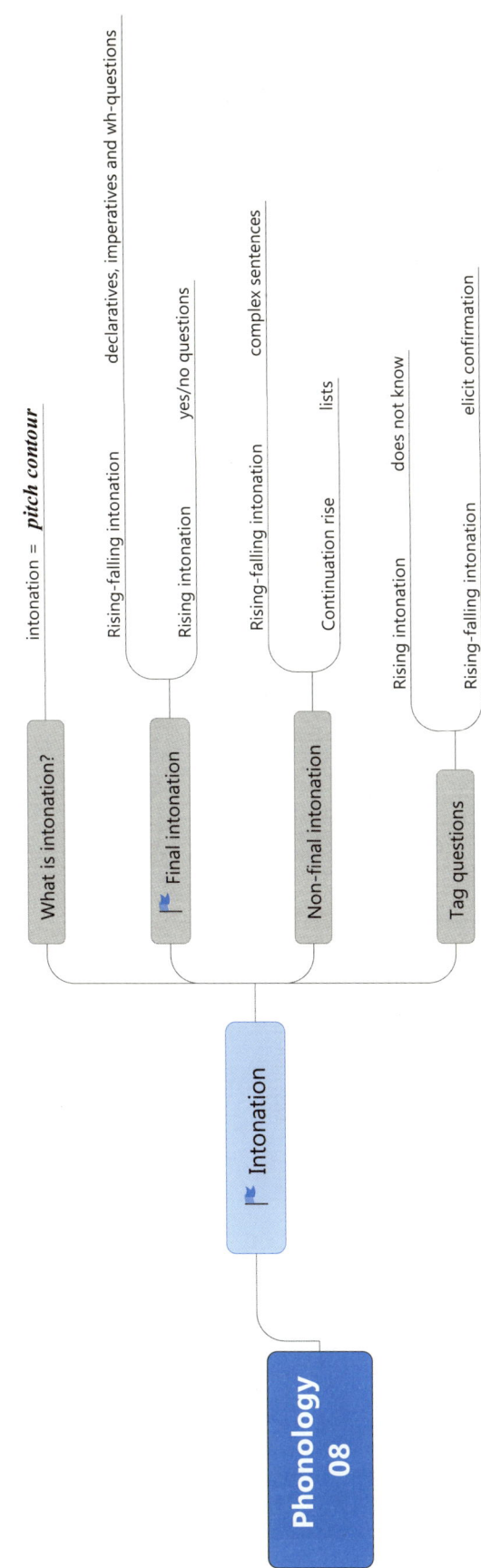

Phonology 09-1 mind map

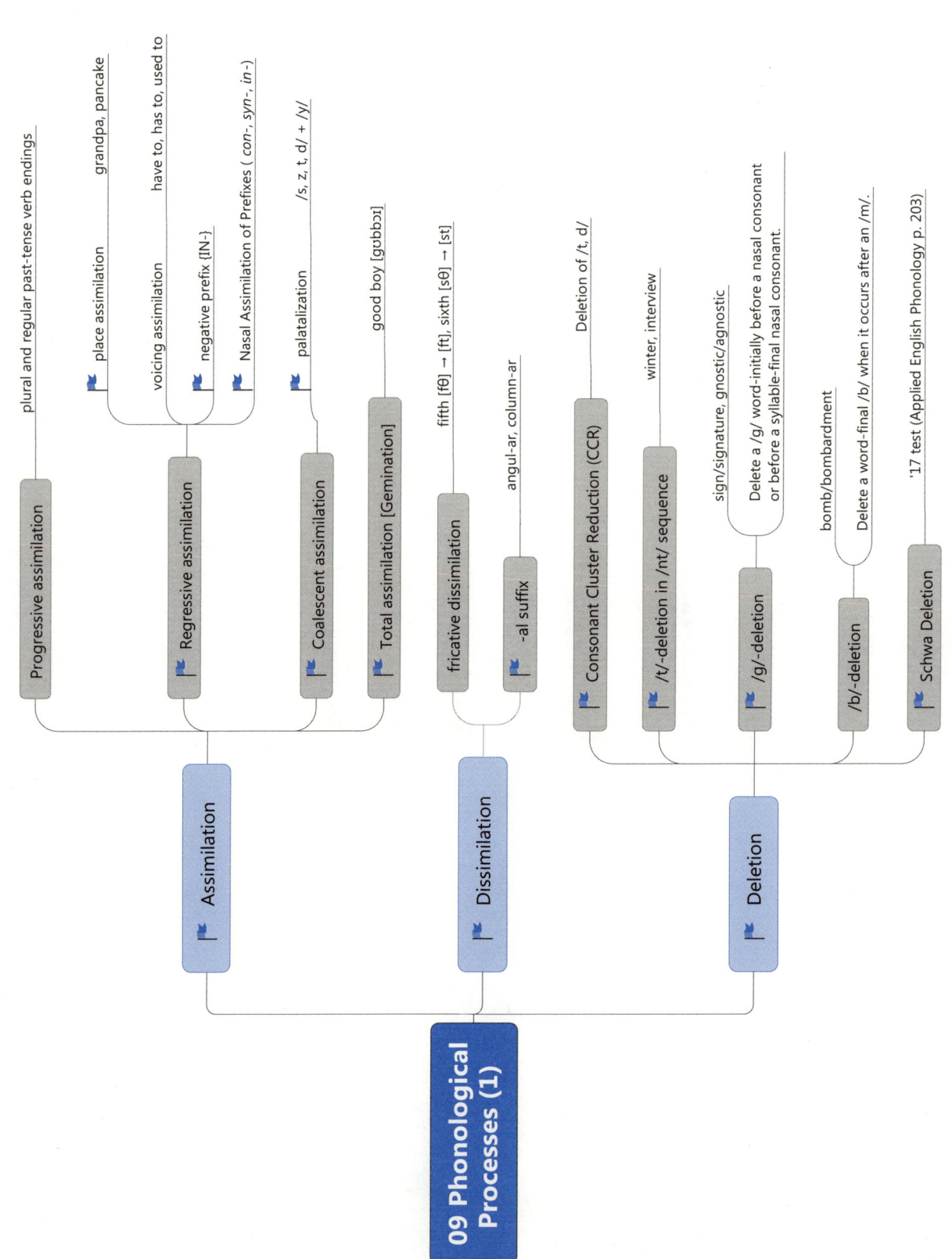

Phonology 09-2 mind map

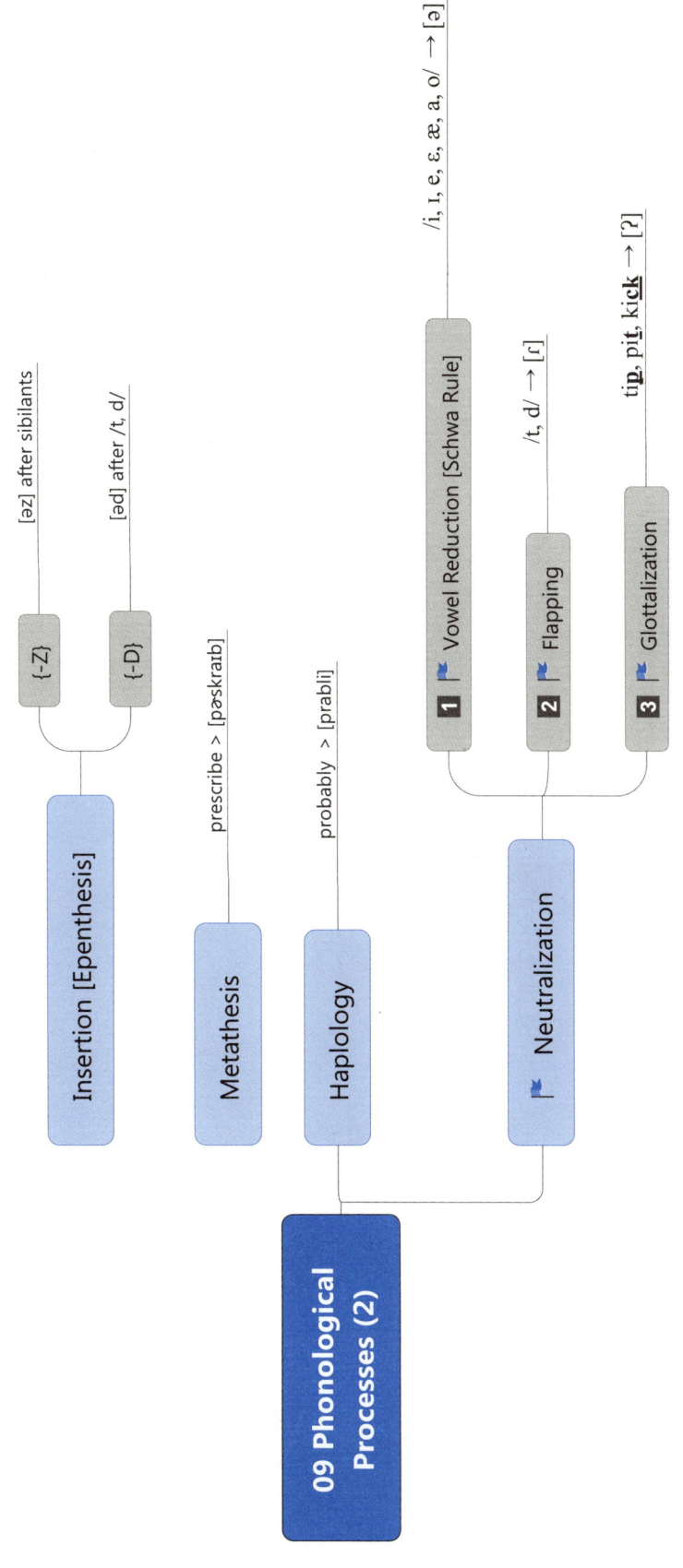

Phonology 10 mind map

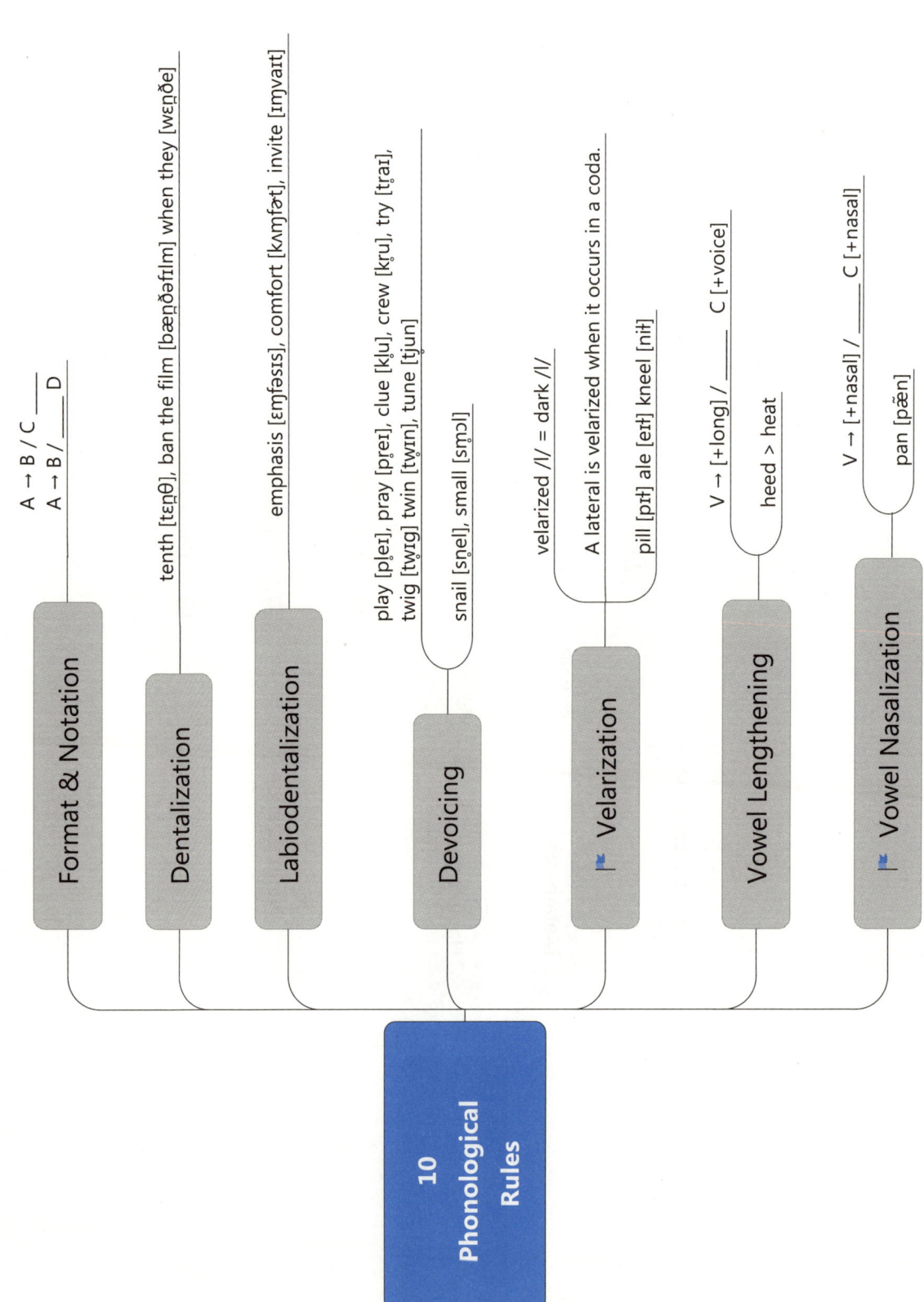

Chapter 01 Phonology

최진호 영어학 INTERMEDIATE

01 Consonants

Note the phonetic notations in the table below before starting the discussion.

Table 1. English consonant and vowel symbols with example words

Phonetic Symbol	Word positions		
	Initial	Medial	Final
Consonants			
ʃ (š)	*sh*ine	ma*ch*ine	ca*sh*
ʒ (ž)	—	vi*s*ion	massa*g*e
tʃ (č)	*ch*air	tea*ch*er	whi*ch*
dʒ (ǰ)	*j*ump	lar*g*er	hu*g*e
j (y)	*y*ard	be*y*ond	so*y*
ɹ (r, ɻ)	*r*ain	bo*r*ing	fou*r*
Vowels and diphthongs			
i (ij, iy)	*ea*se	f*ee*t	b*ee*
ɪ	*i*t	s*i*t	—
e (ej, ey, ei, eɪ)	*ei*ght	b*a*ke	s*ay*
ɛ	*e*dge	r*e*d	—
æ	*a*nger	n*a*p	—
ʌ	*o*ven	l*o*ve	—
ə	*a*bove	oft*e*n	Tamp*a*
ɑ	*a*rch	f*a*ther	sp*a*

ɔ	all	hall	saw
o (ow, oʊ)	oat	goat	bow
ʊ	—	book	—
u (uw)	ooze	loose	two
aɪ (aj, ay)	ice	side	buy
ɔɪ (ɔj, ɔy)	oil	voice	boy
aʊ (au, aw)	out	sound	how

※ IPA (International Phonetic Alphabet) and NAPA (North American Phonetic Alphabet):

⟨ IPA: ʃ   ʒ   tʃ   dʒ   j
  NAPA: š   ž   č   ǰ   y ⟩

1 The Vocal Tract

The vocal tract consists of the passageway between the lips and nostrils on one end and the larynx, which contains the vocal cords, on the other. A cross-section of the vocal tract is given in Figure 1.

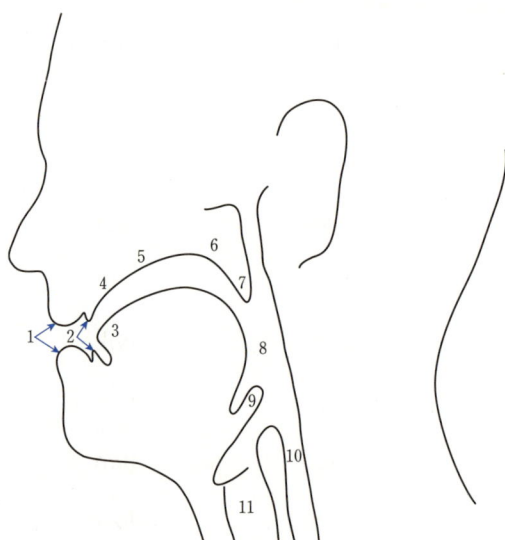

Figure 1. The vocal tract

Let's go over the landmarks in this figure one by one: (1) lips (2) teeth (3) tongue (4) **alveolar ridge**, the bony ridge right behind the upper teeth (5) **palate**, the bony dome constituting the roof of the mouth (6) **velum**, the soft tissue immediately behind the palate (7) uvula, the soft appendage hanging off the velum (you can see it if you open your mouth wide and look in a mirror) (8) pharynx, the back wall of the throat behind the tongue (9) epiglottis, the soft tissue which covers the vocal cords during eating, thus protecting the passageway to the lungs (10) esophagus, the tube going to the stomach (11) **larynx**, containing the vocal cords (12) trachea, the tube going to the lungs.

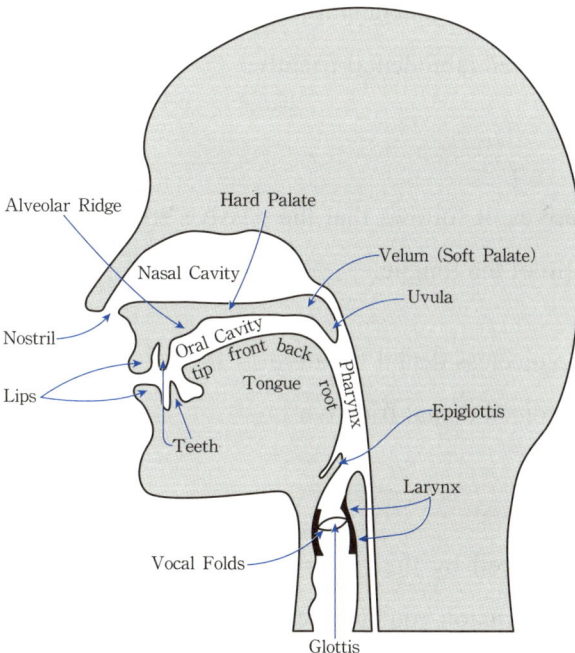

Figure 2. The vocal tract

2 Place of Articulation

For any articulation corresponding to one of these consonant phonemes, the vocal tract is constricted at one of the following points.

(1) Bilabial

For a bilabial sound, the active articulator is the bottom lip, and the passive articulator is the top lip.

/p/	**p**ie	voiceless bilabial plosive
/b/	**b**y	voiced bilabial plosive
/m/	**m**y	voiced bilabial nasal
/w/	**w**itch	voiced labial-velar approximant

(2) Labiodental

For labiodental sounds, the active articulator is again the bottom lip, but this time it moves up to the top front teeth.

/f/	**f**at	voiceless labiodental fricative
/v/	**v**at	voiced labiodental fricative

(3) Interdental

For the two dental fricatives, it follows that the passive articulator is the top front teeth; the active articulator is the tip of the tongue.

[θ]	**th**igh	voiceless dental fricative
[ð]	**th**y	voiced dental fricative

(4) Alveolar

Alveolar sounds are produced by the tip or blade of the tongue moving up towards the alveolar ridge, the bony protrusion you can feel if you curl your tongue back just behind your top front teeth.

/t/	**t**ie	voiceless alveolar plosive
/d/	**d**ie	voiced alveolar plosive
/s/	**s**ip	voiceless alveolar fricative
/z/	**z**ip	voiced alveolar fricative
/n/	**n**igh	voiced alveolar nasal
/l/	**l**ip	voiced alveolar lateral approximant
/r/	**r**ip	voiced alveolar (central) approximant

(5) Palatal

▲ Palato-alveolar (or Postalveolar)

Palato-alveolar [Postalveolar] sounds are produced with the blade of the tongue as the active articulator, and the adjoining parts of the alveolar ridge and the hard palate as the passive one. They include two fricatives, and the affricates introduced in the last section.

/ʃ/	**ship**	voiceless palato-alveolar fricative
/ʒ/	**beige**	voiced palato-alveolar fricative
/tʃ/	**chunk**	voiceless palato-alveolar affricate
/dʒ/	**junk**	voiced palato-alveolar affricate

▲ Palatal

Palatals are produced by the front of the tongue, which moves up towards the hard palate.

/j/	**yes**	voiced palatal approximant

(※ They use either /y/ or /j/ notation for the palatal glide.)

(6) Velar '17

For velar sounds, the active articulator is the back of the tongue, and the passive articulator is the velum, or soft palate.

/k/	**cot**	voiceless velar plosive
/g/	**got**	voiced velar plosive
/ŋ/	**rang**	voiced velar nasal

(7) Glottal

Glottal sounds are in the minority in articulatory terms, since they do not involve the tongue: instead, the articulators are the vocal folds, which constitute a place of articulation as well as having a crucial role in voicing. English has two glottal sounds. The first is an allophone of /t/, namely the glottal stop, [ʔ]. The second, the voiceless glottal fricative [h], is a phoneme in its own right.

/ʔ/ **bu**tt**on**   voiceless glottal stop

/h/ **h**igh   voiceless glottal fricative

◆ Place of articulation (Summary)

Labials (5)	Bilabials	/p, b, m/
	Labiodentals	/f, v/
Dentals (2)	Interdentals	/θ, ð/
	Alveolars (7)	/t, d, s, z, n, l, r/
Palatals (5)	Palato-alveolars	/ʃ, ʒ, tʃ, dʒ/
	Palatals	/j/
	Velars	/k, g, ŋ/
	Glottals	/ʔ, h/

3 Manner of Articulation

(1) Stops

If the active and passive articulators actually touch, stopping airflow through the oral cavity completely for a brief period, the sound articulated is a stop.

| /p/ | **p**ea | /t/ | **t**ea | /k/ | **k**ey |
| /b/ | **b**all | /d/ | **d**og | /g/ | **g**ear |

    Since the definition of a stop involves the complete, transient obstruction of the oral cavity, it also includes nasal sounds, where airflow continues through the nose. English /m/, /n/ and /ŋ/ are therefore nasal stops, although they are typically referred to simply as nasals, as there are no distinctive English nasals involving other manners of articulation. All these nasals are also voiced.

(2) Fricatives

During the production of a fricative, the active and passive articulators are brought close together, but not near enough to totally block the oral cavity. This close approximation of the articulators means the air coming from the lungs has to squeeze through a narrow gap at high speed, creating turbulence, or local audible friction, which is heard as hissing for a voiceless fricative, and buzzing for a voiced one.

/f/	**five**	/v/	**five**	/θ/	**thick**	/ð/	**though**
/s/	**size**	/z/	**size**	/š/	**shell**	/ž/	**genre, measure**

(3) Affricates [20]

The sounds in this group are made by briefly stopping the airstream completely and then releasing the articulators slightly so that friction is produced; these sounds start as stops and finish as fricatives. the affricate sounds are underlined in the following words.

/č/	**cheers**	/ǰ/	**jam**

(4) Nasals

The sounds in this group are made by lowering the velum and letting the airstream pass primarily through the nasal cavity.

/m/	**make**	/n/	**nut**, **bun**	/ŋ/	**sing**

(5) Liquids

The sounds in this group result when an obstruction is formed by the articulators but is not narrow enough to stop the airflow or to cause friction. The /l/ is often described as a ***lateral*** liquid, because for most speakers the tongue touches the roof of the mouth near the alveolar ridge, and air flows around the sides of the tongue. The /r/ is described as a bunched liquid because for most American English speakers the tongue is just that—bunched up under the palate—during the production of the sound.

/l/	**leer**	/r/	**red**

(6) Glides (= Semi-vowels)

The sounds in this group are made with only a slight closure of the articulators—if the vocal tract were any more open, the result would be a vowel.

/y/   **y**ellow   /w/   **w**ash

Table 2. English Consonants

place \ manner	Bilabial	Labio-dental	(Inter-)dental	Alveolar	Palato-alveolar	Palatal	Velar	Glottal
OBSTRUENTS(vl/vd)								
Stop	p b			t d			k g	ʔ
Fricative		f v	θ ð	s z	š ž			h
Affricate					č ǰ			
SONORANTS(vd)								
Nasal	m			n			ŋ	
Liquid				l, r				
Glide	(w)					j	w	

※ Palato-alveolar = Alveopalatal   Palato-alveolar = Palatal

02 Vowels

1 Vowels

English vowel phonemes are described in terms of the following physical dimensions.

(1) Tongue Height

For any articulation corresponding to one of the vowel phonemes, that tongue is either relatively **high** in the mouth (/i, ɪ, u, ʊ/), **mid** (/e, ɛ, ʌ, (ə), o/) **low** (/æ, a, ɔ/). Compare *see* /si/ (high) and *say* /se/ (mid).

(2) Tongue Advancement

For any articulation corresponding to one of the vowel phonemes, that tongue is either relatively ***front*** (/i, ɪ, e, ɛ, æ/) or ***back*** (/ʌ (ə), a, u, ʊ, o, ɔ/). Compare ***see*** /si/ (front) and ***sue*** /su/ (back).

(3) Tenseness '02, '19

For any articulation corresponding to one of the vowel phonemes, the vocal musculature is either relatively ***tense*** (/i, e, a, u, o, ɔ/) or ***lax*** (/ɪ, ɛ, æ, ə, ʌ, ʊ/). Compare ***aid*** /ed/ (tense) and ***Ed*** /ɛd/ (lax).

(4) Lip Rounding

For any articulation corresponding to one of the vowel phonemes, the lips are either relatively ***round*** or ***rounded*** (/u, ʊ, o, ɔ/) or ***unrounded*** (/i, ɪ, e, ɛ, æ, ə, ʌ, a/). Compare ***so*** /so/ (round) and ***say*** /se/ (unrounded).

Table 3 charts the vowel phonemes of English in terms of these four physical dimensions. Thus, for example, /i/ is described as high, front, tense, unrounded vowel. On the other hand, /ɔ/ is described as low, back, tense, rounded vowel.

Table 3. English vowels

		front unrounded	central unrounded	back rounded
high	tense	i (sheep)		u (pool)
	lax	ɪ (ship)		ʊ (pull)
mid	tense	e (paste)		o (low)
	lax	ɛ (pen)	ə ʌ (cup)	ɔ (law)
low	tense		a (cop)	ɑ
	lax	æ (pan)		

※ /ɔ/ is usually regarded as tense. Thus, lax vowels are /ɪ, ɛ, æ, ə, ʌ, ʊ/.

※ ⟨ Tense vowels: long vowels (e, i, o, u) or diphthongs
    Lax vowels + [ɔ/ɑ]: short vowels

2 Diphthongs

> **Diphthongs**
> /aɪ/ /aʊ/ /ɔɪ/ /eɪ/ /oʊ/

A **diphthong** is a sequence of two vowel sounds "squashed" together. Diphthongs are present in the phonetic inventory of many languages, including English. The vowels we have studied so far are simple vowels, called **monophthongs**. The vowel sound in the word *bite* [baɪt], however, is the [a] vowel sound of *father* followed rapidly by the [ɪ] sound of *fit*, resulting in the diphthong [aɪ]. Similarly, the vowel in *bout* [baʊt] is [a] followed by the [ʊ] sound of *put*, resulting in [aʊ]. Another diphthong that occurs in English is the vowel sound in *boy* [bɔɪ], which is the vowel [ɔ] of *bore* followed by [ɪ], resulting in [ɔɪ].

Exercise 1 Cover the answers in the right column with a sheet of paper. Then, write **all** the phonetic representations of the sounds described in the left column:

e.g. voiceless stops: [p, t, k]
   an alveolar nasal: [n]

voiced stops:	voiced stops: [b, d, g]
bilabial stops:	bilabial stops: [p, b]
velar stops:	velar stops: [k, g]
flap:	flap: [ɾ]
a bilabial nasal:	a bilabial nasal: [m]
a velar nasal:	a velar nasal: [ŋ]
a voiceless labiodental fricative:	a voiceless labiodental fricative: [f]
the bilabials:	the bilabials: [p, b, m, (w)]
the labials:	the labials: [p, b, m, f, v]
oral stops:	oral stops: [p, t, k, b, d, g]
nasal stops:	nasal stops: [m, n, ŋ]
alveolar stops:	alveolar stops: [t, d, n]

alveolar fricatives:	alveolar fricatives: [s, z]
alveolar obstruents:	alveolar obstruents: [t, d, s, z]
alveolar sonorants:	alveolar sonorants: [n, l, r]
the sonorants:	the sonorants: [m, n, ŋ, l, r, j, w] + all vowels
affricates:	affricates: [tʃ, dʒ]
a labio-velar glide:	a labio-velar glide: [w]
a palatal glide:	a palatal glide: [j] (=[y])
an alveolar nasal:	an alveolar nasal: [n]
an alveolar lateral:	an alveolar lateral: [l]
the alveolars:	the alveolars: [t, d, s, z, n, l, r]
approximants:	approximants: [r, l, w, j] ※ [j] = [y]
glides:	glides: [w, j]
a glottal stop:	glottal stop: [ʔ]
an alveolar voiced stop:	an alveolar voiced stop: [d]
an alveolar nasal:	an alveolar nasal: [n]
a voiceless velar:	a voiceless velar: [k]
liquids:	liquids: [l, r]
alveolar liquids:	alveolar liquids: [l, r]
a homorganic nasal sound of [p]:	a homorganic nasal sound of [p]: [m]
a homorganic nasal sound of [t]:	a homorganic nasal sound of [t]: [n]
a homorganic nasal sound of [k]:	a homorganic nasal sound of [k]: [ŋ]
homorganic stops of [n]:	homorganic stops of [n]: [t, d]

> **Exercise 2** Cover the answers in the right column with a sheet of paper. Then, write the descriptive labels for the phonetic representations of the sounds given in the left column:

e.g. [k]: a voiceless velar stop
    [č, ǰ]: palato-alveolar affricates
        (palatal affricates)

[ŋ]:	[ŋ]: a velar nasal
[l, r]:	[l, r]: liquids
[n]:	[n]: a (voiced) alveolar nasal
[b]:	[b]: a voiced bilabial stop
[d]:	[d]: a voiced alveolar stop
[k, g]:	[k, g]: velar stops (or velars)
[p, b]:	[p, b]: bilabial stops (or bilabials)
[p, b, m]:	[p, b, m]: bilabial stops (or bilabials)
[t, d]:	[t, d]: alveolar stops (or alveolars)
[t, d, n]:	[t, d, n]: alveolar stops (or alveolars)
[g]:	[g]: a voiced velar stop
[f]:	[f]: a voiceless labiodental fricative
[θ, ð]:	[θ, ð]: interdental fricatives (or dentals)
[p, b, m, f, v]:	[p, b, m, f, v]: labials
[s]:	[s]: a voiceless alveolar fricative
[z]:	[z]: a voiced alveolar fricative
[w]:	[w]: a labio-velar glide (or a velar glide)
[j] (=[y]):	[j] (=[y]): a palatal glide
[h]:	[h]: a glottal fricative
[š, ž, č, ǰ, y]:	[š, ž, č, ǰ, y]: palatals
[k, g, ŋ]:	[k, g, ŋ]: velar stops (or velars)

03 Distinctive Features '14, '15, '16

1 Distinctive Features (1)

(1) Syllabic (syl)

Segment that constitute a syllable peak are syllabic [+syl], while those that do not constitute a syllable peak are non-syllabic [–syl]. When non-vowels constitute a syllable peak (e.g. [l̩] in *riddle* [rɪdl̩] and [n̩] in *button* [bʌʔn̩]), they are specified as [+syl].

[+syl]: all vowels, and sometimes [m, n, ŋ, l, r]
[–syl]: all consonants

(2) Soronant (son) '14, '15

Sonorant sounds are typically produced without an extreme degree of oral cavity constriction. Vowels, nasals, liquids (*r*, *l*) and glides (*w*, *y*) are usually considered [+son], while sounds with more radical cavity constriction, such as stops, fricatives and affricates (**obstruents**), are specified as [–son].

(3) Consonantal (cons)

Consonantal sounds are produced with obstruction along the center line of the oral cavity. All the consonants are [+cons]. The only non-consonantal sounds ([–cons]) are the Vowels and the Glides *w* and *y*.

(4) Continuant (cont)

Continuant sounds are characterized by continued air movement through the oral cavity during the production of the sounds. **Non-continuants** are produced with complete obstruction in the oral cavity. Thus, stops, including *m*, *n*, and *ŋ*, are [–cont], while fricatives, glides and so forth are [+cont]. The affricates *č* and *ǰ* are also [–cont] since they contain a stop onset.

[–cont]: [p, b, t, d, k, g, m, n, ŋ, č, ǰ]
        (Stops + Nasals + Affricates = **non-continuants**)

[+cont]: [f, v, θ, ð, s, z, š, ž, h, l, r, w, y]
(Fricatives + Liquids + Glides = **continuants**)

(5) Strident (str)

Strident sounds are produced with an obstruction in the oral cavity which allows air to come through a relatively narrow constriction. As the air escapes, the turbulence produces "white" noise (**a hissing sound**).

The fricatives *f, v, s, z, š, ž* (excluding *θ, ð*) and the affricates *č* and *ǰ* are [+str]. The affricates are distinguished from the strident fricatives by the specification [−continuant] because of the stop onset. ⇒ affricates [+str, −cont]

[+str]: [f, v, s, z, š, ž, č, ǰ] (fricatives + affricates) ▶ strident = sibilant + f, v

cf Sibilants: [s, z, š, ž, č, ǰ] ▶ sibilant = [+strident, +coronal] '05
'**sibilants**': A fricative or an affricate that is produced with a high-frequency energy, usually by means of a groove in the tongue.

(6) Delayed Release (d.r.)

Delayed release specifies the manner in which consonants are released. Stops are released instantaneously ([−d.r.]); affricates, fricatives, and other sounds are released gradually ([+d.r.]). This feature is important in distinguishing stops from affricates. Thus, in English *č* and *ǰ* are [+d.r.], and *t* and *d* [−d.r.], although they share the specification [−cont].

[−d.r.]: [p, b, t, d, k, g] (Stops)
[+d.r.]: [f, v, θ, ð, s, z, š, ž, h, č, ǰ] (Fricatives + Affricates)

※ '**delayed release**' is a distinctive feature representing how quickly the closure in a **non-continuant** consonant is released. It separates stops, which are [−delayed release], from affricates, which are [+delayed release].

(7) Nasal (nas)

Nasal sounds are characterized by the opening of the velum so that air can escape through the nasal passage.

[+nas]: [m, n, ŋ]

[−nas]: [p, b, t, d, k, g, f, v, θ, ð, s, z, š, ž, h, č, ǰ, l, r, w, y] (all the others)

(8) Lateral (lat) '20

Lateral sounds are the ones in which the air moves through the side of the oral cavity while the tongue blocks the middle of it. In English, only *l* is lateral.

[+lat]: [l]

[−lat]: all the others

(9) Anterior (ant) '14

Anterior sounds are produced with a primary obstruction located at or in front of the alveolar region of the mouth.

[+ant]	bilabials, labiodentals, interdentals, alveolars	
[−ant]		alveopalatals, palatals, velars, glottals

(10) Coronal (cor) '16

Coronal sounds are produced with the front (tip or blade) of the tongue raised from neutral position. This includes articulations from the interdental through the palatal positions. Sounds that are produced without raising the front of the tongue are [−cor].

[+cor]		interdental, alveolars, alveopalatals, palatals	
[−cor]	bilabials, labiodentals		velars, glottals

The features [cor] and [ant] distinguish four natural classes of segments:

labials   [−cor, +ant]
dentals/alveolars   [+cor, +ant]
alveopalatals/palatals   [+cor, −ant]
velars/glottals   [−cor, −ant]

(11) Dorsal

Dorsal sounds are articulated by raising the dorsum of the tongue. All vowels are dorsal sounds. Dorsal consonants include palatal, velar and uvular consonants. ⇒ [+dorsal]: /k, g, ŋ/ (velars)

※ [+coronal] is contrasted with [+labial] and [+dorsal].
  ⎧ [+labial] (= bilabials + labiodentals): **/p, b, m, f, v/**
  ⎩ [+dorsal] (= velars): **/k, g, ŋ/**

  ⎧ [+coronal] = articulated with the tongue blade and/or tip.
  ⎩ [+dorsal] = articulated with the tongue body.

(12) [± voice]

[+voice] sounds involve vibration of the vocal cords; [−voice] do not.

(13) [± labial]

[+labial] sounds have rounding or constriction at the lips. They are therefore <u>bilabial</u> and <u>labiodental</u> consonants and rounded vowels.

(14) [± sibilant]

[+sibilant] fricatives (/s, z, ʃ, ʒ, tʃ, dʒ/) are those with large amounts of acoustic energy at high frequencies.

(15) [± tense]

[+tense] vowels are long vowels, produced with greater tension; [−tense] (short) vowels are also called lax.

Natural Class

A **natural class** of sounds is <u>a complete set of sounds that share one or more features</u>. For example, /m/, /n/, and /ŋ/ in English form a natural class because they constitute the complete set of sounds that share the feature [+nasal]. Likewise, /p/, /t/, and /k/ form a natural class in English because they constitute all the [+stop, −voiced] sounds of language.

Table 4. Consonants of English (with three features)

		[+ant]				[−ant]			
	place\manner	Bilabial	Labio-dental	(Inter-)dental	Alveolar	Palato-alveolar	Palatal	Velar	Glottal
[−son]	Stop	p b			t d			k g	ʔ
	Fricative		f v	θ ð	s z	š ž			h
	Affricate					č ǰ			
[+son]	Nasal	m			n			ŋ	
	Liquid				l, r				
	Glide						j	w	
				[+cor]					
		[−cor]						[−cor]	

※ Palato-alveolar = Alveopalatal   Palato-alveolar = Palatal

Exercise 3

Some Distinctive Features for Consonants

Distinctive Features	Labials	Dentals/ Alveolars	Palato- alveolars	Velars
[anterior]	+	+	−	−
[coronal]	−	+	+	−

Distinctive Features	Nasal stops	Oral stops	Fricatives	Liquids/ Glides
[sonorant]	+	−	−	+
[continuant]	−	−	+	+

Cover the answers in the right column below with a sheet of paper. Then, consulting the feature table above, write **only one** feature with a plus/minus value that the given sounds in the left column have in common.

[n, r]:	[n, r]: [+sonorant] (or [+coronal])
[n, t]:	[n, t]: [−continuant] (or [+coronal])
[r, s]:	[r, s]: [+continuant] (or [+coronal])
[θ, v, t]:	[θ, v, t]: [+anterior] (or [−sonorant])
[k, ʧ]:	[k, ʧ]: [−anterior] (or [−sonorant])

Table 5. Distinctive Features for English Consonants

Features	p	b	m	t	d	n	k	g	ŋ	f	v	θ
Consonantal	+	+	+	+	+	+	+	+	+	+	+	+
Sonorant	−	−	+	−	−	+	−	−	+	−	−	−
Syllabic	−	−	−/+	−	−	−/+	−	−	−/+	−	−	−
Nasal	−	−	+	−	−	+	−	−	+	−	−	−
Voiced	−	+	+	−	+	+	−	+	+	−	+	−
Continuant	−	−	−	−	−	−	−	−	−	+	+	+
Labial	+	+	+	−	−	−	−	−	−	+	+	−
Alveolar	−	−	−	+	+	+	−	−	−	−	−	−
Palatal	−	−	−	−	−	−	−	−	−	−	−	−
Anterior	+	+	+	+	+	+	−	−	−	+	+	+
Velar	−	−	−	−	−	−	+	+	+	−	−	−
Coronal	−	−	−	+	+	+	−	−	−	−	−	+
Sibilant	−	−	−	−	−	−	−	−	−	−	−	−

Features	ð	s	z	ʃ	ʒ	tʃ	dʒ	l	r	j	w	h
Consonantal	+	+	+	+	+	+	+	+	+	−	−	−
Sonorant	−	−	−	−	−	−	−	+	+	+	+	−
Syllabic	−	−	−	−	−	−	−	−/+	−/+	−	−	−
Nasal	−	−	−	−	−	−	−	−	−	−	−	−
Voiced	+	−	+	−	+	−	+	+	+	+	+	−
Continuant	+	+	+	+	+	−	−	+	+	+	+	+
Labial	−	−	−	−	−	−	−	−	−	−	+	−
Alveolar	−	+	+	−	−	−	−	+	+	−	−	−
Palatal	−	−	−	+	+	+	+	−	−	+	−	−
Anterior	+	+	+	−	−	−	−	+	+	−	−	−
Velar	−	−	−	−	−	−	−	−	−	−	+	−
Coronal	+	+	+	+	+	+	+	+	+	+	−	−
Sibilant	−	+	+	+	+	+	+	−	−	−	−	−

※ The phonemes /r/ and /l/ are distinguished by the feature [lateral], not shown here.
  /l/ is the only phoneme that would be [+lateral].

2 Distinctive Features (2)

(1) Distinctive Features: Major classes [Sonorant], [Continuant] and [Consonantal]

[Sonorant]: A sonorant is a sound whose phonetic contest is predominantly made up by the sound waves with voicing.

Approximants and nasals are [+sonorant], fricatives and oral stops [–sonorant]. Members of the latter category are referred to as 'obstruent'.

[Continuant]: A continuant is a sound during whose production the air stream is not blocked in the oral cavity.

Continuant sounds are characterized by continued air movement through the oral cavity during the production of the sounds. **Non-continuants** are produced with complete obstruction in the oral cavity. Approximants and fricatives are [+continuant], nasal and oral stops (that is, 'stops' in general) are [–continuant].

[–continuant]: S+N+A
[+continuant]: F+L+G

The four possible combinations of these two binary features ([Sonorant] and [Continuant]) express four major classes of sounds; the two features are for that reason often referred to as 'major class features'. Here are the four classes:

(1) $\begin{bmatrix} +\text{sonorant} \\ +\text{continuant} \end{bmatrix}$ = 'Approximants'

$\begin{bmatrix} -\text{sonorant} \\ +\text{continuant} \end{bmatrix}$ = 'Fricatives'

$\begin{bmatrix} +\text{sonorant} \\ -\text{continuant} \end{bmatrix}$ = 'Nasal stops'

$\begin{bmatrix} -\text{sonorant} \\ -\text{continuant} \end{bmatrix}$ = 'Oral stops'

Here is a definition of the feature [Consonantal]:

> [Consonantal]: Consonantal sounds are produced with a radical obstruction in the vocal tract.

Vowels as well as /j, w/ are [−consonantal], all other sounds are [+consonantal].

Table 6. The major class features

	Nasal stop	Oral stop	Fricative	Approximant		Vowel
				Liquid	Semivowel	
[Sonorant]	+	−	−	+	+	+
[Continuant]	−	−	+	+	+	+
[Consonantal]	+	+	+	+	−	−
Examples	m n ŋ	p t k b d g	f v θ ð	l r	j w	i u

◆ **distinctive feature—yes or no?**

Distinctive feature: [± **sonorant**], [± **coronal**], [± **anterior**], [± labial], [± nasal], [± lateral], [± approximant], [± strident], [± sibilant], etc.

Not a distinctive feature: obstruent ([−sonorant]), liquid ([+approximant]), glide ([+approximant]), fricative, affricate, alveolar ([+coronal]), palatal ([+coronal]), velar ([+dorsal]), etc.

Distinctive feature but not as an answer of a test: stop, retroflex ([−lateral]), approximant

 cf Some phoneticians do not regard sibilants as a feature. They describe sibilants as [+strident, +coronal].

04 Phonemes vs. Allophones '05, '15 (allophone)

There is something about the t-sounds in 'tuck', 'stuck' and 'cut' that is the same, in the sense that speakers of English group these together as 't-sounds'. At the same time, we recognize that phonetically these t-sounds are different. In the same way consider the t-sounds in 'tea', 'steam' and 'sit': the 't' in 'tea' is likely to be aspirated, the 't' in 'steam' unaspirated and the 't' in 'sit' may be unreleased (indicated by ˺).

(1) t-sounds: tea [tʰi:]   steam [sti:m]   sit [sɪt˺]

It is not difficult to find other groupings of sounds that are both the same and different in just the same way. In parallel with the t-sounds we find that English also has a set of p-sounds—those in 'pea', 'spin' and 'sip'—and a set of k-sounds—those in 'key', 'skin' and 'sick'.

(2) p-sounds: pea [pʰi:]   spin [spɪn]   sip [sɪp˺]
    k-sounds: key [kʰi:]   skin [skɪn]   sick [sɪk˺]

These sets of p-sounds also represent phonetically different speech sounds, yet can clearly be grouped together as p-sounds and k-sounds. The fact that native speakers of English often do not realize that [p], [pʰ] and [p˺] differ also suggests that there may be some relationship between them. While it is not a crucial piece of evidence that the t-sounds, p-sounds and k-sounds *are* groups of related sounds, it does say something about how speakers of English feel about their relatedness.

These groupings like English [t], [tʰ] and [t˺], with respect to their simultaneous unity and diversity, have traditionally been dealt with in terms of two levels of representation. That is to say that at a concrete physical level the members of these groups of sounds *are* different phonetically—they have different phonetic properties—but that abstractly it is useful to group them together as being related. In fact, grouping them together this way reflects the intuition of the native speaker that these sounds are 'the same' in some sense. Taking this view, we can say that abstractly English has a 't' and that concretely the pronunciation of this 't' depends on the context in which it occurs. That is, if the 't' of English appears at the beginning of a word it is pronounced as [tʰ], if it appears as part of a consonant cluster following [s] it is pronounced as [t], if it appears at the end of a word it may be pronounced as [t˺] (or indeed as [ʔ] or [t]). In the same way, we can say that English 'p' has several concrete representatives: [p], [pʰ] and [p˺].

In order to make clear which level of representation we are dealing with, abstract or concrete, the convention is to use square brackets—[ ]—to enclose the symbol(s) for concrete speech sounds as they are pronounced—phonetic material—and to use slashes—/ /—to enclose the symbols representing the abstract elements—underlying material. Taking again the p-sounds of English, we can say that the group is represented abstractly by /p/, which is pronounced concretely as [p], [pʰ] or [p`], depending on where it occurs in a word. In this same way, the k-sounds consist of /k/, representing the group which is pronounced [k], [kʰ] or [k`].

By using this approach, we can distinguish between the surface sounds of a language—those that are spoken—and the underlying organizing system. If we know, for instance, that we're talking about underlying /p/, we can predict for English which member of the group of phonetic p-sounds—[p], [pʰ] or [p`]—will occur in a particular position. The abstract underlying units are known as **phonemes** while the predictable surface elements are known as **allophones**. In these terms we can say that the phoneme /p/ is realized as the allophone [pʰ] word-initially, as the allophone [p] in an initial cluster following [s] and as the allophone [p`] at the end of a word. The relationship can be shown graphically as in (3).

(3)

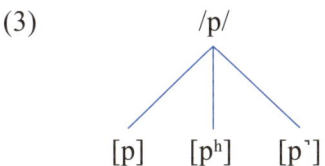

Knowing, for instance, that English contains [b], [p], [pʰ] and [p`]—a list—tells us nothing about any possible phonological relationships between these sounds, that is that [p], [pʰ] and [p`] are allophones of a single phoneme, /p/, and that [b] is an allophone of a contrasting phoneme, /b/.

It is important to recognize that this kind of abstraction from the concrete to the underlying is not unique to linguistics and is, in fact, a familiar concept from the natural sciences. Consider water. We all know certain facts about water. First of all, we know that, abstractly, it is composed of two hydrogen molecules and an oxygen molecule, which we represent formally as H_2O. We also know that at a temperature below 0ºC H_2O appears as ice; between 0ºC and 100ºC H_2O appears as liquid water and above 100ºC H_2O appears as water vapor. Just as the p-sounds [p], [pʰ] and [p`] are underlyingly /p/, water, ice and water vapor are underlyingly H_2O.

(4)

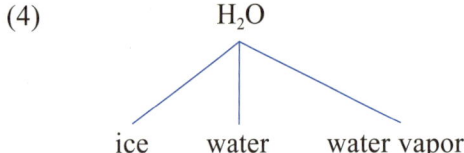

What this means is that in both cases, the phonological and the physical, we have a single entity—i.e. /p/ and H_2O—that occurs in various forms in specific environments. If we chose not to view phonology in this way we would be forced to say that [p], [pʰ] and [p˺] are not related to single abstract entity, which would be analogous to saying that water, ice and water vapor are not related to H_2O.

1 Finding phonemes and allophones [Distribution of Sounds] '12, '17

We need first to be able to determine the phonemes then relate them to their allophones. Phonemes are most often established by finding a contrast between speech sounds. These contrasts can be most easily seen in minimal pairs.

(1) Minimal pairs and contrastive distribution '12 Choice, '17

The clearest sort of contrast is a **minimal pair**, that is, a pair of words which differ by just one sound and which are different lexical items. By 'different lexical items' we mean distinct items of vocabulary, regardless of their meaning. If we compare 'bat' and 'mat', for example, we know as speakers of English that they are two different lexical items and we can see that they differ from each other by precisely one sound, the initial [b] versus [m]. Therefore, we can say that [b] and [m] **contrast**. On the basis of that contrast we can suggest that [b] and [m] are allophones of separate phonemes, /b/ and /m/ (remembering that allophones are the actual speech sounds appearing in square brackets). If we then compare the initial sound in 'fat' we see that there is a contrast with both [b] and [m], since 'fat', 'bat', and 'mat' are different lexical items and since each differs from the other by only one sound. Thus, [f] commits with [b] and [m]. Therefore, we can say that [b], [m] and [f] are each allophones of separate phonemes, /b/, /m/ and /f/ respectively.

Minimal pairs rest on **contrastive distribution**, as we have just seen with the initial consonants in 'fat', 'bat' and 'mat' which contrast with each other. We saw this contrast by means of a **commutation test**, i.e., a substitution of one sound for another yielding a different lexical item. Contrastive distribution can show a contrast anywhere in the word, however, not just initially. This means that 'rub' and 'rum' or 'robed' and 'roamed' are just as much minimal pairs as 'bat' and 'mat' since in each case the sounds in question appear in identical phonetic environments and constitutes the only phonetic difference between the two lexical items. Compare (5), in which we see that except for the sounds in question, [b] and [m], the phonetic structures of the words are the same.

(5)   [b]   [m]
     rub   [rʌ_]   rum   [rʌ_]
     robed   [roʊ_d]   roamed   [roʊ_d]

Sometimes in a given language there are no minimal pairs to contrast for a specific pair of sounds, yet we can still establish phonemes. Consider the [ʃ] of 'shoe' and the [ʒ] of 'leisure'. Word-initial position does not help us find a contrast since in English [ʒ] does not occur word-initially (apart from a very few loanwords). Word-finally the occurrence of [ʒ] is also limited, e.g. 'beige'. Word-medially both sounds occur: [ʃ] 'fissure', 'usher', [ʒ] 'measure', 'leisure'. But even in this position we do not find a true minimal pair, that is, we do not find two lexical items differing by only one speech sound. What we can find, however, is a **near minimal pair**, such as 'mission' and 'vision'. Note that with this pair the immediate phonetic environment of the two sounds concerned, [ʃ] and [ʒ], is identical, i.e. between a stressed [ɪ] and a [ə]: [ˈmɪʃən] vs. [ˈvɪʒən] (Superscript ˈ indicates stress.)

(6)   [ʃ]   [ʒ]
     mission   ˈɪ_ə   vision   ˈɪ_ə

So, even though this is not a true minimal pair (because the lexical items differ by more than one speech sound) it is convincing evidence of a contrast since the sounds we are comparing occur in identical phonetic environments.

(2) Complementary Distribution '12 Choice

Notice that a minimal pair or commutation test will not help us at all with the kinds of sound groups we discussed above, that is the p-sounds, the k-sounds, the t-sounds. This is because in the environment where we find one of the p-sounds we won't find any of the other p-sounds: [pʰ] at the beginnings of words but not in clusters following [s], we find [p̚] at the ends of words but not word-initially. This state of affairs, in which two sounds do not occur in the same environment, is referred to as **complementary distribution**. It is precisely because we cannot get the p-sounds to contrast with each other that we know they belong to the same phoneme, that is, they are allophones of a single phoneme. Referring to the water analogy again, at a temperature at which we find water we do not find ice and at a temperature at which we find ice we do not find steam. The three related manifestations of H_2O, like the three related p-sounds, do not appear in the same environment. Note that we ***do*** find contrasts between members of different groups of sounds—[pʰ] and [kʰ] contrast, as do [p] and [k] and so on—but we find no contrasts among the members of a group.

Above we referred to allophones as being predictable sounds. We can now see what is meant by that. Taking the p-sounds again, we know that we find [pʰ] word-initially and [p] in clusters following [s]. Therefore, if we know that we are dealing with a p-sound, i.e. one of the set of allophones of /p/, we can predict ***which*** p-sound will be pronounced in which context. This is what we mean by allophones being predictable. As an example, take the following word of English which is missing the initial consonant:

(7) [__ɛt]

Without knowing what word it is supposed to be, we cannot guess whether the initial consonant should be [m] or [b] or [pʰ] or [l] or [g] or a number of other consonants. However, if we are told that the blank must be filled in with a p-sound, we know which one it will be: [pʰ]. The phoneme is unpredictable but the allophone, once we know which phoneme is involved, ***is*** predictable.

(3) Free variation '12 Choice

While the distinction between allophones and phonemes is quite clear cut, there are some phenomena which can obscure the identification of phonemes. One of these is so-called free variation. In our discussion of the t-sounds we have indicated in a number of places that a voiceless stop may be unreleased at the end of a word, e.g. [mæt̚]. But we have also indicated in passing that /t/ has other realizations at the end of a word, including unaspirated release [mæt] and glottal stop [mæʔ]. Given that these are three phonetically different speech sounds in the same position one might suggest that they are related to different phonemes. But note that these do not contrast: [mæt̚], [mæt] and [mæʔ] are three different pronunciations of the *same* lexical item. Since they involve the same lexical item, we can say that the three sounds are in **free variation**, since there are no minimal pairs. We can thus maintain that <u>they are allophones of a single phoneme</u>.

(8) Distribution of Sounds

① **Overlapping Distribution**	**Contrastive**	minimal pairs	different phonemes	bat - mat rub - rum
	Non-contrastive	free variation	allophones of a single phoneme	mat [mæt̚] or [mæt] or [mæʔ]
② **Complementary Distribution**			allophones of a single phoneme	pit, spit, tip [pʰ] [p] [p̚]

(9) The Phonemic Principle

Two or more sounds are realization of *the same* phonemes if:

① they are in **complementary distribution**

and

② they are **phonetically similar**

Two or more sounds are realization of the *different* phonemes if:

① they are in **overlapping distribution**

and

② they serve to signal a **semantic contrast**

2 Diacritical Marks

Table 7. Common Diacritical Marks Used in the Narrow Transcription of English

Diacritical Mark	Meaning	Examples
[̥]	voiceless	ply [pl̥aɪ], clam [kl̥æm], true [tr̥u]
[ʰ]	aspirated	tin [tʰɪn], cat [kʰæt], pot [pʰat]
[ʷ]	labialized	cool [kʷul], toward [tʷɔrd], dough [dʷo]
[~]	velarized	pal [pæɫ], elk [ɛɫk], vulgar [vʌɫgɚ]
[̪]	dental	eighth [et̪θ], width [wɪd̪θ], breadth [brɛd̪θ]
[ʔ]	unreleased	kite [kaɪʔt], stop [staʔp], lick [lɪʔk]
[ʲ]	palatalized	key [kʲi], keel [kʲil], gears [gʲirz]
[̃]	nasalized	man [mæ̃n], mango [mæ̃ŋgo], slim [slĩm]
[ː]	long	have [hæːv], loathe [loːð], major [meːdʒɚ]
[̩]	syllabic	puddle [pʌdl̩], shuffle [šʌfl̩], button [bʌtn̩]

※ diacritical marks ⇒ allophones of a phoneme

05 Consonant Allophones

1 Aspiration '11 Choice, '13 Choice

> Voiceless stops are aspirated when they are <u>at the beginning of a stressed syllable.</u>

One example of how environment can affect the articulation of a sound involves the stop consonants /p, t, k/. Thus far, we have distinguished these sounds from /b, d, g/ in terms of voicing. However, an additional significant feature of voiceless stop consonants in English is **aspiration**, the brief puff of air that accompanies the allophones of /p, t, k/ in words such as *p̲an*, *t̲an*, and *k̲ey*. The presence or absence of aspiration is easier to demonstrate with the bilabial stops /p/ and /b/. If an English speaker says **pie**, the aspiration will often extinguish a lighted match or move a strip of paper placed in front of the speaker's mouth. If the same speaker says **buy**, it will not noticeably affect the flame or the paper. Since /t/ and /k/ are articulated farther back in the mouth than /p/, the aspiration is harder to demonstrate visually than for /p/ but it is nonetheless present and salient.

In general, then, we can say that the voiced stop consonants are not aspirated whereas the voiceless stop consonants are. However, we need to further qualify this statement, since the occurrence of aspiration with /p, t, k/ depends on the position of the consonant within a word. Try saying the following words, in which /p, t, k/ occur word initially (column 1) and <u>at the beginning of a stressed syllable</u> (column 2):

	Column 1	**Column 2**
[pʰ]	peal	rePEAL
[tʰ]	test	deTEST
[kʰ]	kin	aKIN

Notice how the stop consonant is aspirated both at the beginning of the words in column 1 and at the beginning of the stressed (i.e., second) syllable in column 2.

Now compare the unaspirated [p] and [k] that occur at the beginning of unstressed syllables (column 1) with the aspirated [pʰ] and [kʰ] at the beginning of the stressed syllables (column 2) (the consonant /t/ will be discussed separately):

Column 1	**Column 2**
[p]	[pʰ]
opus	opPOSE
opal	apPALL

Column 1	**Column 2**
[k]	[kʰ]
REcord (n.)	reCORD (v.)
Ochre	ocCUR

Notice the aspiration when these stop consonants begin a stressed syllable.

We can further see this difference in aspiration when there is a stress shift due to a derivational ending, as in the following case:

    [p]   [pʰ]
    RApid   raPIDity

Again here, there is a noticeable difference between the unaspirated [p] in ***rapid*** and the aspirated [pʰ] in ***rapidity***—clear evidence of the role positional variation plays in determining the aspiration of voiceless stop consonants.

◆ **Allophones of /p/, /t/ or /k/**

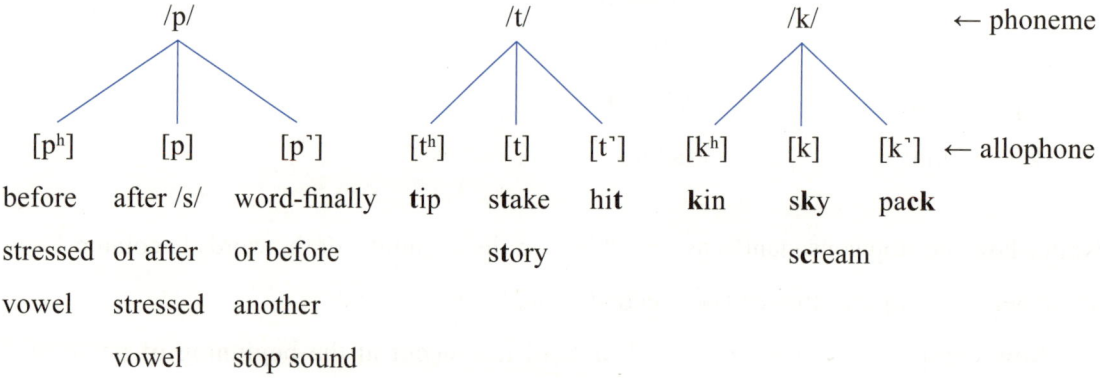

※ Allophones of /p/ are in complementary distribution.

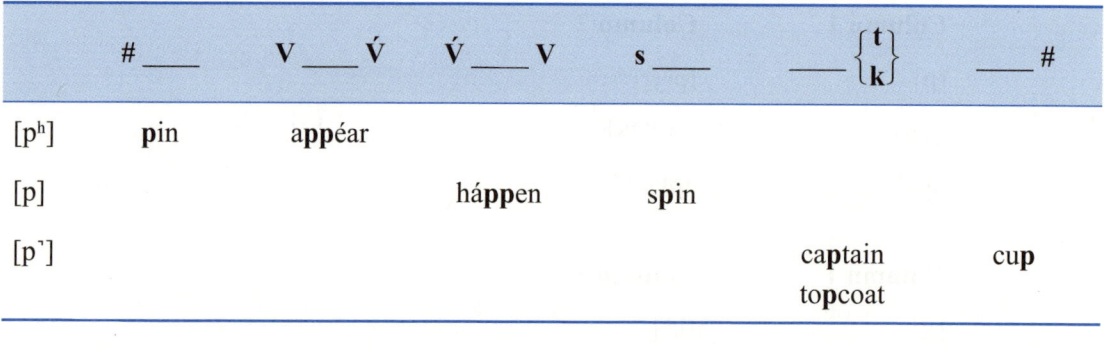

Aspiration Rule

$$\begin{bmatrix} +stop \\ -voice \end{bmatrix} \rightarrow [+aspirated] \: / \: \$ \underline{\qquad} \underset{[+stress]}{V}$$

2 Glottal Stop Replacement [Glottalization] '13, '15

> The glottal stop replacement can take place when the target /t/ is in a syllable-final position.

A glottal stop is the sound that occurs when the vocal cords are held tightly together. Consider the following.

(1) Batman [bæʔmæn]   atrocious [ətɹoʃəs] (not *[əʔɹoʃəs])
    Hitler [hɪʔlɚ]   attraction [ətɹækʃən] (not *[əʔɹækʃən])
    atlas [æʔləs]
    Atlanta [əʔlæntə]
    he hit me [hihɪʔmi]
    eat well [iʔwɛl]
    hot water [hɑʔwɑɾɚ]

In most speakers of American and British English (AE, BE), glottal stops or the preglottalized /t/ are commonly found as allophones of /t/ in words in the left column of (1). While the glottal stop can replace the /t/ in these words, it is not allowed in the right column words. The reason for this is that the glottal stop replacement requires the target /t/ to be in a syllable-final position ([bæʔ.mæn], [əʔ.læn.tə]). The words that do not allow the replacement have their /t/ in the onset position ([ə.tɹo.ʃəs], [ə.tɹæk.ʃən]), as /tɹ/ is a permissible onset in English.

The glottal stop replacement of syllable-final /t/ is also observable before syllabic nasals (e.g. beaten [biʔn̩], kitten [kɪʔn̩]).

◆ **Allophones of /t/**

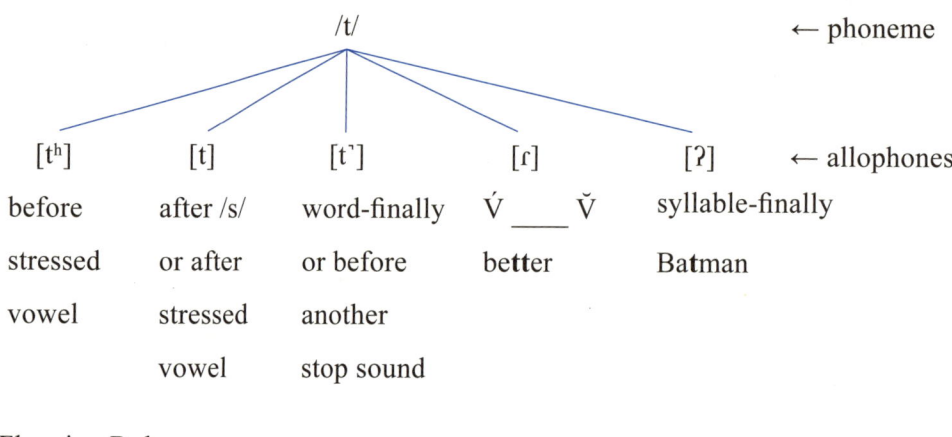

Flapping Rule

$\begin{Bmatrix} /t/ \\ /d/ \end{Bmatrix} \rightarrow [ɾ] / \acute{V} \underline{\quad} \check{V}$

3 Velar Nasal /ŋ/

While /ŋ/ is typically represented by the ng sequence orthographically, this is a unidirectional relationship. While some words with orthographic ng in the middle have the pronunciation /ŋ/ only, others will have /ŋg/. Morphology seems to be a factor. For example, while ng in the words in column A stands for /ŋg/, it stands for /ŋ/ in the words in column B.

A		B		C	
finger	[fɪŋgɚ]	singer	[sɪŋɚ]	sing	[sɪŋ]
mango	[mæŋgo]	hanger	[hæŋɚ]	hang	[hæŋ]
anger	[æŋgɚ]	wrongful	[ɹɔŋfʊl]		

The difference between the two groups of words is that while the former are monomorphemic words, the latter have two morphemes. There are, however, other monomorphemic words in column C in which ng stands for /ŋ/ ([sɪŋ], [hæŋ]). Thus, the generalization will have to be made in the following manner: the orthographic *ng* stands for /ŋ/ **at the end of a morpheme**, or when **inside a polymorphemic word**. Such a generalization will have one notable exception related to comparative and superlative suffixes. Contrast the two groups of words in column D and E below.

	D		**E**
long	[lɔŋ]	longer	[lɔŋɚ]
strong	[stɹɔŋ]	stronger	[stɹɔŋɡɚ]
		longest	[lɔŋɡəst]
		strongest	[stɹɔŋɡəst]

While adjectives such as ***long***, ***strong*** are pronounced with a /ŋ/ ([lɔŋ], [stɹɔŋ]), their comparatives and superlatives have /ŋg/ ([lɔŋɚ], [stɹɔŋɚ], and [lɔŋɡəst], [stɹɔŋɡəst]).

4 Clear l and Dark l '14, '19

We will consider the allophones of /l/, which shows the complementary distribution of clear [l] and dark [ɫ].

(1) clear l, #___   clear l, V___V   dark l, ___#

    lip [lɪp]   pillow [pɪ.loʊ]   pill [pɪɫ]

    lay [leɪ]   halo [heɪ.loʊ]   ale [eɪɫ]

    lean [lin]   kneeler [ni.lə]   kneel [niɫ]

We found [l] word-initially and between vowels, whereas [ɫ] occurs word-finally. Given the syllable boundaries, we can reformulate this generalization in such a way that it becomes much simpler: [l] occurs in syllable onsets, and [ɫ] occurs in codas. Interestingly, this formulation is not only shorter; it also makes strong and better predictions concerning the distribution of clear and dark l in contexts. Consider, for example, the words ***Hilton*** and ***poultry***, as well as ***Henley*** and ***hotly***. The contexts specified in (1) say nothing about which allophone of /l/ should appear here. But our syllable-based generalization does so: In ***Hilton*** and ***poultry***, /l/ is in coda position and should thus be realized as [ɫ]. In ***Henley*** and ***hotly***, by contrast, /l/ is in onset position and should thus be realized as [l].

(2) Syllabification and /l/ in **Hilton** and **poultry**

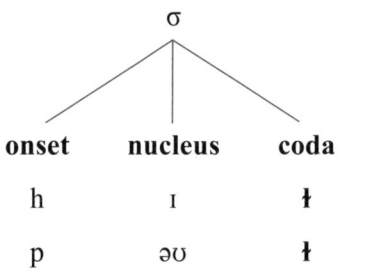 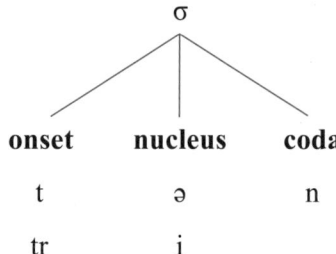

(3) Syllabification of /l/ in **Henley** and **hotly**

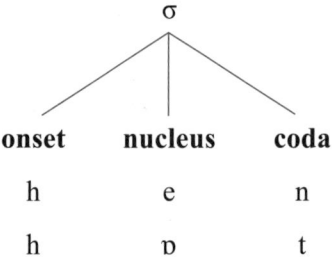 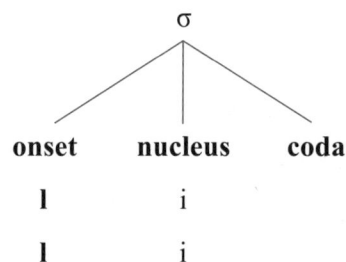

The rule that governs the distribution of clear and dark l has not only become simpler than the one that was postulated in (1), it has also become more comprehensive, covering all contexts in which /l/ can occur in English. In addition to the word-medial contexts discussed above, we can now also explain why dark [ɫ] appears in words like the following: *cold* [kəʊɫd], *realm* [reɫm], *elk* [eɫk]. Again our generalization from (1) says nothing about these words: /l/ is not word-final. By contrast, our syllable-based generalization predicts dark [ɫ] for the words—[ɫ] is in coda position in *cold*, *realm*, and *elk*.

(1) Velarized /l/ = dark [ɫ]

The data below show different realization of /l/ in different phonetic contexts.

(4)

#__	C[-voice]__V	V__V	__#
lip [lɪp]	clip [kl̥ɪp]	miller [mɪlə]	pill [pɪɫ]
lay [leɪ]	clay [kl̥eɪ]	silly [sɪli]	ale [eɪɫ]
lean [lin]	clean [kl̥in]	kneeler [nilə]	kneel [niɫ]

/l/ has three different realizations: [l], [l̥], and [ɫ]. The allophone [l] occurs in words like *lap*, i. e. at the beginning of words, whereas [l̥] occurs in words like *clap*, i.e. after voiceless consonants.

The third realization of /l/ found in (4), [ɫ], is what is called a **velarized** realization of /l/, also termed **dark l**. The non-velarized realization [l] is termed **clear l**. So before we consider the distribution of clear and dark l, let us clarify what the new variant, 'dark l', is. The terms 'clear l' and 'dark l' refer to the auditory impression of [l] and [ɫ], in that the latter somehow sounds darker. The term 'velarized l' refers to the articulatory properties of [ɫ], which may in fact be more helpful here. 'Velarized' comes from 'velum', which is, as you know, the very soft, back part of the so-called soft palate. But what has the velum, which is located far beyond the alveolar ridge, got to do with an l-sound, which is an alveolar sound? Figure 1 illustrates the answer to this question, by comparing the position of the tongue in clear and dark l.

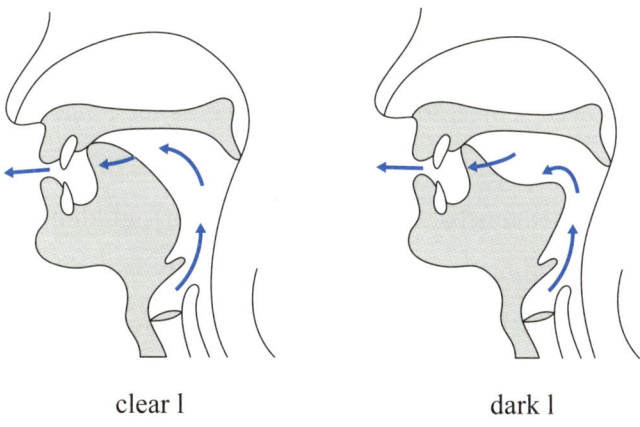

clear l   dark l

Figure 1. Clear l and dark l

You see that, whereas the tip of the tongue touches the alveolar ridge, the back of the tongue is still free to do something. So both [l] and [ɫ] are alveolar sounds. But during the production of [ɫ] the back of the tongue is raised towards the velum (which it does not touch). When producing 'clear l', by contrast, the back of the tongue is relaxed and remains in a lower position.

5 Syllabic Consonants

(1) Syllabic Nasals '07

Nasals, together with liquids, can be syllabic in English. In words such as **sudden**, **button**, **open**, **taken**, and **chasm**, the second syllables may be represented solely by nasal consonants ([sʌdn̩], [bʌtn̩], [opm̩], [tekŋ̩], [kæzm̩]). Although these forms are possible, and indeed are preferable over the ones with an [ə] in the second syllables in running speech, the same is not possible in words such as **felon**, **carom**, which are pronounced only as [fɛlən] and [kæɹəm] (not [fɛln̩] and [kæɹm̩]) respectively. Neither is it possible to have a syllabic nasal in **film** or **charm**. Why? The key issue appears to be the manner of articulation of the segment preceding the nasal. For a nasal to be syllabic, it has to be immediately preceded by an obstruent. Since the segments preceding the nasal in **film** and **charm** are sonorants, the nasals cannot be syllabic. It should also be stated that when the consonant preceding the nasal is preceded by another consonant, the nasal tends not to be syllabic, as we normally insert an [ə] in that syllable, as exemplified by **piston** [pɪstən] not [pɪstn̩], **Lincoln** [lɪŋkən] not [lɪŋkn̩].

One issue that has been subject to some controversy is the homorganicity of the syllabic nasal and the preceding obstruent. The overwhelming majority of examples of syllabic nasals come from **homorganic** sequences such as **bidden** [bɪdn̩], **golden** [goldn̩], **Latin** [lætn̩], **kitten** [kɪtn̩], etc. Indeed, the motivation for **homorganicity** is further revealed by examples such as **ribbon** [ɹɪbən] vs. [ɹɪbm̩], **open** [opən] vs. [opm̩], **bacon** [bekən] vs. [bekŋ̩], **broken** [brokən] vs. [brokŋ̩], in which the syllabic nasal assimilates to the place of articulation of the preceding obstruent in colloquial speech. While these examples support the homorganicity view, it should be pointed out that we can also encounter words such as **madam** [mædm̩] and **modem** [modm̩] with [dm̩], and **chasm** [kæzm̩] and **prism** [pɹɪzm̩] with [zm̩], which present notable exceptions, because their syllabic nasals are not homorganic with the preceding obstruent, and they are not subject to further assimilation to become *[mædn̩] *[modn̩], *[kæzn̩], *[pɹɪzn̩].

(2) Syllabic Liquids '09 Choice

The liquids, /l, r/, differ from the glides in one important respect: they can be syllabic in English. The conducive environment for the syllabicity of the liquids is similar, but not identical, to that of the nasals we examined earlier. Nasals required an obstruent as the preceding segment to become syllabic, while liquids can accept any consonant for this condition. For example, in words such as **channel** [tʃænl̩], **kennel** [kɛnl̩], the final syllable has the syllabic liquid after a sonorant consonant. Also worth mentioning is the lack of the requirement of homorganicity between the syllabic liquids and the preceding consonant. Unlike nasals, which overwhelmingly require homorganicity with the preceding obstruent, syllabic liquids have the freedom to occur after consonants with different places of articulation, as exemplified by **apple** [æpl̩], **removal** [ɹəmuvl̩], **pickle** [pɪkl̩], **eagle** [igl̩].

We should also add, in parallel to what was said in relation to nasals, that whenever the consonant that precedes the lateral is preceded by another consonant, we normally insert an [ə] between the liquid and the consonant preceding it, and thus, the liquid does not become syllabic. Examples such as **pistol** [pɪstəl] not [pɪstl̩], **tingle** [tɪŋgəl] not [tɪŋgl̩], and **candle** [kændəl] not [kændl̩] illustrate this clearly.

◆ Summary

Syllabic Nasals	Syllabic Liquids
① For a nasal to be syllabic, it has to be immediately preceded by an obstruent.	① A syllabic liquid can accept any consonant for its immediately preceding consonant.
② When the consonant preceding the nasal is preceded by another consonant, the nasal tends not to be syllabic, as we normally insert an [ə] in that syllable. e.g. **piston** [pɪstən] not [pɪstn̩], **Lincoln** [lɪŋkən]	② the same e.g. **pistol** [pɪstəl], **tingle** [tɪŋgəl], **candle** [kændəl]
③ the homorganicity of the syllabic nasal and the preceding obstruent e.g. **bidden, golden, Latin, kitten ribbon** [ɹibm̩], **open** [opm̩], **bacon** [bekŋ̩], **broken** [brokŋ̩] exceptions) madam, modem, chasm, prism	③ lack of the requirement of homorganicity e.g. **apple** [æpl̩], **removal** [ɹəmuvl̩], **pickle** [pɪkl̩], **eagle** [igl̩]

06 Syllables

1 The Syllable Structure '14 (rhyme), '15 (onset), '18 (onset)

The syllable is composed of a nucleus (usually a vowel) and its associated nonsyllabic segments. Native speakers of a language demonstrate their awareness of this unit of phonological structure whenever they count syllables in a word. No English speaker would hesitate to say that the word *accident* has three syllables, and most speakers would feel confident that it could be broken up into the syllables /æk.sə.dənt/ (the '.' marks syllable divisions informally).

Speakers also demonstrate knowledge that syllables have internal structure as well. The organization of a syllable is shown in Figure 2 with the monosyllabic English word *sprint*.

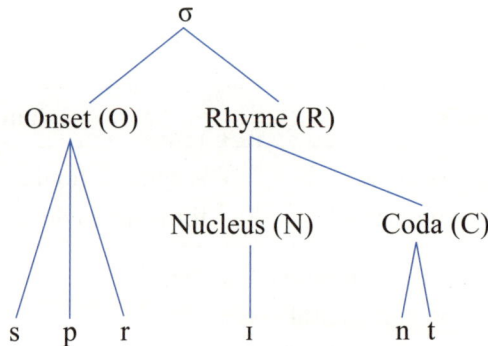

Figure 2. Internal structure of a syllable

A complete description of the internal structure of a syllable requires four subsyllabic units. The **nucleus** (abbreviated **N**) is the syllable's only obligatory member; it is a syllabic element that forms the core of a syllable. The **coda** (**C**) consists of those elements that follow the nucleus in the same syllable. The **rhyme** (**R**) is made up of the nucleus and coda. The **onset** (**O**) is made up of those elements that precede the rhyme in the same syllable.

2 Sonority Sequencing Principle (SSP) '13 Choice

The nature of the syllabic nucleus, and indeed the order of segments within the syllable as a whole, is in part governed by the notion of **sonority**. Every speech sound has a degree of sonority, which is determined by factors like its loudness in relation to other sounds, the extent to which it can be prolonged, and the degree of stricture in the vocal tract: the more sonorant a sound, the louder, more sustainable and more open it is. Voicing is also relevant here, in that voiced sounds are more sonorant than voiceless ones. In acoustic terms, sonority is related to formant patterns; the more sonorant a sound, the clearer, more distinct its formant structure. Based on these definitions, the most sonorant sounds are low vowels like [ɑ]; the least sonorant class is the voiceless stops, e.g. [t]. Speech sounds can be arranged on a scale of relative sonority, known as the **sonority hierarchy**, as shown below:

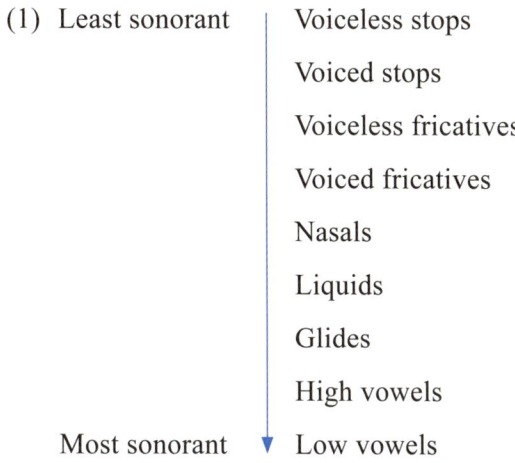

(1) Least sonorant — Voiceless stops
Voiced stops
Voiceless fricatives
Voiced fricatives
Nasals
Liquids
Glides
High vowels
Most sonorant — Low vowels

This scale has an important role to play in determining the selection of the nucleus of a syllable and the order of segments within the onset and coda.

In general, the most sonorous sounds are selected as syllabic nuclei, with sonority increasing within the onset, and decreasing within the coda. This means that the nucleus forms a high point of sonority (hence the alternative term 'peak' for nucleus), with the margins (onset and coda) as slopes of sonority falling away on either side. So the English syllable 'crank' might be represented graphically as

(2)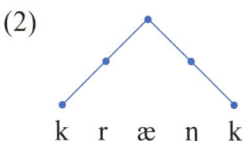

k r æ ŋ k

This idea of rising then falling sonority within the syllable helps explain certain cross-linguistic phonotactic restrictions. For instance, the reason that a sequence like [rkækŋ]) is impossible as a *single* syllable in English (or any other language) is that what would be the onset shows falling sonority, [r] being more sonorant than [k], and the coda shows increasing sonority, [k] being less sonorant than [ŋ].

It should be borne in mind, however, that not all phonotactic statements can be ascribed to sonority violations. For example, the ban on word-initial *[kn] in English has nothing to do with sonority, since the sequence adheres to the principle of rising sonority within the onset, and is perfectly acceptable in languages like Danish or German; its ungrammaticality is simply an arbitrary fact about English, unrelated to sonority.

On the other hand, it is clear that the sonority hierarchy is not always conformed to within syllables: it is possible in many languages to find acceptable syllables in which the segments in the onset or coda are in the 'wrong' order. So, for example, English has words like 'stoat' and 'skunk', with a fricative before a stop in the onset, i.e. *falling* sonority; and the codas in 'fox' and 'adze' exhibit *rising* sonority, with stop before fricative. Similarly, German allows words such as **Sprache** 'language' with initial [ʃp] or **Strauss** 'ostrich' with initial [ʃt]. While such forms are clearly counter to any generalization based on sonority, they do appear to form a specific set of exceptions, in that they don't seem to involve just any random sequences of segments; the segment which is 'out of place' is typically a member of the class known as the *sibilant* fricatives [s, z, ʃ, ʒ].

◆ **Summary**

The sonority hierarchy

high sonority   *low sonority*

Vowels > Glides > Liquids > Nasals > Fricatives > Stops

                  Affricates

example sounds: [a, i]   [w, j]   [l, r]   [m, n]   [f, s]   [p, t]

Sonority Sequencing Principle (SSP)

Onset consonants rise in sonority towards the nucleus.

Coda consonants fall in sonority away from the nucleus.

(That is, the sonority has to fall toward both edges of the syllable).

3 Syllabification

While the sonority hierarchy is useful in deciding the internal organization of syllables, it is less helpful when it comes to deciding where one syllable ends and another begins. If we represent a polysyllabic word like 'parrot' in terms of a sonority graph, as we did with 'crank' in (2) above, we get the following:

(3)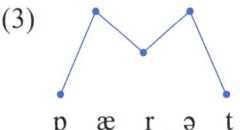
p æ r ə t

While this successfully identifies two sonority peaks at [æ] and [ə], and thus indicates that there are two syllables, it does not tell us where the boundary between them falls. We can surmise that the medial [r] is on the boundary, since it constitutes a sonority trough, but we cannot tell whether it is in the coda of the first syllable or the onset of the second.

To determine the location of the boundary, we need to appeal to the **Maximal Onset Principle**. Some languages insist on the presence of an onset, and no languages require the presence of a coda. This can be interpreted as indicating that languages prefer onsets — that they are in some sense 'more important' than codas. What this means for syllable boundary placement (syllabification) is that where possible, consonants should be syllabified in onsets rather than codas. So, in the 'parrot' example in (3) the boundary comes *before* the [r], which thus forms the onset of the second syllable. Interestingly, this division generally corresponds to native speakers' intuitions about where the boundary should lie.

Now consider the pair of words 'plastic' and 'frantic'; where is the boundary between the first and second syllables in these words? The word 'plastic' is straightforward; the Maximal Onset Principle predicts that both the [s] and the [t] will be in the onset of the second syllable:

'pla.stic'. But with 'frantic' most speakers would agree that the boundary is between the two consonants: 'fran.tic'. This is because medial clusters can only be assigned to onsets to the extent that such sequences are possible word-initially in the language in question. In English, [st] is a possible word-initial cluster, as in 'stag', but *[nt] is not; there are no words beginning with [nt] in English. This means that the Maximal Onset Principle does not apply blindly, assigning all medial consonants to onsets, but takes into account language-specific phonotactic restrictions on permitted onsets. Any medial consonants which cannot be part of a licit word-initial sequence are assigned to the coda of the preceding syllable, as with the [n] in 'frantic' above, or the [k] in 'extra' [ɛk.strə] (since while [str] is a permitted initial sequence (as in 'string'), *[kstr] is not). It may be the case that more than one of the medial consonants must be assigned to the preceding coda, as in 'ant.ler', since English allows neither *[ntl] or *[tl] initially.

4 Phonotactics '09 Choice

Phonotactics, the set of constraints on how sequences of segments pattern, forms part of a speaker's knowledge of the phonology of his or her language.

(1) Onset constraints

The following table contains examples of the possible syllable-initial consonant sequences of English that contain a voiceless stop consonant. These sequences are all illustrated in word-initial position to make them easier to pick out.

Table 1. Initial consonant clusters in English containing a voiceless stop

Labial + liquid or glide		Alveolar + liquid or glide		Velar + liquid or glide	
[pl]	please	[tl]	—	[kl]	clean
[pr]	proud	[tr]	trade	[kr]	cream
[pw]	—	[tw]	twin	[kw]	queen
[pj]	pure	[tj]	tune	[kj]	cute
[spl]	splat	[stl]	—	[skl]	sclerosis
[spr]	spring	[str]	strip	[skr]	scrap
[spw]	—	[stw]	—	[skw]	squeak
[spj]	spew	[stj]	stew	[skj]	skewer

The examples in Table 1 show that the first segment of a word-initial three consonant cluster in English is always *s*; the second consonant in the series is always a voiceless stop, and the third is either a liquid or a glide. These sound patterns can be formally represented as follows:

$$\sigma\,[s\ \begin{Bmatrix} p \\ t \\ k \end{Bmatrix}\ \begin{Bmatrix} (l) \\ r \\ (w) \\ j \end{Bmatrix}$$

In this formalization, σ indicates the boundary of a syllable, and the curly braces designate 'either/or'. The sounds in parentheses are not found in all combinations. An important observation about the types of onsets that are allowed in English is that the consonant combinations are not random: sonorant consonants (here liquids and glides) are closer to the nucleus than are stops and fricatives.

5 Accidental and systematic gaps

Some gaps in the inventory of possible English words include **snool**, **splick**, **sklop**, **fliss**, **trock**, and **kriff**, although none of these forms violates any constraints on onset combinations found in English. Gaps in a language's inventory of forms that correspond to nonoccurring but possible forms are called **accidental gaps**. Occasionally, an accidental gap will be filled in by the invention of a new word. The word **Kodak** is one such invented word. Borrowed words such as **perestroika** (from Russian), **taco** (from Spanish), and **Zen** (from Japanese) are readily accepted by English speakers as long as their syllable structures conform to the phonotactic patterns of the language.

Table 1 has shown which syllable-initial consonant clusters involving voiceless stops are permissible in English. Gaps in the occurring syllable structures of a language that result from the exclusion of certain sequences are called **systematic gaps**. Certain onset sequences like /bz/, /pt/, and /fp/ are systematic gaps in the pattern of English. They are outright unacceptable to English speakers, and never occur in spoken English. Instead, such sequences will be adjusted phonologically when they are pronounced in spontaneous speech. This can be seen in the case of borrowings from other languages into English. Many Greek words beginning with **ps-** and **pt-** have been absorbed into English, as the spellings of **psychology**, **psoriasis**, and **pterodactyl** attest. In all of them, the impermissible syllable-initial clusters ***ps-** and ***pt-** have been reduced to **s-** or **t-** onsets of spoken English.

◆ gaps

accidental gaps	systematic gaps
= possible words (comply with phonological/morphological rules)	= impossible words (violate phonological/morphological rules)
blick	*bnick

07 Stress '03, '05, '07, '08, '10, '16, '17, '18, '19, '21

Syllable names		
antepenult **antepenultimate**	**penult** **penultimate**	**ult** ultimate (✕)
third syllable from the last	second syllable from the last	the last syllable the final syllable

1 Word Stress '07, '08, '18

There are some general rules, as in (1), which do allow stress placement to be predicted in many English words.

(1) a. Noun rule: stress the penultimate syllable if heavy.

　　　　　　　　If the penultimate syllable is light, stress the antepenult.

　　　　　　　　a.ró.ma　　　a.gén.da　　　dí.sci.pline

　　b. Verb rule: stress the final syllable if heavy.

　　　　　　　　If the final syllable is light, stress the penultimate syllable.

　　　　　　　　o.béy　　　u.súrp　　　a.tóne　　　tá.lly　　　hú.rry

These stress rules depend crucially on the weight of the syllable: a syllable will be heavy if it has a branching rhyme, composed of either a long vowel or diphthong, with or without a coda, or a short vowel with a coda. A syllable with a short vowel and no coda will be light. As (1a) shows, English nouns typically have stress on the penultimate syllable, so long as that syllable is heavy, which it is in *aroma* (with a long [o:] vowel or a diphthong [oʊ] depending on your accent), and in *agenda*, where the relevant vowel is short [ɛ], but followed by a consonant, [n]; this must be in the coda of syllable two rather than the onset of syllable three, since there are no *[nd] initial clusters in English. However, in *discipline* the penultimate syllable is light [sɪ]; the following [pl] consonants can both be in the onset of the third syllable, since there are initial clusters of this type in *play*, *plant*, *plastic* and so on. Since [sɪ] has only a short vowel and no coda consonants, it fails to attract stress by the Noun Rule, and the stress instead falls on the previous, initial syllable.

A similar pattern can be found for verbs, but with stress falling consistently one syllable further to the right. That is, the Verb Rule preferentially stresses final syllables, so long as these are heavy. So, **obey** (with a final long vowel or diphthong), has final stress, as do **usurp** (having a final syllable [ʌrp], with a short vowel and two coda consonants), and **atone** (with a long vowel or diphthong plus a consonant in the coda). However, both **tally** and **hurry** have final light syllables, in each case consisting only of a short vowel in the rhyme. It follows that these cannot attract stress, which again falls in these cases one syllable further left.

2 Suffixes & Stress '10 Choice, '16

Since the addition of prefixes does not change word stress, our presentation will be on the varying effects of suffixes on word stress. We can classify the suffixes as:

(a) stress-bearing (attracting) suffixes;

(b) stress-shifting (fixing) suffixes;

(c) stress-neutral suffixes.

(1) Stress-bearing (attracting) suffixes

These suffixes attract stress. Below are some common derivational suffixes:

-ade	lémon–lemonáde
-aire	míllion–millionaíre
-ation	réalize–realizátion '16
-ee	ábsent–absentée (exception: commíttee)
-eer	móuntain–mountainéer '16
-ese	Japán–Japanése
-esque	pícture–picturésque '16
-ette	kítchen–kitchenétte
-itis	lárynx–laryngítis
-ific	hónor–honorífic

Expectedly, these stress-bearing suffixes always constitute heavy syllables. The items above with suffixes should not be confused with the same/similar-looking monomorphemic forms such as ***brigade, jamboree, grotesque, brunette, bursitis,*** etc.

(2) Stress-neutral suffixes

These suffixes never make any difference to the stress pattern of the resulting word. Such suffixes include all eight inflectional suffixes (plural; possessive; third person singular present tense <u>-s</u>; progressive <u>-ing</u>; past <u>-ed</u>; past participle <u>-en</u>/<u>-ed</u>; comparative <u>-er</u>; and superlative <u>-est</u>), and several derivational ones:

-al	arríve–arríval
-ant	ascénd–ascéndant '16
-cy	célibate–célibacy
-dom	frée–frédom
-er	pláy–pláyer
-ess	líon–líoness
-ful	gráce–gráceful
-hood	nátion–nátionhood '16
-ish	gréen–gréenish
-ism	álcohol–álcoholism
-ist	húman–húmanist
-ive	submít–submíssive
-ize	spécial–spécialize
-less	bóttom–bóttomless
-ly	fríend–fríendly
-ment	aménd–améndment
-ness	fránk–fránkness '16
-ship	fríend–fríendship
-some	búrden–búrdensome
-wise	clóck–clóckwise
-th	grów–grówth
-ty	cértain–cértainty

-y   sílk–sílky '16

We should point out that the last item, adjective-forming suffix -y, should not be treated in the same way as the noun-forming -y, which shifts the stress to the antepenultimate, as in homophone–homophony, photograph–photography, etc.

 While the above-listed suffixes do not normally change the location of the stress, when several unstressed syllables are piled up to the right of the stress, we see that the stress moves to the antepenult.

móment–mómentary *but* momentárily

(3) Stress-shifting (fixing) suffixes '10 Choice, '16

 A multiplicity of derivational suffixes, when added to a root, shift the stress from its original position **to the syllable immediately preceding the suffix**. Below are some of the common ones in this group:

-ean	Áristotle–Aristotélian
-ial	súbstance–substántial '10 Choice
-ian	líbrary–librárian
-ical	geómetry–geométrical
-icide	ínsect–insécticide '10 Choice
-ic	périod–periódic (exceptions: Árabic, lúnatic)
-ify	pérson–persónify
-ious	lábor–labórious '10 Choice
-ity	húmid–humídity
-ometer	spéed–speedómeter
-ual	cóntext–contéxtual '10 Choice
-ous	móment–moméntous
-y	hómonym–homónymy '10 Choice, '16

We need to point out that if the original stress is on the last syllable of the root (the syllable immediately before the suffix), no change in location of the stress will result, because it is already where it should be (e.g. divérse–divérsify, absúrd–absúrdity, obése–obésity).

There is also a group of suffixes that put the stress on the syllable immediately before them if that syllable is heavy (i.e. has branching rhyme). The suffix *-al* in refusal, recital, and accidental is an example of this phenomenon. **The stress falls on the syllable that is immediately before the suffix, because that syllable is heavy** (long vowel, diphthong, and closed syllable, respectively). However, **if the syllable in question is not heavy, then the stress moves one more syllable to the left** (e.g. séasonal, práctical). The same is observable in the suffix *-ency* of emérgency and consístency on the one hand, and présidency and cómpetency on the other. While in the first two words the stress is on the syllable immediately before the suffix (closed syllable), it falls on the syllable one more position to the left in the last two words because the syllable before the suffix is light.

It is worth pointing out that there are some other endings that seem to vacillate between the different suffix types, of which *-able* is a good example. This suffix behaves like stress-neutral suffixes in most cases, as in quéstion–quéstionable, adóre–adórable, mánage–mánageable. However, in several disyllabic stems with final stress, it shifts the stress one syllable left (to stem-initial), as in admíre–ádmirable, compáre–cómparable, prefér–préferable. To complicate things further, *-able* may also shift the stress one syllable to the right, as in démonstrate–demónstrable.

Another interesting case is the *-ive* suffix. When added to a monosyllabic root, the stress, expectedly, is on the root (*-ive* cannot bear stress) as in áct–áctive. However, in words with three or more syllables, we may see the stress falling on the syllable before it (e.g. decísive, offénsive), or moving one more to the left (e.g. négative, sédative), or even to one further left (e.g. génerative, méditative).

3 Sentence Stress [Tonic Accent] '00

> **(Major) Sentence Stress [Tonic Accent]**
> ① The major sentence stress falls on **the last content word** within a sentence.
> ② The major sentence stress is placed on **the information focus** of the sentence.
> ③ The major sentence stress falls on **the contrasted element**.

(1) Content vs. Function Words

For students to produce sentences that have the appropriate stress patterns and thus the appropriate English rhythm, it is necessary that they know which words of a sentence are stressed and which are not stressed.

English words can be divided into two groups: **content words** and **function words**. Content words are those words that express independent meaning. Included in this group are:

1. Nouns
2. Main Verbs
3. Adjectives
4. Adverbs
5. Question Words (e.g. why, when, what)
6. Demonstratives (this, that, these, those)

Content words are usually stressed.

Function words are words that have little or no meaning in themselves, but which express grammatical relationships. Function words include:

1. Pronouns (e.g. her, him, it, them)
2. Conjunctions (e.g. and, or, as, that)
3. Prepositions (e.g. at, to, of)
4. Articles (e.g. a, an, the)
5. Auxiliaries (e.g. will, have, be)
6. Relative pronouns (e.g. that, which, who)

Function words are usually unstressed, unless they are to be given special attention.

(2) Placement of main stress in sentences

While all content words receive major word stress, one content word within a particular sentence will receive greater stress than all the others. We refer to this as the **major sentence stress**. In most cases the major sentence stress falls on the last content word within a sentence. Consider the pronunciation of the sentences below:

    Susan bought a new sweater at Creeds.

    I walked home in the rainstorm.

    Peter likes your suggestion.

In each of these sentences, the stressed syllable of the final content word receives the major sentence stress.

    With individual words, we distinguished between three levels of stress: major, minor, and unstress. With sentences, we must distinguish between four levels of stress: major sentence stress, major word stress, minor word stress, and unstress. Thus, in the sentence 'I walked home in the rainstorm', 'I', 'in', and 'the' are function words and are unstressed; 'walked', 'home', and 'rainstorm' are content words and receive major word stress; and 'rainstorm', in addition, receives the major sentence stress. As 'rain' is the syllable of this content word that receives major word stress, it is also the syllable receives major sentence stress. This makes 'rain' both louder and longer than 'walked' and 'home'. Since 'rainstorm' is a compound, 'storm' receives minor word stress.

    In some cases, major sentence stress will not fall on the major stressed syllable of the final content word of a sentence. That is, when a speaker wishes to direct the hearer's attention to some other content word in the sentence, this word will receive major sentence stress. Consider the following dialogue:

Speaker A   What did you buy at Creeds?

Speaker B   I bought a new sweater at Creeds.

Notice that the second sentence does not receive major sentence stress on 'Creeds', but rather on the stressed syllable of 'sweater'. This is the element of the sentence that Speaker B is directing Speaker A's attention to. We call this element the *information focus* of the sentence. Generally, it is the stressed syllable of the content word representing information focus that receives major sentence stress. Most often, the information focus occurs at the end of a sentence. Indeed, a more natural response to Speaker A's question above would be: 'I bought a new sweater', or simply 'A new sweater'.

(3) Contrastive stress

It is also possible for major sentence stress to function contrastively. Consider the following short dialogues. In the first, the contrast takes the form of a contradiction. In the second, the contrast takes the form of a choice between alternatives. (We use capital letters to represent contrastive stress.)

Speaker A	I hear that Susan bought another second-hand sweater.
Speaker B	No, she bought a NEW sweater.
Speaker A	Did Susan buy a new sweater or a second-hand one?
Speaker B	She bought a NEW sweater.

We might expect the major sentence stress in Speaker B's responses to fall on 'sweater' because it is the final content word of both sentences. However, notice that it is the contrasted information in Speaker B's responses that receives major sentence stress, i.e., the fact that the sweater is new. This contrastive stress can be even heavier and louder than the normal major sentence stress, particularly in sentences where a contradiction is being made.

4 Emphatic Stress '05

Compare these sentences:

(1) / Harry studied painting in **Pa**ris, / **too**. /

(2) / Harry studied **pain**ting in Paris, / **too**. /

(3) / Harry **stu**died painting in Paris, / **too**. /

(4) / **Ha**rry studied painting in Paris, / **too**. / '05

What is the meaning of *too* (or *also*)? Its 'meaning' is to indicate that what has been said previously with the use of one word or term applies as well with the use of another word of the same part of speech, the accented word in the tone unit which *too* follows. The first sentence, then, emphasizes that Harry studied painting in Paris as well as in some other place; the second sentence says that Harry studied painting as well as some other, previously mentioned subject; the third tells us that Harry studied painting in addition to some other activity connected with painting; and the fourth that Harry, as well as some other person or persons, studied painting in Paris.

5 Stress Shift

Poetry also provides an excellent illustration of the English preference for alternating stress. It does not especially matter whether we have sequences of SWSWSWSW, or SWWSWWSWWSWW; but what does matter is avoiding either lapses, where too many unstressed syllables intervene between stresses, or clashes, where stresses are adjacent, with no unstressed syllables in between at all. The English process of Iambic Reversal seems designed precisely to avoid **stress clashes** of this kind. It affects combinations of words which would, in isolation, have final stress on the first word, and initial stress on the second. For instance, (1) shows that the citation forms (that is, the formal speech pronunciation of a word alone, rather than in a phrase) of *thirteen* and *champagne* have final stress.

(1) A: How many people turned up?
    B: ˌThirˈteen.
    A: What are you drinking?
    B: ˌChamˈpagne.

However, when final-stressed words like *thirteen* and *champagne* form phrases with initial-stressed ones like *players* or *cocktails*, the stress on the first word in each phrase moves to the left, so that in ˈthirˌteen ˈplayers and ˈchamˌpange ˈcocktails, both words have initial stress. This is clearly related to the preference of English speakers for eurhythmic alternation of stronger and weaker syllables, as illustrated in (2).

(2) W S   S W   S W   S W
   thirteen   players   →   thirteen   players

     W S   S W   S W   S W
   champagne cocktails   →   champagne cocktails

If these words retained their normal stress pattern once embedded in the phrases, we would find clashing sequences of WSSW, as shown on the left of (2), in violation of eurhythmy; consequently, the prominence pattern of the first word is reversed, changing from an iamb to a trochee—hence the name Iambic Reversal. The result is a sequence of two trochaic feet, giving SWSW and ideal stress alternation.

6 Foot '05, '21

The normally accepted definition is that <u>each phonological foot starts with a stressed syllable, and continues up to, but not including, the next stressed syllable</u>. This means that ***cat in a hat*** consists of two feet, the first containing ***cat in a***, and the second, ***hat***. Although ***cat flap*** consists of only two words (or indeed one, if we agree this is a compound), as opposed to four in ***cat in a hat***, it also consists of two feet, this time one for each syllable, since both ***cat*** and ***flap*** bear some degree of stress. Indeed, because English is a stress-timed language, allowing approximately the same amount of time to produce each foot (as opposed to syllable-timed languages, like French, which devote about the same amount of time to each syllable regardless of stress), ***cat in a hat*** and ***cat flap*** will have much the same phonetic duration. The same goes for ***the cat sat on the mat***, with rather few unstressed syllables between the stressed ones, and ***as snug as a bug in a rug***, with a regular pattern of two unstressed syllables to each stress. This isochrony of feet, whereby feet last for much the same time regardless of the number of syllables in them, is responsible for the characteristic rhythm of English.

Like syllables, feet can also be contrasted as stronger and weaker. Sometimes, there will be more than one foot to the word; for instance, a word like ˈ***raider***, with primary stress on the first syllable and no stress on the second, can be opposed to ˈ***raˌdar***, with primary versus secondary stress. It is not possible to capture this distinction using only syllable-based trees, since both **raider** and **radar** have a stronger first syllable and a weaker second syllable. However, these two W nodes are to be interpreted in two different ways, namely as indicating no stress in **raider**, but secondary stress in **radar**. To clarify the difference, we must recognize the foot. **Raider** then has a single foot, while **radar** has two, the first S and the second W. Recall that small sigma (σ) indicates a syllable, and capital sigma (Σ), a foot.

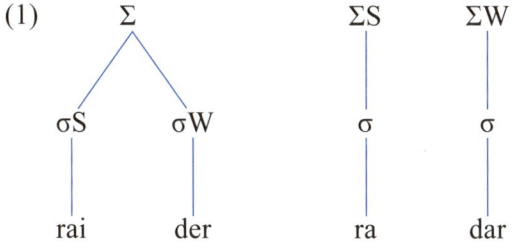

In other cases, the same number of feet may be spread over more than, one word, so that ˈcat ˌflap has two feet, related as S versus W, while ˌcat in a ˈhat also has two feet, although here the first foot is larger, including **in a** as well as **cat**, and the prominence relationship of W S reflects the fact that **cat flap** is a compound bearing initial primary stress, while **cat in a hat** is a phrase, with main stress towards the end.

7 Full Forms and Reduced Forms

◆ The Pronunciation of Function Words '06

When function words are spoken in isolation, they are stressed; that is, they are pronounced in their strong form. In connected speech, where function words are normally unstressed, they are pronounced in their weak form. In the following list of words, compare the pronunciation of the strong forms to the pronunciation of the weak forms.

	Strong form	Weak form
can	[kæn]	[kən]
will	[wɪl]	[wəl], [əl]
have	[hæv]	[əv], [v]

to	[tu]	[tə]
he	[hi]	[i]
them	[ðɛm]	[ðəm], [əm]
and	[ænd]	[ən], [n]

Below we list the specific ways in which strong forms of function words are modified in connected speech.

(1) The vowel is reduced to schwa in function words such as 'to', 'them', 'the', 'a', 'and', 'as', and 'of'.

Give them a break.	[gɪv əm ə breɪk]
A cup of coffee.	[ə kʌp əv kafi]
He went to the store.	[hi wɛnt tə ðə stor]
Apples and oranges.	[æpəlz ənd orəndʒəz]
As sweet as sugar.	[əz swit əz ʃʊgər]

(2) An initial consonant can be lost, as with the pronouns 'he', 'him', 'her', and 'them'.

I watched them last night.	[aɪ wɑtʃt əm læst naɪt]
I watched her do it.	[aɪ wɑtʃt ər du ɪt]
Where did he go?	[wɛr dɪd i goʊ]
Have you seen him today?	[hæv yu sin əm tədeɪ]

(3) Some function words lose their final consonants. This is particularly true of 'of' and 'and'.

A cup of coffee.	[ə kʌp ə kafi]
Now and then.	[naʊ ən ðɛn]
A lot of nonsense.	[ə lɑt ə nɑnsɛns]
Cream and sugar.	[krim ən ʃʊgər]

08 Intonation '04, '08, '12 Choice

1 What is intonation?

Intonation is often called the melody of language since it refers to the pattern of ***pitch*** changes that we use when we speak. If you listen to someone speaking, you will notice that there are many changes in pitch. These pitch changes are called ***intonation patterns*** [***pitch contour***] and play an important role in conveying meaning. Languages that use pitch to signal a difference in meaning between words are referred to as tone languages. English does not use pitch in this way. Nevertheless, pitch changes do contribute significantly to the meaning of English sentences. These changes in pitch in English occur over entire clauses or sentences and different pitch patterns can signal very different meanings for the same sentence.

In the following sections, we introduce some of the basic intonation patterns of English. We represent these patterns with arrows.

2 Final intonation '12 Choice

(1) Rising-falling intonation

Listen to yourself when you say the following sentence:

Susan bought a new sweater.

Notice that the pitch of your voice rises at the major sentence stress, the first syllable of the word 'sweater', and falls over the second syllable of this word. The pitch of the entire sentence is referred to as the ***intonation pattern***. The pattern in this sentence is ***rising-falling***. It is the most common intonation pattern in English and is characteristic of simple <u>declarative sentences</u>, <u>commands</u> and <u>questions that begin with a **wh**-word</u>, such as 'who', 'what', 'when', 'where', 'why', or 'how'. Say the sentences below, concentrating on the pitch change at the word receiving major sentence stress.

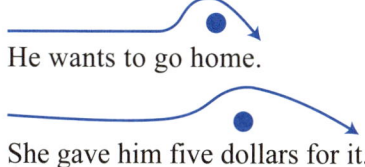
He wants to go home.

She gave him five dollars for it.

Give her a sweater.

What do you want to do with it?

In each case, the pitch rises at the major sentence stress and falls over the remaining part of the sentence. This descent in pitch can be rather abrupt, especially when it must be accomplished over just one syllable as is the case with 'home' in the first sentence. When the voice falls to the bottom of the pitch range, it usually indicates that the speaker has finished speaking.

(2) Rising intonation

Listen to the pitch of your voice when you say the following sentence:

Did Susan buy a new sweater?

Notice again that the pitch of your voice rises at the major sentence stress. However, rather than a sharp decline in pitch level after the stressed syllable, as with the rising-falling intonation pattern, the voice continues to rise. The intonation pattern in this case is ***rising*** and is characteristic of questions that require a simple yes or no answer.

In order to familiarize yourself with this pattern, say the following sentences, concentrating on the pitch of your voice. We represent this intonation pattern with a rising arrow.

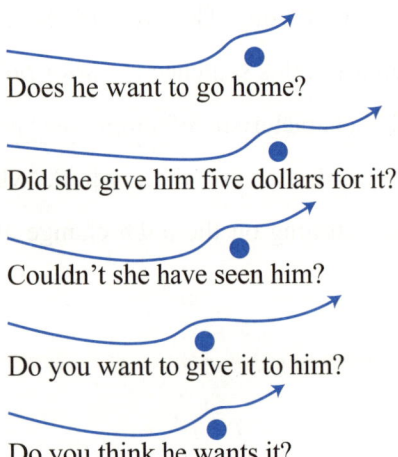

Does he want to go home?

Did she give him five dollars for it?

Couldn't she have seen him?

Do you want to give it to him?

Do you think he wants it?

This intonation contour is used to express doubt. That is, the speaker is not sure what the answer to the question is and would like the information supplied. We can turn a simple statement into a yes/no question through the use of rising intonation. For example, if we say:

John left town.

with a rising intonation, we are not making a statement. We are expressing some doubt regarding the truth of the statement, indicating to the listener that a response is required. Thus, we can see that intonation patterns can contribute to sentence meaning in English.

3 Non-final intonation

(1) Rising-falling intonation

Complex sentences often have two separate intonation patterns. An example of such a sentence is provided below.

   Because of his athletic ability, he was given a scholarship.

Here the pitch rises and falls on the word 'ability', and also on the word 'scholarship'. On 'scholarship', the pitch drifts to the bottom of the pitch range, while on 'ability', the pitch does not fall nearly as far. The intonation contour on the first half of the sentence is a ***non-final rising-falling contour***. The following sentences usually have two intonation contours—the non-final contour on the first phrase and the final contour on the second. We represent these contours slightly differently, as shown by the arrows. The arrow on the non-final contour does not go as far down as it does for the final contour. (We indicate that there should be two separate contours by the use of //.)

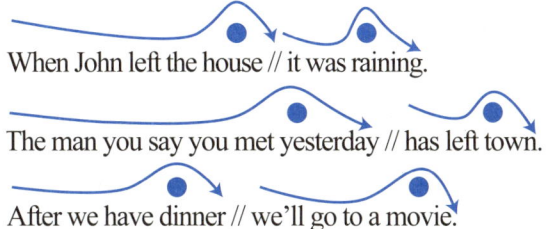
When John left the house // it was raining.
The man you say you met yesterday // has left town.
After we have dinner // we'll go to a movie.

Thus, a fall at the end of the sentence to the lowest pitch possible indicates that our thought is complete, and a fall that is not to the bottom of the pitch range indicates that we still have more to say. It is very useful to bear this in mind when listening to your students' pronunciation. Our experience is that if a student does not have a large enough drop in pitch in ending a sentence, native speakers will expect that there is more to come. This can lead to embarrassing silences and communication breakdowns.

(2) Continuation rise

Say the following sentence.

    Susan bought a new sweater, new shoes, and a new dress.

This intonation contour of this sentence is termed a ***continuation rise*** and is often used with lists. The pitch of the voice rises slightly on each noun of the list, indicating that we are not yet finished speaking. On the final noun of the list, we find the familiar rise-fall. Pronounce the following sentences in order to familiarize yourself with this pattern.

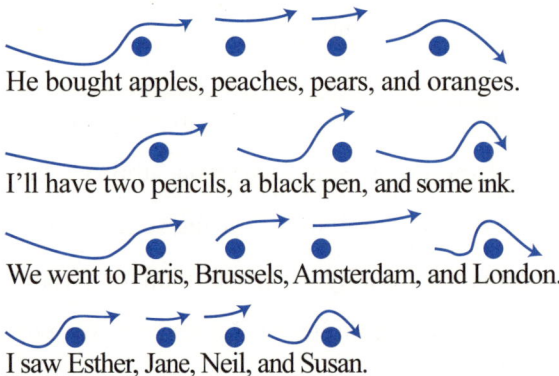

Some complex sentences display a continuation rise on the first half rather than a rise-fall.

In this sentence, the intonation may rise slightly on the word 'ahead'. Following a slight pause, we find the rising-falling contour on the next clause.

4 Tag questions

Tag questions can display either final rising-falling or final rising intonation contours. Their meaning will differ depending on which of these contours is used. Pronounce the following tag questions with the intonation contours indicated:

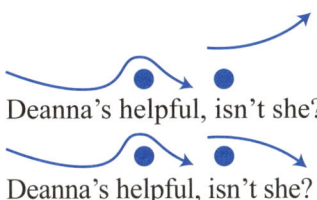

The first sentence, with a rising contour, indicates that the speaker genuinely <u>does not know</u> whether Deanna is helpful and wants the listener to provide this information. The second sentence, with a rising-falling contour, indicates that the speaker believes that Deanna is helpful and is merely <u>eliciting confirmation</u> from the listener.

Tag questions with rising-falling intonation are very often used to begin conversations. For example, in attempting to begin a conversation with a stranger, one might say:

In uttering this sentence, the speaker is not demanding an answer to a question but rather opening the lines of communication.

◆ **Summary**

What is intonation?

intonation = *pitch change/contour*

	Intonation Patterns	When to use
Final intonation	Rising-falling intonation	declaratives, imperatives, ***wh***-questions
	Rising intonation	yes/no questions
Non-final intonation	Rising-falling intonation	complex sentences
	Continuation rise	lists
Tag questions	Rising intonation	does not know
	Rising-falling intonation	elicit confirmation

◆ **Attitudinal Function of Intonation (Applied English Phonology pp. 172~176)**

falling intonation (= rising-falling intonation)	rising intonation
finality (completion)	incompletion
certainty	uncertainty (lack of assurance)

09 Phonological Processes '02, '07, '08, '09, '10, '11, '12, '13, '15, '16, '17, '18, '19, '20, '21,

1 Assimilation '02, '07, '08, '09, '10, '12, '18, '19, '20

An example of an adjustment in connected speech is the process of **assimilation**, during which a given sound (the assimilating sound) takes on the characteristics of a neighboring sound (the conditioning sound). There are three types of assimilation in English: (1) *progressive* (or perseverative), (2) *regressive* (or anticipatory), and (3) *coalescent*.

(1) Progressive assimilation

In **progressive assimilation** the conditioning sound precedes and affects the following sound. Examples of progressive assimilation in English are the regular plural /s/ vs. /z/ alternation, in which the final sound of the stem conditions the voiced or voiceless form of the suffix. This type of assimilation also occurs in the regular past tense /t/ vs. /d/ alternation:

(1) Assimilation in plural and regular past-tense verb endings

	Conditioning sound	Assimilated sound
-s ending		
bags	/g/	/bæg → **z**/
backs	/k/	/bæk → **s**/
-d ending		
moved	/v/	/muv → **d**/
fished	/ʃ/	/fiʃ → **t**/

For the plural -*s* ending, the voiced /g/ of **bags** conditions the voiced form of the -*s* ending, causing it to be pronounced /z/, whereas the voiceless /k/ of **back** conditions the /s/ pronunciation of the ending. Notice that the same type of conditioning occurs in the -*d* endings.

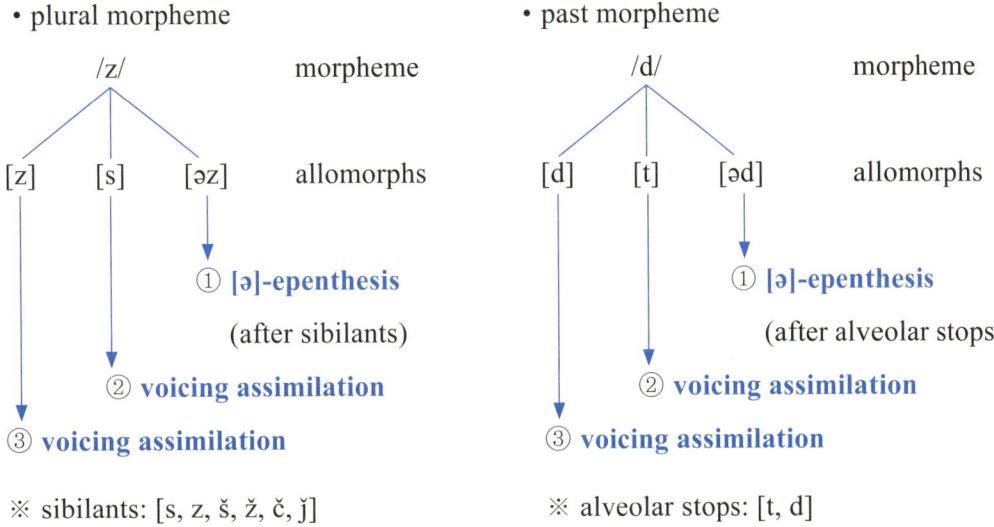

(2) Regressive assimilation

In English, **regressive assimilation** is more pervasive as a purely phonological process than is progressive assimilation. In regressive assimilation, the assimilated sound precedes and is affected by the conditioning sound. Examples of this type of phenomenon are the following:

grandpa: the /p/ causes the /nd/ to be articulated as /m/: /græmpɑ/
pancake: the /k/ causes the /n/ to become /ŋ/: /pæŋkejk/
can buy: the /b/ in *buy* causes the final /n/ in *can* to be articulated as /m/: /kæmbaj/
can go: the /g/ in *go* causes the final /n/ in *can* to be articulated as /ŋ/: /kæŋgoʊ/

Regressive assimilation occurs commonly in the periphrastic modals **has**/**have to** (when expressing obligation) and **used to** (when expressing former habitual action):

(2) Regressive assimilation in periphrastic modals

have	+	to	→	hafta
/hæv/		/tu/		/hæftə/
has	+	to	→	hasta
/hæz/		/tu/		/hæstə/
used	+	to	→	usta
/juzd/		/tu/		/justə/

In these examples, the voiceless /t/ of *to* is the conditioning sound that causes the voiced /v/, /z/, and /d/ preceding it to assimilate and become voiceless /f/, /s/, and /t/:

Assimilated sound	←	Conditioning sound
/hæf	←	tə/
/hæs	←	tə/
/jus	←	tə/

◆ negative prefix {IN-} '10 Choice, '20

Regressive assimilation helps explain the various allomorphic forms of the English negative prefix: *in-*, *im-*, *ir-*, *il-*. Note that the unmarked allomorph *in-* occurs in all cases except when the following sound is a bilabial or a liquid: ***indecent, inept, invalid***. However, when the following sounds is a bilabial, the organs of speech approach a position closer to that of the conditioning sounds to produce ***im-***, as in ***impossible*** or ***immobile***. Similarly, when followed by the liquids /l/ and /r/, the negative prefix is conditioned or changed to ***il-*** and ***ir-*** respectively, as in ***illogical*** and ***irrational***.

(3) Allomorphic forms of the English negative prefix

in-	*im-*	*il-*	*ir-*
inoperative	impossible	illogical	irreplaceable
inflexible	imbalanced	illegal	irresponsible
indifferent	immeasurable	illegitimate	irrelevant
inexcusable	immobile	illegible	irrational
intangible	impartial	illiberal	irregular

negative prefix /in-/			
/in/ → [in]	/ ____ alveolars or vowels	(ex indirect, inactive)	
/in/ → [im]	/ ____ bilabials	(ex impossible, imbalanced, immobile)	
/in/ → [iŋ]	/ ____ velars	(ex incongruous, incorrect)	
/in/ → [il]	/ ____ [l]	(ex illogical, illegible)	
/in/ → [ir]	/ ____ [r]	(ex irreplaceable, irrelevant)	
allomorphs			

Regressive assimilation can be further categorized into two types: place assimilation and manner assimilation.

① **Place assimilation**

With stop consonants, a final /t/ or /d/ may assimilate to a following initial /p, k/ or /b, g/, respectively (i.e., the place of articulation changes but the voiced or voiceless quality of the segment remains constant):

good boy   good girl
  [b:]   [g:]
 /gʊbɔj/   /gʊgɜrl/

at peace   pet kitten
  [p:]   [k:]
 /æpis/   /pɛkɪtn̩/

Notice that final nasal consonants, especially /n/, may also adjust their place of articulation according to that of a following conditioning consonant:

He's in pain.   They're in Kansas.
   [m]   [ŋ]
 /ɪmpejn/   /ɪŋkænzəs/

It rains in May.   Be on guard!
    [m]   [ŋ]
  /ɪmej/   /əŋgɑrd/

② **Manner assimilation**

There are also some cases of regressive assimilation with a change in manner of articulation.

    Could you give me a call?
              [m:]
            /gɪmi/

    Let me do that for you.
      [m:]
     /lɛmi/

(3) Coalescent assimilation '07, '12, '20

The third type of assimilation, **coalescent assimilation**, is a type of reciprocal assimilation. The figure in (4) illustrates how the first sound and second sound in a sequence come together and mutually condition the creation of a third sound with features from both original sounds.

    (4) The process of coalescent assimilation

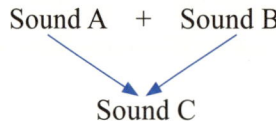

The most frequent type of coalescent assimilation is **palatalization**, during which the final alveolar consonants /s, z, t, d/ or final alveolar consonant sequences /ts, dz/ are followed by initial palatal /y/. The figure in (5) shows how, in the resulting process of coalescent assimilation, these alveolar sounds become the palatalized fricatives /ʃ, ʒ/ or affricates /tʃ, dʒ/, respectively:

(5) Palatalization

Rule		Examples
/s/	/ʃ/	issue
		He's coming this year.
/z/	/ʒ/	pleasure
		Does your mother know?
/t/	/tʃ/	stature
	+ /y/ →	Is that your dog?
/ts/	/tʃ/	He hates your mother.
		She lets you stay up late.
/d/	/dʒ/	procedure
		Would you mind moving?
/dz/	/dʒ/	She needs your help.
		He never heeds your advice.

(4) Total assimilation [Gemination] '09 Choice

When an assimilation process results in contiguous identical consonants, it is called **gemination**. There are a number of cases of gemination in English which typically take place in more casual and rapid speech styles, as shown in (6).

(6) give me [gɪmmi]   let me [lɛmmi]

There is an interesting case of gemination in English in which alveolar stops may assimilate to a following bilabial or velar stop, as shown in (7).

(7) good bye [gʊbbaɪ]   good boy [gʊbbɔɪ]
    right poor [raippʊə]   right corner [raikkɔrnɚ]
    pet cat [pɛkkæt]   bad guess [bæggɛs]

◆ Summary

Partial assimilation: ① progressive ② regressive ③ coalescent   [Direction of Change]
　　　　　　　　　① place ② manner ③ voicing　　　　　　　　[Consonant Change]
Total assimilation: gemination

◆ Total assimilation

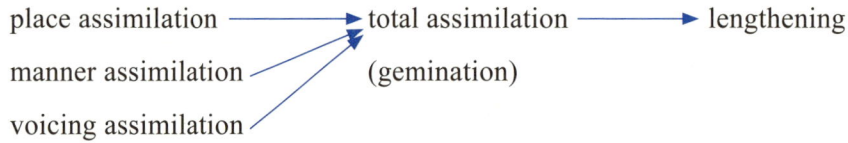

2 Dissimilation '11, '20

The process of **dissimilation** occurs when adjacent sounds become more different from each other (rather than more similar, as is the case with assimilation).

(1) fricative dissimilation

fifth [fθ] → [ft]　　　　　　　sixth [sθ] → [st]

An example of easing pronunciation through dissimilation is found in some varieties of English, in which there is a fricative dissimilation rule. This rule applies to sequences /fθ/ and /sθ/, changing them to [ft] and [st]. Here the fricative /θ/ becomes dissimilar to the preceding fricative by becoming a stop.

(2) *-al* suffix '11, '20

A classic example of the same kind of dissimilation occurred in Latin, and the results of this process show up in the derivational morpheme /-ar/ in English. In Latin a derivational suffix *-alis* was added to nouns to form adjectives. When the suffix was added to a noun that contained the liquid /l/, the suffix was changed to *-aris*; that is, the liquid /l/ was changed to the dissimilar liquid /r/. These words came into English as adjectives ending in *-al* or in its dissimilated form *-ar*, as shown in the following examples:

-al	-ar
anecdot-al	angul-ar
annu-al	annul-ar
ment-al	column-ar
pen-al	perpendicul-ar
spiritu-al	simil-ar [11]
ven-al	vel-ar [20]

All of the *-ar* adjectives contain /l/, and as ***columnar*** illustrates, the /l/ need not be the consonant directly preceding the dissimilated segment.

3 Deletion [08, '09 Mock, '11, '17, '19]

Rules of **deletion** cause a segment present at the phonemic level to be deleted at the phonetic level of a word.

The following are some of the most typical environments for deletion:

(1) Consonant Cluster Reduction (CCR) [08]

> /t/ or /d/ is deleted when they occur second in a sequence of three consonants.

- **Loss of /t/ or /d/** when they occur second in a sequence or cluster of three consonants:
  /t/   res̸tless, lis̸tless, exac̸tly
  /d/   win̸dmill, kin̸dness, han̸ds

- **Deletion of word-final /t/ or /d/** in clusters of two at a word boundary when the following word begins with a consonant. Note that when the following word begins with a vowel, resyllabification occurs in place of deletion.

  (1) **Deletion of /t, d/**   **Resyllabification**
                                     (before vowel)

      Eas̸t side   Eas/t end
      blin̸d man   blin/d eye

wild boar wil/d ass

old boyfriend ol/d age

(2) /t/-deletion in /nt/ sequence '09 Mock, '11

> /t/ is lost when following a /n/ and at an unstressed syllable or before a syllabic [l̩].

Loss of /t/ when /nt/ is between two vowels or before a syllabic [l̩]:

/t/   winter, Toronto, enter, mantle

/t/ is deleted only in an unstressed syllable. /t/ following an /n/ cannot be deleted in contain, interred, entwined, etc.

(3) /g/-deletion '11

Consider the following examples:

A		B	
sign	[sãɪn]	signature	[sɪgnətʃər]
design	[dəzãɪn]	designation	[dɛzɪgneʃə̃n]
paradigm	[pʰærədãɪm]	paradigmatic	[pʰærədɪgmærək]

In none of the words in column A is there a phonetic [g], but in each corresponding word in column B a [g] occurs. Our knowledge of English phonology accounts for these phonetic differences. The "[g]–no [g]" alternation is regular and is also seen in pairs like *gnostic* [nastɪk] and *agnostic* [ægnastɪk]. This rule may be stated as:

Delete a /g/ word-initially before a nasal consonant or before a syllable-final nasal consonant.

Given this rule, the phonemic representations of the stems in ***sign/signature***, ***design/designation***, ***malign/malignant***, ***phlegm/phlegmatic***, ***paradigm/paradigmatic***, ***gnostic/agnostic***, and so on will include a /g/ that will be deleted by the regular rule if a prefix or suffix is not added. By stating the class of sounds that follow the /g/ (nasal consonants) rather than any specific nasal consonant, the rule deletes the /g/ before both /m/ and /n/.

(4) /b/-deletion

Silent	Pronounced
bomb	bombardment
limb	limbic

The rule may be stated as:

Delete a word-final /b/ when it occurs after a /m/.

(5) Schwa Deletion '17

4 Insertion [Epenthesis]

Epenthesis is the insertion of a vowel or consonant segment within an existing string of segments. Although less frequent than deletion English, epenthesis is by no means uncommon. The most important type of epenthesis in English occurs in certain morphophonological sequences such as the regular plural and past tense endings. Here an epenthetic schwa /ə/ is added to break up clusters of sibilants or alveolar stops. Progressive assimilation alone will not make the morphological endings sufficiently salient. Thus for the plural endings, for which we can posit an underlying {Z} morpheme, we have:

Assimilation	Epenthesis
plate + {Z} = /pleyts/	place + {Z} = /pleysəz/
bag + {Z} = /bægz/	buzz + {Z} = /bʌzəz/

And for regular past tense, for which we can posit an underlying {D} morpheme, we have:

Assimilation	Epenthesis
look + {D} = /lukt/	plant + {D} = /plæntəd/
grin + {D} = /grɪnd/	hand + {D} = /hændəd/

5 Metathesis

Metathesis is a process <u>that reorders a sequence of segments</u>. Metathesis often results in a sequence of phones that is easier to articulate. It is common to hear metathesis in the speech of children, who often cannot pronounce all the consonant sequences that adults can. For example, some English-speaking children pronounce ***spaghetti*** as ***pesghetti*** [pəskɛɾi]. In this form, the initial sequence [spə], which is often difficult for children to pronounce, is metathesized to [pəs]. Another example found in many dialects is the form [æks] for [æsk].

The pronunciations of ***prescribe*** and ***prescription*** as ***perscribe*** and ***perscription*** are often-cited examples of metathesis in adult speech. In these cases, metathesis facilitates the pronunciation of two successive consonant-r sequences in each word.

(1) Metathesis

original word		the switching of two units
irrelevant	>	irrevelant
elevator	>	evelator
tragedy	>	tradegy
rejuvenate	>	rejunevate
I asked him	>	[aɪ ækst ɪm]
prescribe	>	[pɚ-skraɪb]
pronounce	>	[pɚ-naʊns]
hundred	>	[hʌndɚd]

6 Haplology

Haplology is a process of the elimination of a syllable when two consecutive identical or similar syllables occur.

(1) Haplology

haplology	>	haplogy
February	>	Febury, Febuary
library	>	[laɪbrɪ]
Mississippi	>	[mɪsɪpi]

probably   >   [prabli]
similarly   >   [siməli]
particularly >   particuly

7 Neutralization '08, '13, '15, '16, '17

Phonemes that are contrastive in certain environments may not be contrastive in all environments. In the environments where they do not contrast, the contrast is said to be **neutralized**. The elimination of certain distinctive features of phonemes in certain environments is called **neutralization**.

(1) Vowel Reduction [Schwa Rule]

> Vowels become a reduced vowel (schwa) when in an unstressed syllable.

Consider the vowels in the following pairs of words:

	A			B	
/i/	compete	[i]	competition	[ə]
/ɪ/	medicinal	[ɪ]	medicine	[ə]
/e/	maintain	[e]	maintenance	[ə]
/ɛ/	telegraph	[ɛ]	telegraphy	[ə]
/æ/	analysis	[æ]	analytic	[ə]
/a/	solid	[a]	solidity	[ə]
/o/	phone	[o]	phonetic	[ə]

In column A, all the boldfaced vowels are stressed vowels with a variety of vowel phones; in column B, the boldfaced vowels are without stress, or **reduced**, and are pronounced as schwa [ə]. In these cases, the stress pattern of the word varies because of the different suffixes. The vowel that is stressed in one form becomes unstressed in a different form and is therefore pronounced as [ə]. The phonemic representations of all of the root morphemes contain a stressed vowel such as /i/ or /e/ that becomes phonetically [ə] when it is destressed. We can conclude, then, that [ə] is an allophone of all English vowel phonemes. The rule to derive the schwa is simple to state:

Change a vowel to a [ə] when the vowel is unstressed (reduced).

◆ **Vowel Reduction & [ɪ]** '17

Although we have consistently used [ə] in reduced syllables, it is not uncommon to find an [ɪ] in people's speech. That is, for a word such as implication we can get [ɪmplɪkeʃən] as well as [ɪmpləkeʃən]. In general, [ɪ] is found before palato-alveolars (e.g. selfish [sɛlfɪʃ], sandwich [sændwɪtʃ], marriage [mæɹɪdʒ]) and velars (e.g. metric [mɛtɹɪk], running [ɹʌnɪŋ]). It should be noted, however, that the syllable structure is also a factor. The influence of palato-alveolar/velar consonants is more visible when there is tautosyllabicity. For example, we tend to find [ɪ] in topic [tɑpɪk], which is likely to change to an [ə] in a related word such as topical [tɑpəkəl], because the velar, [k], is the onset of the following syllable. Individuals should check their pronunciation of such syllables and transcribe the vowels accordingly. However, since reduced syllables are necessarily unstressed, and [ə] cannot appear in a stressed syllable (but [ɪ] can), we encourage our students to use [ə] for such vowels, for practical reasons.

(2) Flapping '08, '16

> Intervocalic alveolar stops become a flap when followed by an unstressed vowel.

Consider the following English words, each of which is accompanied by its phonemic and phonetic representations.

ride	/ráɪd/	[ráɪd]	writer	/ráɪtər/	[ráɪɾər]
dire	/dáɪr/	[dáɪr]	lender	/léndər/	[léndər]
rider	/ráɪdər/	[ráɪɾər]	Easter	/ístər/	[ístər]
write	/ráɪt/	[ráɪt]	attack	/ətǽk/	[ətǽk]
tire	/táɪr/	[táɪr]	adobe	/ədóbi/	[ədóbi]

In these data, both /t/ and /d/ become [ɾ] (an alveolar flap) under certain circumstances. Our task is to determine under what conditions /t/ and /d/ become [ɾ]. We might begin by noting that /t/ and /d/ never become [ɾ] when they begin or end a word. Thus, the relevant alveolar stops (/t/ and /d/) must be those that occur somewhere in the middle of the word. This narrows the field to *rider*, *writer*, *lender*, *Easter*, *attack*, and *adobe*. Of these, only the alveolar stops in *rider* and *writer* become [ɾ]. What is different about the environment of /t/ and /d/ in these words? First of all, they occur between vowels. (Compare *lender* and *Easter*, where the stop occurs between a consonant and a vowel.) Second, the vowel to the left is stressed and that to the right is unstressed. (Compare *attack* and *adobe*, where the vowel to the left of the stop is unstressed and that to the right is stressed.) Now we are in a position to propose a rule: /t/ and /d/ become [ɾ] when they occur between two vowels, the first of which is stressed and the second of which is unstressed. This rule accurately accounts for all of the [ɾ]'s in our data. That is, it predicts exactly those cases where /t/ and /d/ become [ɾ]; and, by exclusion, it also predicts where they remain unchanged.

The Flapping Rule, in turn, can be formalized as follows.

$$\begin{bmatrix} +\text{stop} \\ +\text{alveolar} \end{bmatrix} \rightarrow [ɾ] \ / \ \underset{[+\text{stress}]}{V} \ \underline{\quad} \ \underset{[-\text{stress}]}{V}$$

As usual, there are variations on this notation. You might also see this rule written as follows.

$$\left\{ \begin{matrix} /t/ \\ /d/ \end{matrix} \right\} \rightarrow [ɾ] \ / \ \acute{V} \ \underline{\quad} \ \breve{V}$$

A breve (˘) above a vowel indicates that it is unstressed.

Flapping is a special case of **neutralization,** a process that obliterates the contrast between two segments in a particular environment.

(3) Glottalization '13, '15 ⇒ See 05. Consonant Allophones

◆ Summary

Neutralization	
① Vowel Reduction	/i, ɪ, e, ɛ, æ, a, o/ → /ə/
② Flapping	/t, d/ → [ɾ]
③ Glottalization	ti**p**, pi**t**, ki**ck** → [ʔ]

10 Phonological Rules

1 Format & Notation

A → B / C _____

(Sound A changes to have the features B in the environment after C.)

A → B / _____ D

(Sound A changes to have the features B in the environment before D.)

A → B / C _____ D

(Sound A changes to have the features B in the environment between C and D.)

A: The underlying sound that is changed.

B: The resulting sound, or the individual features that change.

The slash (/) is a shorthand notation for "in the environment where …". It means that the notation to the right describes where the phonological rule is applied.

_____ : The location of the sound that is going to be changed.

For example, the flapping rule of American English: e.g. [bɪɾər]

/t/ → [ɾ] / V _____ $\begin{bmatrix} +syll \\ -stress \end{bmatrix}$

(1) Parenthesis Notation

( ) is used to include optional elements in rules.

A → B / X (Y) _____ Z

The rule for 'l-velarization'; e.g. 'fell', 'bulk'

/l/ → [ɫ] / _____ (C) #

(2) Brace Notation

{ } represents an either/or relationship between two environments.

$$A \rightarrow B / \left\{ \begin{matrix} X \\ Z \end{matrix} \right\} \_\_ Y$$

The rule for glottalizing /t/ as in 'cat' or 'atlas':

$$/t/ \rightarrow [ʔ] / \_\_ \left\{ \begin{matrix} C \\ \# \end{matrix} \right\}$$

(3) Alpha Notation

Alpha notation is used for feature matching generalization. The α represents either '+' or '−' value of features.

$$/n/ \rightarrow \begin{bmatrix} \alpha \text{ ant} \\ \beta \text{ cor} \end{bmatrix} / \_\_ \begin{bmatrix} +\text{cons} \\ \alpha \text{ ant} \\ \beta \text{ cor} \end{bmatrix}$$

2 Dentalization

> Alveolar sounds are dentalized before an interdental sound (/θ, ð/).

The alveolar lateral liquid, /l/, which is produced with varying degrees of 'velarization' (i.e. raising the back of the tongue), is articulated in a more forward (dental) fashion when it is followed by an interdental fricative (e.g. wealth [wɛl̪θ], kill them [kɪl̪ðɛm]).

The alveolar nasal, /n/, is articulated in a more forward fashion (dental) when it is followed by an interdental (/θ, ð/): tenth [tɛn̪θ], ban the film [bæn̪ðəfɪlm], when they [wɛn̪ðe].

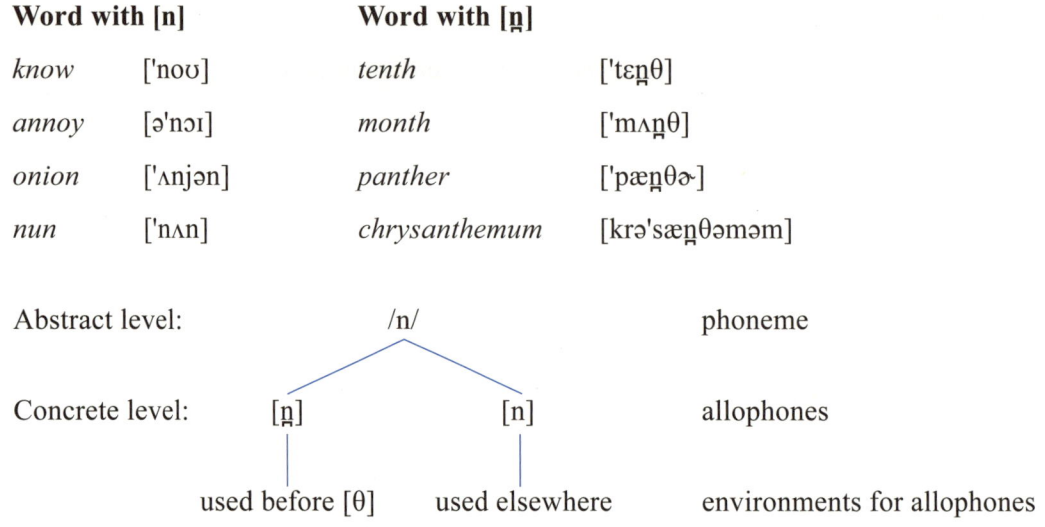

3 Labiodentalization

Bilabial and alveolar nasals become labio-dentals when they are followed by a labio-dental sound, as in emphasis [ɛɱfəsɪs], comfort [kʌɱfɚt], invite [ɪɱvaɪt], infant [ɪɱfənt]. This assimilation is not restricted to the adjacent sounds in the same word and still occurs when the labio-dental fricative is at the beginning of the next word, for example come first [kʌɱ fɚst], on fire [aɱ faɪr], warm feet [wɔrɱ fit].

Table 1. English Consonants

place manner	Bilabial	Labio-dental	(Inter-)dental	Alveolar	Palato-alveolar	Palatal	Velar	Glottal
OBSTRUENTS(vl/vd)								
Stop	p b			t d			k g	ʔ
Fricative		f v	θ ð	s z	š ž			h
Affricate					č ǰ			
SONORANTS(vd)								
Nasal	m	ɱ	n̪	n			ŋ	
Liquid				l, r				
Glide	(w)					j	w	

※ [ɱ] is an allophone of /m/ or /n/. [n̪] is an allophone of /n/.

4 Devoicing

> Approximants are partially devoiced when they follow a voiceless aspirated stop.
> e.g. play [pl̥eɪ], pray [pɹ̥eɪ], clue [kl̥u], crew [kɹ̥u], try [tɹ̥aɪ], twig [tw̥ɪg] twin [tw̥ɪn], tune [tj̥un]

/m/ and /n/ are also subject to progressive assimilation in cases of partial devoicing after the voiceless obstruent /s/, as in snail [sn̥el], small [sm̥ɔl].

Word with [ɫ]		Word with [l̥]		Word with [l̪]		Word with [l]	
file	['faɪɫ]	slight	['sl̥aɪt]	wealth	['wɛl̪θ]	listen	['lɪsən]
fool	['fuɫ]	flight	['fl̥aɪt]	health	['hɛl̪θ]	lose	['luz]
all	['ɔɫ]	plow	['pl̥aʊ]	filthy	['fɪl̪θi]	allow	[ə'laʊ]
ball	['bɔɫ]	cling	['kl̥ɪŋ]	tilth	['tɪl̪θ]	aglow	[ə'gloʊ]
fell	['fɛɫ]	discipline	['dɪsəpl̥ən]	stealth	['stɛl̪θ]	blend	['blɛnd]
feel	['fiɫ]						

This pattern can be described as follows:

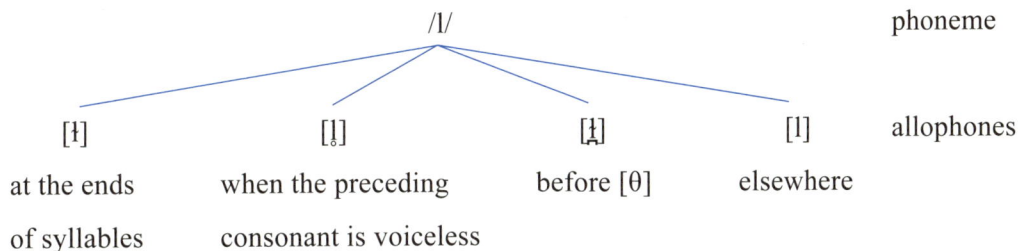

		/l/		phoneme
[ɫ]	[l̥]	[l̪]	[l]	allophones
at the ends of syllables	when the preceding consonant is voiceless	before [θ]	elsewhere	

5 Velarization '14

> A lateral is velarized when it occurs in a coda.

/l/ is velarized when it occurs in a coda. (velarized /l/ = dark /l/)
e.g. *pill* [pɪɫ] *ale* [eɪɫ] *kneel* [niɫ]

(1) Allophones of phoneme /l/

/l/ Devoicing

/l/ → [l̥] / $\begin{bmatrix} +\text{consonant} \\ -\text{voice} \end{bmatrix}$ ___

Partially devoice /l/ after a voiceless consonant.

/l/ Dentalization

/l/ → [l̪] / ___ θ

/l/ is rendered as velarized and dental before [θ].

/l/ Velarization

/l/ → [ɫ] / ___ $

/l/ is velarized syllable-finally.

Table 2. Common Diacritical Marks Used in the Narrow Transcription of English

Diacritical Mark	Meaning	Examples
[̥]	voiceless	ply [pl̥aɪ], clam [kl̥æm], true [tr̥u]
[ʰ]	aspirated	tin [tʰɪn], cat [kʰæt], pot [pʰat]
[ʷ]	labialized	cool [kʷul], toward [tʷɔrd], dough [dʷo]
[~]	velarized	pal [pæɫ], elk [ɛɫk], vulgar [vʌɫgɚ]
[̪]	dental	eighth [et̪θ], width [wɪd̪θ], breadth [brɛd̪θ]
[ʔ]	unreleased	kite [kaɪʔt], stop [staʔp], lick [lɪʔk]
[ʲ]	palatalized	key [kʲi], keel [kʲil], gears [gʲirz]
[˜]	nasalized	man [mæ̃n], mango [mæ̃ŋgo], slim [slĩm]
[ː]	long	have [hæːv], loathe [loːð], major [meːdʒɚ]
[̩]	syllabic	puddle [pʌdl̩], shuffle [šʌfl̩], button [bʌtn̩]

※ diacritical marks ⇒ allophones of a phoneme

6 Vowel Lengthening

> A vowel becomes lengthened when it precedes a voiced consonant.

Consider the following English words, each of which is accompanied by its phonemic and phonetic representations.

heat	/hit/	[hit]
seize	/siz/	[si:z]
keel	/kil/	[kʰi:l]
leaf	/lif/	[lif]
heed	/hid/	[hi:d]
cease	/sis/	[sis]
leave	/liv/	[li:v]

In these data, /i/ has two allophones, [i] and [i:] (a colon after a vowel indicates that it is lengthened). Once again, our task is to determine under what conditions /i/ becomes [i:]. We might begin by hypothesizing that some property of the consonant to the *left* of the vowel causes it to lengthen. This hypothesis, however, must clearly be wrong. Consider, for example, *seize* [si:z] and *cease* [sis]. The former has a long vowel and the latter has a short vowel, yet in both cases the vowel is preceded by [s]. Thus, the consonant to the left of the vowel obviously has no effect upon the length of the vowel, since here the same consonant precedes both a long vowel and a short vowel.

Alternatively, we might hypothesize that some property of the consonant to the *right* of the vowel causes it to lengthen, here we have more luck. Note that the vowels in *heat*, *leaf*, and *cease* are short, and each one is followed by a voiceless consonant ([t], [f], and [s] are [–voice]). In contrast, the vowels in *heed*, *leave*, *seize*, and *keel* are long and each one is followed by a voiced consonant ([d], [v], [z], and [l] are [+voice]). Now we are in a position to propose a rule: /i/ becomes [i:] when it precedes a voiced consonant. This rule accurately accounts for our data. It predicts exactly those cases where /i/ becomes [i:] and, by exclusion, it also predicts where /i/ remains unchanged.

Let's go one step further and formalize our rule as follows.

/i/ → [+long] / _____ C
　　　　　　　　　　[+voice]

This rule states that the phoneme /i/ becomes lengthened when it precedes a voiced consonant (C). As in our Aspiration Rule discussed earlier, there are variations on this notation. You might also see this rule written as follows.

/i/ → [iː] / _____ C
　　　　　　　　[+voice]

In addition, if we were to go beyond the data on which we have based this rule and include examples containing allophones of the other vowels in English, we would see that *all* vowels become lengthened under the same conditions, namely when they precede a voiced consonant. Thus, we can state the Vowel Lengthening Rule as follows.

V → [+long] / _____ C
　　　　　　　　　[+voice]

Once again, we can see that phonological rules apply to *classes* of segments (e.g., vowels) rather than to individual segments (e.g., /i/, /e/, /æ/, and so on).

7 Vowel Nasalization '12 Choice

> Vowels are nasalized when followed by a nasal consonant.

Consider the following English words, each of which is accompanied by its phonemic and phonetic representations.

map	/mæp/	[mæp]
pan	/pæn/	[pæ̃n]
pad	/pæd/	[pæd]
Pam	/pæm/	[pæ̃m]

gnat	/næt/	[næt]
pang	/pæŋ/	[pæ̃ŋ]

In these data, /æ/ has two allophones, [æ] and [æ̃]. (A tilde over a vowel indicates that it is nasalized. A nasalized vowel is perceived as being pronounced with the velum lowered.) As before, our task is to determine under what conditions /æ/ becomes [æ̃]. Before getting started, however, note that the vowels in **pan**, **pad**, **Pam**, and **pang** should be long (i.e., [æː]), since they each precede a voiced consonant; yet the phonetic transcription does not indicate this. Pay this no mind; it is common practice in phonology to ignore phonetic details irrelevant to the particular task at hand. In this case, vowel lengthening has nothing to do with vowel nasalization, so it has been ignored. Likewise, the aspiration notation in this data has been omitted, since aspiration has nothing to do with vowel nasalization.

Let's now return to the problem of determining under what conditions /æ/ becomes [æ̃]. First of all, we might assume, naturally enough, that since English has no nasalized vowel phonemes, a phonetically nasalized vowel is the result of being adjacent to a nasal consonant, /m/, /n/, or /ŋ/. Thus, our task is simplified. Is it the preceding or the following nasal consonant that is causing the vowel to become nasalized? The answer is straightforward. Since **map** [mæp] and **gnat** [næt] both contain a preceding nasal consonant but no nasalized vowel, vowel nasalization must not be caused by a preceding nasal consonant. On the other hand, since **pan** [pæ̃n], **Pam** [pæ̃m], and **pang** [pæ̃ŋ] each contain a nasalized vowel followed by a nasal consonant, it must be the following nasal consonant that is causing the vowel nasalization. We are now in a position to propose a rule: /æ/ becomes [æ̃] when it is followed by a nasal consonant. This rule accurately predicts exactly the cases where /æ/ becomes [æ̃]; and, by exclusion, it also predicts where /æ/ remains unchanged.

We can formalize this rule as follows.

/æ/ → [+nasal] / _____ C
                       [+nasal]

Or, alternatively, as follows.

/æ/ → [æ̃] / _____ C
                 [+nasal]

Once again, if we were to go beyond the data on which our rule is based, we would see that all vowels in English become nasalized when they precede a nasal consonant. Thus, we could state the Vowel Nasalization Rule for English as follows.

$$V \rightarrow [+\text{nasal}] / \underline{\hspace{1cm}} C$$
$$[+\text{nasal}]$$

Again, we see that phonological rules apply to classes of segments, rather than to individual segments. It is also worth mentioning that this type of rule, in which a segment becomes more like a neighboring segment in some way, is called an **assimilation** rule. In this case, a vowel becomes more like an adjacent nasal consonant by becoming nasalized itself.

Morphology 01-02 mind map

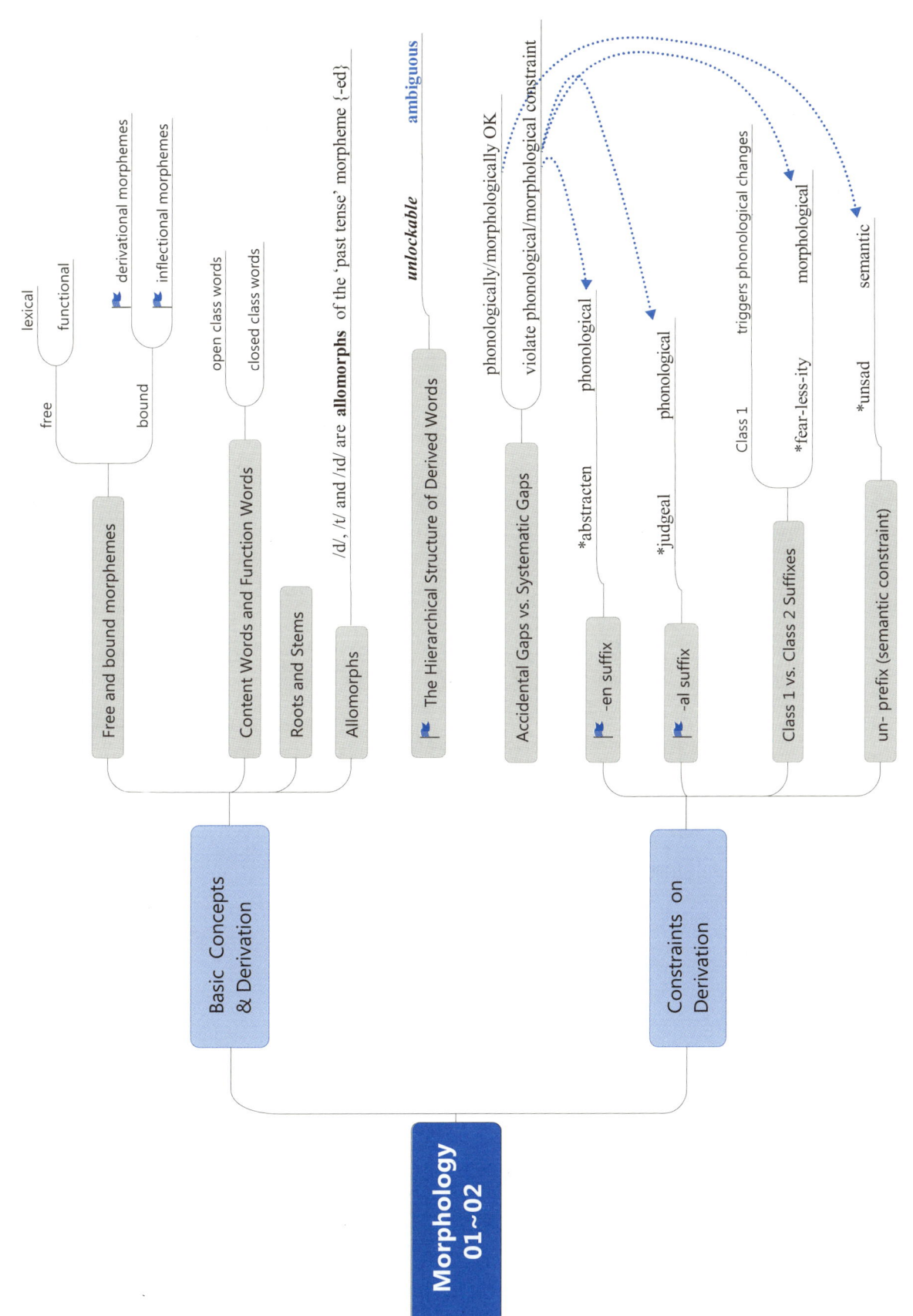

Morphology 03 mind map

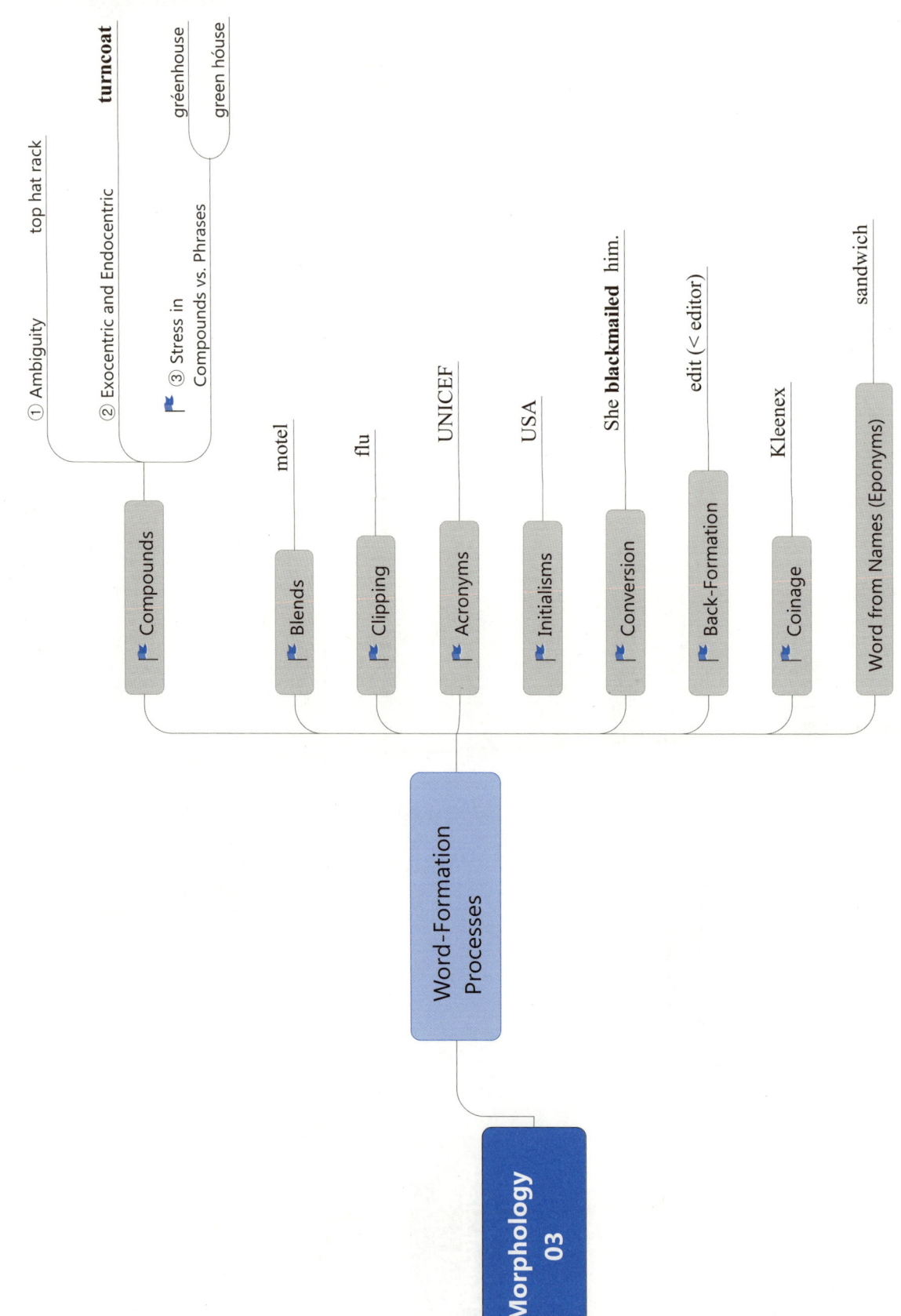

Chapter 02 Morphology

01 Basic Concepts & Derivation

The study of the internal structure of words, and of the rules by which words are formed, is **morphology.**

1 Free and bound morphemes

The **'morpheme'** is defined as the smallest (minimal) unit of meaning. The prefix *un-* means 'not,' as in *undesirable, unhappy*, etc., so *un-* is a morpheme as the remaining meaningful parts *desirable* and *happy* are.

One of the things we know about particular morphemes is whether they can stand alone or whether they must be attached to a base morpheme. Some morphemes like *boy, desire, gentle,* and *man* may constitute words by themselves. These are **free morphemes**. Other morphemes like *-ish, -ness, -ly, pre-, trans-,* and *un-* are never words by themselves but are always parts of words. These **affixes** are **bound morphemes** and they may attach at the beginning or at the end of a word.

(1) derivational morphemes vs. inflectional morphemes '13 Choice, '21

The set of affixes that make up the category of bound morphemes can also be divided into two types. We use these bound morphemes to make new words (**derivational morphemes**) or to indicate aspects of the grammatical function of a word (**inflectional morphemes**).

English has only eight bound inflectional affixes:

	English Inflectional Morphemes	Examples
-s	third-person singular present	She wait-s at home.
-ed	past tense	She wait-ed at home.
-ing	progressive	She is eat-ing the donut.
-en	past participle	Mary has eat-en the donuts.
-s	plural	She ate the donut-s.
-'s	possessive	Disa's hair is short.
-er	comparative	Disa has short-er hair than Karin.
-est	superlative	Disa has the short-est hair.

A useful way to remember all these different types of morphemes is in the following figure.

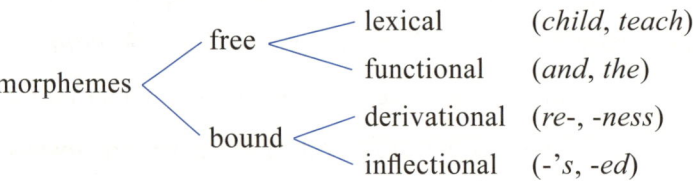

Figure 1. Morpheme classification

◆ Summary

derivational morphemes	inflectional morphemes
can cause category change or meaning change	✕

2 Content Words and Function Words

Languages make an important distinction between two kinds of words—content words and function words. Nouns, verbs, adjectives, and adverbs are the content words. **Content words** are sometimes called the **open class** words because we can and regularly do add new words to these classes, such as *Facebook* (noun), *blog* (noun, verb), *online* (adjective, adverb), etc.

Other classes of words do not have clear lexical meanings or obvious concepts associated with them, including conjunctions such as *and*, *or*, and *but*; prepositions such as *in* and *of*; the articles *the* and *a/an*, and pronouns such as *it*. These kinds of words are called **function words** because they specify grammatical relations and have little or no semantic content. Function words are sometimes called **closed class** words. This is because it is difficult to think of any conjunctions, prepositions, or pronouns that have recently entered the language.

Content words and Function words (with interchangeable terms)

Content words	Function words
Lexical morphemes	**Functional** morphemes
Open class words	Closed class words
e.g. girl, man, house, tiger, sad, long, yellow, sincere, open, look, follow, break	e.g. and, but, when, because, on, near, above, in, the, that, it, them

3 Roots and Stems

Morphologically complex words consist of a morpheme **root** and one or more affixes. Some examples of English roots are *paint* in *painter*, *read* in *reread*, *ceive* in *conceive*, and *ling* in *linguist*. A root may or may not stand alone as a word (*paint* and *read* do; *ceive* and *ling* don't). The latter is called a bound root.

The **stem** is that part of a word that is in existence before any *inflectional* affixes (i.e., those affixes whose presence is required by the syntax such as markers of singular and plural number in nouns, tense in verbs, etc.) have been added.

Noun stem	Plural suffix
cat	-s
worker	-s

In the word-form *cats*, the plural inflectional suffix *-s* is attached to the simple stem *cat*, which is a bare **root**, that is, the irreducible core of the word. In *workers*, the same inflectional *-s* suffix comes after a slightly more complex stem consisting of the root *work* plus the suffix *-er*, which is used to form agentive nouns from verbs. Here *work* is the root, but *worker* is the stem to which *-s* is attached.

When a root morpheme is combined with an affix, it forms a **stem**. Other affixes can be added to a stem to form a more complex stem, as shown in the following:

root	believe	verb
stem	believe + able	verb + suffix
word	un + believe + able	prefix + verb + suffix
root	system	noun
stem	system + atic	noun + suffix
stem	un + system + atic	prefix + noun + suffix
stem	un + system + atic + al	prefix + noun + suffix + suffix
word	un + system + atic + al + ly	prefix + noun + suffix + suffix + suffix

With the addition of each new affix, a new stem and a new word are formed.

Finally, a **base** is any unit whatsoever to which affixes of any kind can be added. The affixes attached to a base may be **inflectional** affixes selected for syntactic reasons or **derivational** affixes which alter the meaning or grammatical category of the base. In the preceding example, *system*, *systematic*, *unsystematic*, and *unsystematical* are bases.

4 Allomorphs

If different morphs represent the same morpheme, they are grouped together and they are called **allomorphs** of that morpheme. So, /d/, /t/ and /ɪd/ are **allomorphs** of the 'past tense' morpheme {-D} in English. Likewise, /z/, /s/ and /ɪz/ are **allomorphs** of the 'plural' morpheme {-Z} in English. Also, /ɪn/, /ɪm/ and /ɪŋ/ are **allomorphs** of the negative prefix morpheme {IN-} in English.

(1) Plural Morpheme {-Z}

Many morphemes have two or more different pronunciations, called **allomorphs**, the choice between them being determined by the context.

Morpheme	Allomorph	Context
{-Z}	[ɪz]	when the preceding sound is a **sibilant** (as in *horse*, *rose*, *bush*, *church* and *judge*)
	[s]	otherwise, when the preceding sound is **voiceless** (as in *cat*, *rock*, *cup* or *cliff*)
	[z]	otherwise, after a **vowel** or a **voiced consonant** (as in *dog* or *day*)

(2) Past Tense {-D}

Morpheme	Allomorph	Context
{-D}	[ɪd]	when the verb ends in [d] or [t] (e.g. *wanted*, *mended* and *painted*)
	[t]	after a verb ending in any **voiceless consonant** other than [t] (as in *parked* or *missed*)
	[d]	after a verb ending in any **voiced sound** other than [d] (as in *cleaned* or *weighed*)

5 The Hierarchical Structure of Derived Words '06, '08

The hierarchical organization of words is even more clearly shown by structurally **ambiguous** words, words that have more than one meaning by virtue of having more than one structure. Consider the word ***unlockable***. Imagine you are inside a room and you want some privacy. You would be unhappy to find the door is ***unlockable***—'not able to be locked.' Now imagine you are inside a locked room trying to get out. You would be very relieved to find that the door is ***unlockable***—'able to be unlocked.' These two meanings correspond to two different structures, as follows:

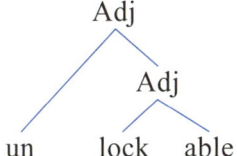
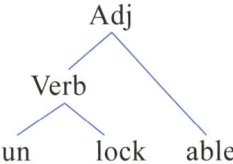

In the first structure, the verb **lock** combines with the suffix **-able** to form an adjective **lockable** ('able to be locked'). Then the prefix **un-**, meaning 'not,' combines with the derived adjective to form a new adjective **unlockable** ('not able to be locked'). In the second case, the prefix **un-** combines with the verb **lock** to form a derived verb **unlock**. Then the derived verb combines with the suffix **-able** to form **unlockable**, 'able to be unlocked.'

An entire class of words in English follows this pattern: **unbuttonable**, **unzippable**, and **unlatchable**, among others. The ambiguity arises because the prefix **un-** can combine with an adjective, or it can combine with a verb, as in **undo, unstaple, unearth**, and **unloosen**.

02 Constraints on Derivation

1 Accidental Gaps vs. Systematic Gaps

Lexical gaps are divided into two: accidental gaps and systematic gaps. "Words" that conform to the rules of word formation but are not truly part of the vocabulary are called accidental gaps. In other words, accidental gaps are well-formed (thus, possible) but non-existing words. On the other hand, the impossible words are called systematic gaps because they violate phonological or morphological rules of the language.

accidental gaps		systematic gaps	
*blick, *slarm	*unsad, *undirty	*bnick, *srick	*unsystem, *needlessity, *fastly
phonologically OK	morphologically OK	violate phonological constraint (phonotactics)	violate morphological constraint

2 -en suffix '06

Constraints on derivation include three kinds of constraints: phonological, morphological and semantic constraints. The **-en** suffix and **-al** suffix shows phonological constraints on derivation while Class 1 vs. Class 2 suffixation morphological constraints. We will see that the **un-** prefix is controlled by a semantic constraint.

Sometimes, a derivational affix is able to attach only to bases with particular phonological properties. A good example of this involves the English suffix **-en**, which combines with adjectives to create verbs with a causative meaning ('cause to become X'). As the following examples illustrate, however, there are many adjectives with which **-en** cannot combine.

Restrictions on the use of *–en*

Acceptable	Unacceptable
whiten	*abstracten
soften	*bluen
madden	*angryen
quicken	*slowen
liven	*greenen

The suffix **-en** is subject to a phonological constraint. In particular, it can only combine with a **monosyllabic** base that ends in an **obstruent**. Hence it can be added to **white**, which is both monosyllabic and ends in an obstruent, but not to **abstract**, which has two syllables, or to **blue**, which does not end in an obstruent.

◆ Summary

-en suffix	
VC [+obs]	monosyllable
*VC [+son]	disyllables (✗)

3 -al suffix '14

According to Siegel (1974), for a verb base to be eligible for the suffixation of **-al**, it must meet these phonological requirements:

1. The verb base <u>must end in a stressed syllable</u>.
2. The verb base must end phonologically in either a vowel, or a single consonant, or at most two consonants.
3. If the base does not end in a vowel, its final consonant must be made in the front of the mouth (i.e. it must be a labial or alveolar consonant).

These conditions are exemplified in (1). (Consider the pronunciation, not the spelling):

(1) a. -*al* suffix after <u>vowel-final bases</u>
   trial denial betrayal renewal
   b. -*al* after verb bases ending in a <u>labial</u> consonant
   revival arrival approval removal
   c. -*al* after verb bases ending in a <u>dental</u> or <u>alveolar</u> consonant
   betrothal appraisal acquittal recital referral
   d. -*al* after verb bases ending in <u>an (alveolar) consonant preceded by another consonant</u>
   rehearsal dispersal reversal rental

However, if a verb ends in a palatal or velar consonant as in (2), suffixation of this -***al*** is blocked:

(2) *judgeal *attackal *approachal *rebukal *encroachal

The stress on the final syllable is always a vital factor. A base that otherwise meets the conditions for -***al*** suffixation will be ineligible if stress is not on the last syllable. Hence the ill-formedness of *****áudital***, *****cómbatal*** and *****límital***.

As Siegel's analysis predicts, a base like *****attémptal***, which ends in a three-consonant cluster, cannot take the suffix either even though it has got stress in the right place, on the final syllable.

◆ Summary

-al suffix	
V __ V́	(1a)
V __ V́C 　　　[+ant]	(1b, c) (2)
V __ V́CC 　　　[+son][+ant]	(1d)

4 Class 1 vs. Class 2 Suffixes

It is common to distinguish between two types of derivational affixes in English. **Class 1** affixes are characterized by the fact that they often trigger changes in the consonant or vowel segments of the base and may affect the assignment of stress. In contrast, **Class 2** affixes tend to be phonologically neutral, having no effect on the segmental makeup of the base or on stress assignment.

Table 1. Typical effects of Class 1 affixes

Affix	Sample word	Change triggered by affix
-ity	sane – sanity públic – publícity	vowel in the base changes from /e/ to /æ/ final consonant of the base changes from /k/ to /s/ stress shifts to second syllable
-y	démocrat – demócracy	final consonant of the base changes from /t/ to /s/, stress shifts to second syllable
-ive	próduct – prodúctive	stress shifts to second syllable
-(i)al	part – partial	final consonant of the base changes from /t/ to /ʃ/
-ize	public – publicize	final consonant of the base changes from /k/ to /s/
-ious	audacity – audacious	final consonant of the base changes from /s/ to /ʃ/
-ion	native – nation	final consonant of the base changes from /t/ to /ʃ/

Table 2. Some typical Class 2 affixes

Affix	Sample word	Change triggered by affix
-ness	prompt-ness	None
-less	hair-less	None
-ful	hope-ful	None
-ly	quiet-ly	None
-er	defend-er	None
-ish	self-ish	None

When **Class 1** and **Class 2** affixes appear in the same word, the former type of morpheme normally occurs closer to the root than the latter. Moreover, while a **Class 1** affix can follow another **Class 1** affix and while a **Class 2** affix can precede another **Class 2** affix, a **Class 2** affix usually cannot come before a **Class 1** affix. The various possibilities are illustrated below.

relat-ion-al	audac-ious-ness	*fear-less-ity	fear-less-ness
root 1 1	root 1 2	root 2 1	root 2 2

Notice that in the form that is ruled out (*fearlessity) a **Class 1** affix follows a **Class 2** affix.

◆ **Summary**

Class 1 affix	Class 2 affix
phonological changes ① often trigger changes in the **segments** of the base and ② may affect **stress assignment**	**phonologically neutral**
Class 1 + Class 1 Class 2 + Class 2 Class 1 + Class 2 Class 2 + Class 1 (✗)	

◆ Class I suffixes & Class II suffixes

Class I suffixes:	-ity, -ive, -al, -ize, -ous, -ion, -ism, -ize, -ify, -ic, -ate, -ible, -y (noun-forming -y) e.g. profanity, solidify, Icelandic, vacate, legible, democracy
Class II suffixes:	-ness, -less, -ful, -ly, -hood, -like, -some, -ment, -y (adjective-forming -y) -er (agent), -ish e.g. kindness, useless, gruesome, inducement, summery

5 *un-* prefix (semantic constraint)

The use of the italicized words in the dialogue below is odd. What would be the natural and preferred word choices that one would probably use instead of *unill*, *unsad*, *unpessimistic* and *undirty*? Why?

(3) SURGEON: How are you today, Leslie?
PATIENT: I am feeling much better. It's just wonderful to be so *unill* again.
SURGEON: Oh, I'm so *unsad* to see you making such good progress. I am very *unpessimistic* about your chances of making a full recovery. The main thing now is to make sure we keep the wound *undirty* to avoid infection.

This example illustrates how semantics may restrict the application of morphological rules. If there are two adjectives with opposite meanings, one of which has a more positive meaning than the other, normally the negative prefix **un-** attaches to the **positive adjective** (see (4a)). If **un-** is attached to the negative member of the pair, as in (4b), the resulting word is usually ill-formed.

(4) a. unwell   b. *unill
    unloved   *unhated
    unhappy   *unsad
    unwise   *unfoolish
    unclean   *unfilthy, *undirty
    unoptimistic   *unpessimistic

As shown, if there are words representing the two poles of the same semantic dimension, we tend to prefer treating the positive end as **unmarked** (i.e., as normal or basic). We are happier to derive the **marked** (i.e., 'unusual'), less favorable meaning by prefixing the negative prefix to a positive base than doing the reverse. That is why a *happy* person is not said to be **unsad*. To make the dialogue in (3) normal, the marked words, which are italicized, must be replaced by their unmarked counterparts *well*, *happy*, *optimistic*, and *clean*, respectively.

◆ Summary

un- + Adj ─── unmarked adjectives (= positive meaning) ○
              marked adjectives (= negative meaning) ✕
              ex) *unsad, *unfoolish, *undirty

03 Word-Formation Processes

1 Compounds

Two or more words may be joined to form new, **compound** words. English is very flexible in the kinds of combinations permitted, as the following table of compounds shows.

	Adjective	Noun	Verb
Adjective	bittersweet icy-cold red-hot worldly wise	poorhouse	whitewash
Noun	headstrong	homework girlfriend fighter-bomber paper clip elevator-operator landlord mailman	spoonfeed
Verb	feel-good	pickpocket	sleepwalk

Some compounds that have been introduced fairly recently into English are ***Facebook***, ***YouTube***, ***android apps***, and ***crowdsourcing*** (the practice of obtaining information from a large group of people who contribute online).

In English, the rightmost word in a compound is the **head** of the compound. The head is the part of a word or phrase that determines its broad meaning and grammatical category. Thus, when the two words fall into different categories, the class of the second or final word determines the grammatical category of the compound: noun + adjective = adjective, as in ***headstrong***; verb + noun = noun, as in ***pickpocket***. On the other hand, compounds formed with a preposition are in the category of the nonprepositional part of the compound, such as (to) ***overtake*** or (the) ***sundown***. This is further evidence that prepositions form a closed-class category that does not readily admit new members.

Although two-word compounds are the most common in English, it would be difficult to state an upper limit. Consider:

Compounds (three words or more)	
three-time loser	man about town
four-dimensional space-time	master of ceremonies
sergeant-at-arms	daughter-in-law
mother-of-pearl	

(1) Ambiguity

Like derived words, compounds have internal structure. This is clear from the ambiguity of a compound like ***top*** + ***hat*** + ***rack***, which can mean 'a rack for top hats' corresponding to the structure in tree diagram (1), or 'the highest hat rack,' corresponding to the structure in (2).

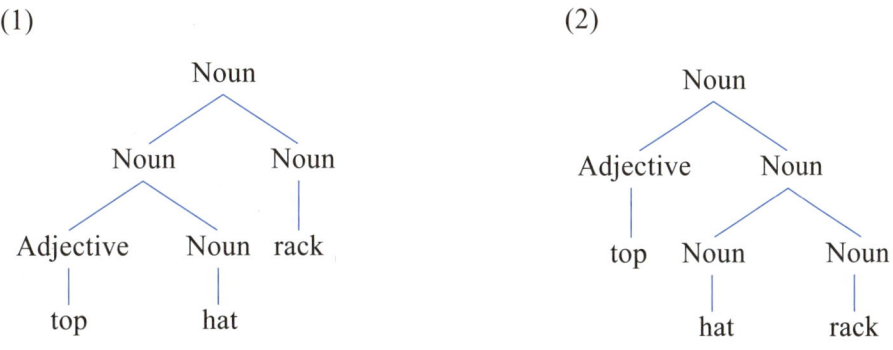

(2) Exocentric and Endocentric Compounds

Two types of compounds

① **exocentric**: their semantic head (or *center*) is 'outside' (*exo*-) the compound.

= headless compound

② **endocentric**: their semantic head (or *center*) is 'inside' (*endo*-) the compound.

The meaning of the entire compound is a hyponym of the meaning of the semantic head.

(e.g. A bed<u>room</u> is a kind of room.)

endocentric compound	exocentric compound
a jumping bean 'a bean that jumps'	"She has a **Redcoat** in her closet" (Redcoat 'British soldier during the American Revolutionary War') ⓒf "She has a **red coat** in her closet" (phrase)
a falling star 'a star that (appears to) fall'	**turncoat** 'traitor'
a magnifying glass 'a glass that magnifies'	**egghead** 'someone who is very intelligent, and only interested in ideas and books'
a boathouse 'a house for boats'	**flat-foot** 'detective'
	butterfingers 'someone who often drops things they are carrying or trying to catch'

The pronunciation of English compounds differs from the way we pronounce the sequence of two words that are not compounded. In an actual compound, the first word is usually stressed and in a noncompound phrase the second word is stressed. Thus we stress **Red** in **Redcoat** but *coat* in *red coat*.

(3) Stress in Compounds vs. Phrases

Adjective-Noun compounds are characterized by a more prominent stress on their first component. In noncompounds consisting of an adjective and a noun, in contrast, the second element is generally stressed.

Compounds vs. Noncompounds

Compound word		Non-compound expressions	
gréenhouse	'an indoor garden'	green hóuse	'a house painted green'
bláckboard	'a chalkboard'	black bóard	'a board which is black'
wét suit	'a diver's costume'	wet súit	'a suit that is wet'

> **Compound Stress Rule (CSR):** Stress on the **first** [left-hand] element.
>
> **Nuclear Stress Rule (NSR):** Stress on the **second** [right-most] word.

2 Blends '07

Blends are similar to compounds in that they are produced by combining two words, but in blends parts of the words that are combined are deleted.

Blending (AB + CD → AD)

the first part of a word + the final part of the other
smoke + fog → **smog**
breakfast + lunch → **brunch**
motor + hotel → **motel**
information + commercial → **infomercial**
urine + analysis → **urinalysis**
iPod + broadcast → **Podcast**
electronic + mail → **e-mail**

3 Clipping '11

Clipping is the abbreviation of longer words into shorter ones by leaving out one or more syllables.

◆ Clipping

Fore-clipping	Back-clipping
omnibus → **bus** caravan → **van** telephone → **phone** influenza → **flu** refrigerator → **fridge**	bicycle → **bike** mathematics → **math** gasoline → **gas** facsimile → **fax** television → **telly** professor → **prof** advertisement → **ad** gymnasium → **gym** pornography → **porn** <person's name> Ronald → **Ron** Elizabeth → **Liz** Susan → **Sue**

4 Acronyms '07

Acronyms are words derived from the initials of several words. Such words are <u>pronounced as a word</u>: **NASA** [næsə] from National Aeronautics and Space Administration, **UNESCO** [junɛsko] from United Nations Educational, Scientific, and Cultural Organization, and **UNICEF** [junəsɛf] from United Nations International Children's Emergency Fund.

5 Initialisms [(Alphabetic) abbreviations] '07

When the string of letters is not easily pronounced as a word, the reduced word is produced <u>by sounding out each letter</u>, as in **NFL** [ɛ̃nɛfɛl] for National Football League, **UCLA** [jusiɛle] for University of California, Los Angeles, and **MRI** [ɛ̃maraɪ] for magnetic resonance imaging. These special kinds of acronyms are sometimes called **alphabetic abbreviations**.

Acronyms	Initialisms [abbreviations]
NASA [næsə]	NFL
UNESCO [junɛsko]	UCLA
UNICEF [junəsɛf]	MRI
radar (radio detecting and ranging)	UN
laser (light amplification by stimulated emission of radiation)	TV
scuba (self-contained underwater breathing apparatus)	DNA
RAM (random access memory)	BBC
AIDS (acquired immune deficiency syndrome)	CNN
MERS (Middle East Respiratory Syndrome)	USA

6 Conversion '02, '07, '21

Consider the examples in (1):

(1) a. The head of the village school has arrived.

b. She will head the village school.

c. She headed that school.

Sometimes we create words by simply assigning them another syntactic category. This word-formation process is called **conversion** or **zero-derivation** (in that there is no affixation involved).

◆ Conversion

N → V		
hammer	hammer	*More examples:*
plant	plant	mother, google, impact, position, process, contrast
ship	ship	
blackmail	blackmail	Stop **mothering** me!
e-mail	e-mail	**Google** it.
fax	fax	She **blackmailed** him for years by threatening to tell the newspapers about their affair.

We also convert adjectives to verbs, as in ***to savage*** or ***to total***, and adjectives to nouns, as in ***a crazy***. ***Laugh***, ***run***, ***buy***, and ***steal*** started out as verbs but can now also be used as nouns.

◆ **Conversion**

V → N	V → N with stress shift	
His first joke got the biggest **laugh** of the night. I go for a **run** every morning. That jacket was a really good **buy**. Best **buys** this week are carrots and cabbages. This suit is **a steal** at $80.	transfér permít convért pervért commúne	tránsfer pérmit cónvert pérvert cómmune

7 Back Formation '11

A new word may enter the language because of an incorrect morphological analysis. For example, *peddle* was derived from *peddler* on the mistaken assumption that the *-er* was the agentive suffix. Such words are called **back-formations**. *Pea* was derived from a singular word, *pease*, by speakers who thought *pease* was a plural.

Back Formation

edit < editor
babysit < babysitter
burgle < burglar
peddle < peddler
swindle < swindler
hawk < hawker

resurrect < resurrection
preempt < preemption
televise < television
orientate < orientation
self-destruct < self-destruction
pea < pease
enthuse < enthusiasm

8 Coinage '11

Sometimes a word may be created from scratch. Called **word manufacture** or **coinage**, this phenomenon is especially common in the case of product names, including ***Kodak***, ***Dacron***, ***Orlon***, and ***Teflon***.

In still other cases, brand names can become so widely known that they are accepted as generic terms for the product with which they are associated. The words ***kleenex*** for 'facial tissue' or ***xerox*** for 'photocopy' are two obvious examples of this.

◆ **Word Coinage**

product/brand name		material name
Kodak	Kleenex	nylon
Dacron	Vaseline	
Teflon	xerox	
Band-Aid	Velcro	
Jell-O		

9 Word from Names (Eponyms)

This is a kind of word coinage. **Eponyms** are words that are coined from proper names.

◆ **Word from Names**

Eponyms	explanation
sandwich	Named for the fourth Earl of Sandwich, who put his food between two slices of bread so that he could eat while he gambled.
boycott	after Charles C. Boycott, English land agent in Ireland who was ostracized for refusing to reduce rents

Syntax 01-02 mind map

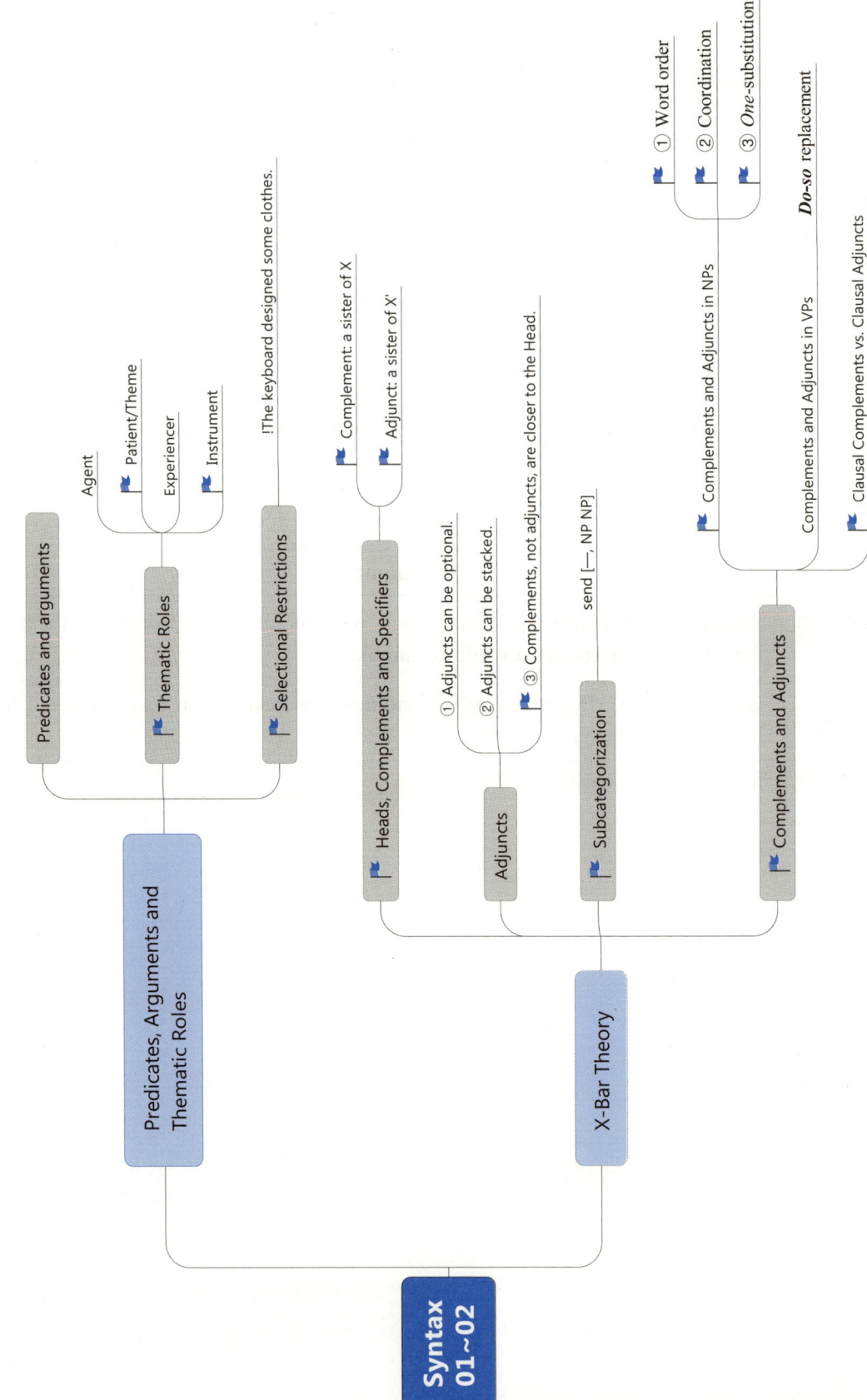

Syntax 03~04 mind map

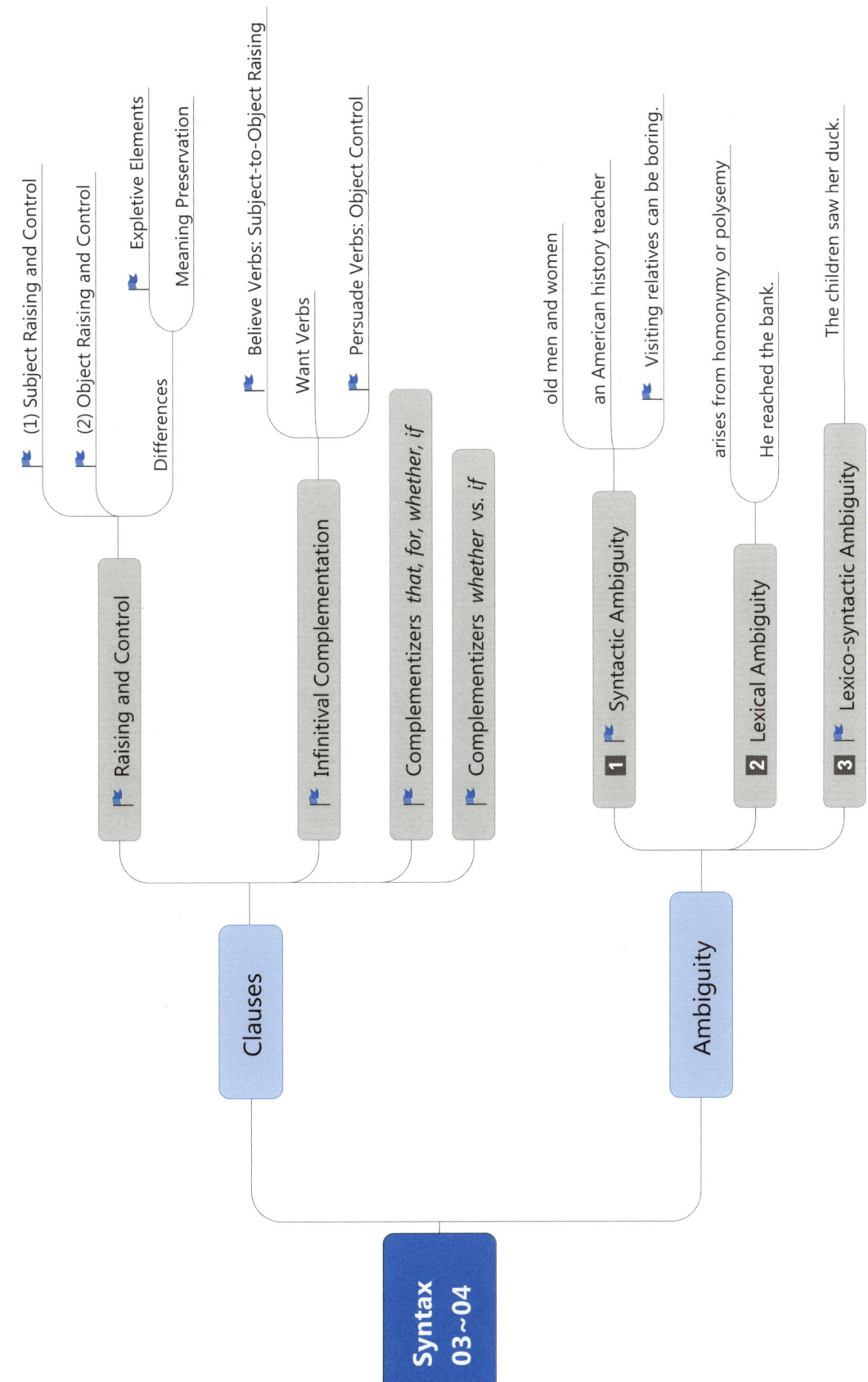

Syntax 05-06 mind map

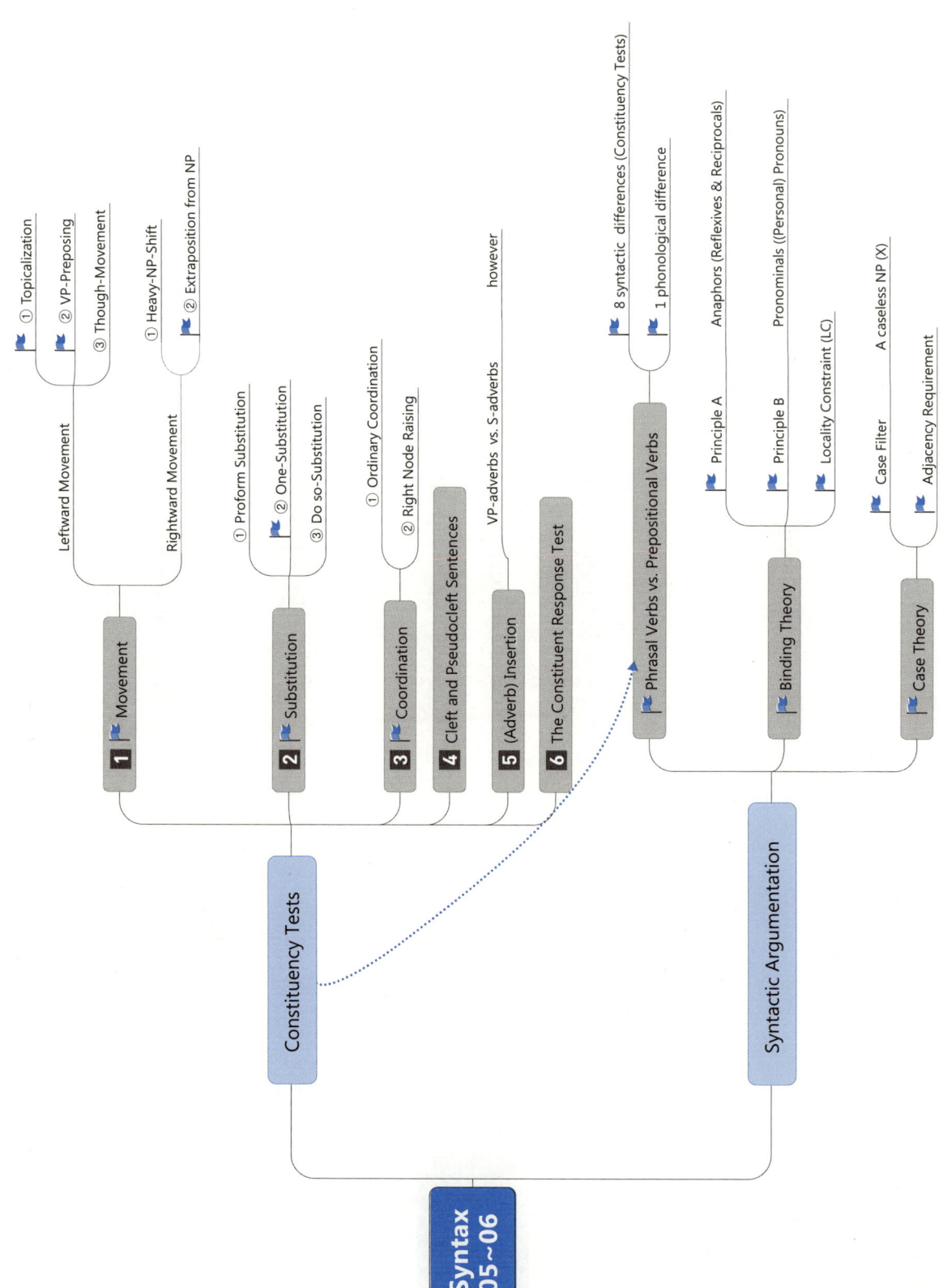

Chapter 03 Syntax

01 Predicates, Arguments and Thematic Roles

1 Predicates and arguments

(1) The crocodile devoured a doughnut.

We will refer to elements that require the specification of the participants in the proposition expressed as predicates (e.g. **devour**), and we will refer to the participants themselves as arguments (**the crocodile**, **a doughnut**). Thus, the sentence (1) can be analyzed as follows.

(2) The crocodile   devoured   a doughnut.
    Argument   Predicate   Argument
    Agent   Patient

Below you will find some further examples of sentences containing argument-taking predicates. Each time the predicates are in bold type and the arguments are in italics.

(3) *Henry* **smiled**.　　　　　　　→ intransitive verb
(4) *The police* **investigated** *the allegation*.　　→ (mono)transitive verb
(5) *Sara* **gave** [*Pete*] [*a parcel*].　　→ ditransitive verb

2 Thematic Roles [θ-roles, Thematic Relations, Semantic Roles] '14

Linguists don't agree exactly how many there are, nor do they agree exactly which roles we should recognize. However, the following thematic roles are widely accepted:

Thematic roles (also known as *theta roles* or *θ-roles*)

Agent	The '**doer**', or **instigator** of the action denoted by the predicate
Patient	The '**undergoer**' of the action or event denoted by the predicate
Theme	The entity that is **moved** by the action or event denoted by the predicate
Experiencer	The **living entity** that experiences the action or event denoted by the predicate
Goal	The **location** or entity in the direction of which something moves
Benefactive	The entity that **benefits from** the action or event denoted by the predicate
Source	The **location** or entity from which something moves
Instrument	The **medium** by which the action or event denoted by the predicate is carried out
Locative	The **place** where the action or event denoted by the predicate is situated

> **Exercise 1** Consider the sentences below and determine which thematic roles the bracketed phrases can be said to carry.

(i) [His mother] sent   [David]   [a letter].
    Agent   Goal   Theme

(ii) [David] smelled   [the freshly baked bread].
     Agent   Patient

(iii) [We] put [the cheese]   [in the fridge].
     Agent   Theme   Goal

(iv) [Frank] threw [himself]   [onto the sofa].
     Agent   Theme/Patient   Goal

(v) [Greg] comes [from Wales].
     Agent   Source

(1) Nonreferential *it* and *there*

Let us now turn to elements in sentences that do not receive thematic roles.

(6) *It* always rains in London.

(7) *There* were six policemen on the bus.

The grammatical Subjects in these sentences are *it* and *there* respectively. We called *it* in (6) *weather it*, because it often occurs in sentences which tell you about the weather, and we called *there* in (7) *existential there*, because it is used in propositions about existence. Notice that unlike referential *it* and locative *there* in (8) and (9) below, the Subjects in (6) and (7) do not refer to entities in the outside world. They are purely Subject slot fillers.

(8) I hate the number 31 bus, *it* is always packed!

(9) I'll put your coffee over *there*.

Remember that unlike referential *it* and *there*, nonreferential *it* and *there* do not receive thematic roles. This concept is important in the later discussion of raising and control construction.

3 Selectional Restrictions '02

Consider the sentences below:

(10) !The keyboard designed some clothes.

(11) !The stapler took a break.

(12) !My colleague broke his feelings.

We refer to the restrictions imposed by the predicates of the sentences above on their arguments as **selectional restrictions**. Linguists have suggested that one way of dealing with selectional restrictions is to assign *features* to predicates and their arguments. For example, we might say that the verb *design* carries a feature [+animate] and that its Subject must also carry this feature. If it doesn't, the resulting sentence in deviant. Clearly, in (10) the Subject expression *the keyboard* is not an animate entity and the sentence is odd as a result. (11) is strange for the same reason. (12) can also be handled in terms of features: we might say that the verb *break* carries the feature [+concrete] which must be matched by a Direct Object that carries the same feature. In (12) the DO is an abstract NP, and this accounts for its peculiarity.

02 X-Bar Theory

1 Heads, Complements and Specifiers '20, '21

In the bracketed phrases in the sentences below the Heads are shown in bold type.

(1) The defendants denied the charge: they claim that they did [$_{VP}$ not **destroy** the garden]

(2) She proposed [$_{NP}$ an **analysis** of the sentence]

(3) Jake is [$_{AP}$ so **fond** of coffee]

(4) They are [$_{PP}$ quite **in** agreement]

(5) My sister cycles [$_{AdvP}$ much **faster** than me]

Specifiers: not, an, so, quite, much

Complements: the garden, of the sentence, of coffee, agreement, than me

Specifiers ('**Spec**') are the elements that specify the Head + Complement sequence. **Complement** denote any constituent whose presence is required by its Head.

(6)
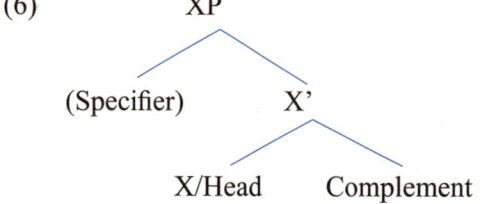

In this tree 'XP' is a phrase headed by X, where X stands for V, N, A, P or Adv. The Specifier is a sister of the node that dominates the Head + Complement sequence, indicated by X'. In (6), X' is at a level that is intermediate between the phrase level XP and the Head level X. Since Head + Complement sequence is a constituent, it is inevitable that we assume the X' or X-bar level.

As seen in (6), the X-bar syntax posits three-level structure for XP, any phrase, which can be described schematically as follows.

(7)   X   <   X'   <   XP
      Head   Intermediate   Phrase
      (lexical)

Also, when we draw tree diagrams, it is useful to remember the sisterhood shown in the following:

(8) Specifier: a sister of X'   Adjunct: a sister of X'
    Complement: a sister of X

2 Adjuncts

Adjuncts refer to a constituent that specifies the 'how', 'when', 'where' or 'why' of the situation expressed by a sentence. Not only VPs can contain adjuncts, but other phrase types as well. Consider the strings below:

(9) [$_{NP}$ an analysis of the sentence *with tree diagrams*]

(10) [$_{AP}$ so fond of coffee *after dinner*]

(11) [$_{PP}$ quite in agreement *about this*]

(12) [$_{AdvP}$ much faster than me *by far*]

Adjuncts can appear *before* the Head.

(13) [$_{NP}$ a *silly* analysis of the sentence]

(14) [$_{AP}$ so *terribly* fond of coffee]

(15) [$_{PP}$ quite *unhesitatingly* in agreement]

(16) [$_{AdvP}$ *clearly* faster than me]

Bear in mind the three following characteristics of Adjuncts:

(1) Adjuncts can be optional.

(17) a. [$_{NP}$ an analysis of the sentence *with tree diagrams*]
     b. [$_{NP}$ an analysis of the sentence]

Both of the sentences above are well-formed, demonstrating the optionality of the adjunct 'with tree diagrams.'

(2) Adjuncts can be stacked.

(18) [$_{NP}$ a ***silly, preposterous*** analysis of the sentence]

(19) [$_{AP}$ so ***terribly*** fond of coffee ***after dinner***]

(20) [$_{PP}$ quite ***unhesitatingly*** in agreement ***with each other***]

(3) Complements, not adjuncts, are closer to the Head '06, '16

Complements are closer to the head of the phrase than are adjuncts. (Complements are sisters of their Heads, while Adjuncts are sisters of the single bar level above the Head.) This property accounts for the ungrammaticality of the following phrases.

(21) * . . . they did [$_{VP}$ not destroy deliberately the garden]

(22) *[$_{NP}$ an analysis with tree diagrams of the sentence]

(23) *[$_{AP}$ so fond in the morning of coffee]

(24) *[$_{PP}$ quite with each other in agreement]

(25) *[$_{AdvP}$ much faster by far than me]

Table 1. Typical Specifiers for the Major Phrase Types NP, VP, AP and PP

Phrase	Specifier	Examples
NP	determiners	[*the* examination] [*this* book] [*those* bicycles] [*our* car] [*many* answers]
VP	negative elements	He does [*not* like planes] She [*never* eats meat]
AP	degree adverbs	[*how* nice] They are [*so* eager to please] He isn't [*that/this* fat] [*too* bad] That's [*rather/quite* disgusting] She is [*as* rich as the Queen]
PP	adverbs	The supermarket is [*right* up your street] The wedding ring went [*straight* down the drain] The office is [*just* to your left]

Table 2. Typical Complements for the Major Phrase Types NP, VP, AP and PP

Phrase	Head	Complement	Examples
NP	N	PP	his *insistence* [_{PP} on the arrangement] (cf. He *insists* on the arrangement.) their *specialization* [_{PP} in wines] (cf. They *specialize* in wines.)
		clause	their *realization* [_{*that*-clause} that all is lost] (cf. They *realize* that all is lost.) her *question* [_{*whether*-clause} whether the expense was worth it] (cf. She *questioned* whether the expense was worth it.) their *requirement* [_{*for*-clause} for all candidates to comply with the rules] (cf. They *requires* all candidates to comply with the rules.)
		NP	a [_{NP} literature] *teacher* (cf. He *teaches* literature / a teacher of literature)

Note: Complement-taking nominal Heads often have a verbal counterpart.

| VP | V | NP | She *placed* [_{NP} an advertisement]. |

		clause	They **know** [_{that-clause} that the sun will shine tomorrow]
		PP	He **looked** [_{PP} at the picture]
		AP	He **is** [_{AP} very healthy]
AP	A	PP	**glad** [_{PP} about your decision] **pleased** [_{PP} with the result] **dependent** [_{PP} on his brother]
		clause	I am so **eager** [_{to-infinitive clause} to work with you] He's **engaged** [_{-ing clause} teaching the students] She's **unsure** [_{wh-clause} what we should do next]
PP	P	NP	**in/under/behind** [_{NP} the car]
		PP	**out** [_{PP} of love] **from** [_{PP} behind the bookcase] **down** [_{PP} by the sea]
		clause	He is uncertain **about** [_{wh-clause} what you said to me]

Table 3. Typical Adjuncts for the Major Phrase Types NP, VP, AP and PP

Phrase	Head	Adjunct	Examples
NP	N	AP	The **warm** summer
		NP	The **woman** busdriver
		PP	The tiles **on the floor**
		clause	My younger sister, **who lives in Italy** The information **that you supplied**
VP	V	AdvP	He **quickly** absconded. She read the prospectus **eagerly**.
		PP	We came here **in the summer**.
		clause	She phoned **because she likes you**.
AP	A	AdvP	We were **unconsolably** disappointed.
		PP	He was abusive **to the extreme**.
PP	P	AdvP	I was **totally** over the moon.
		PP	They designed the museum in tandem **with an Italian architect**.

3 Subcategorization

We saw that the bond between a Head and its Complement is so strong that a Complement must always be adjacent to its Head, and that an Adjunct may not intervene. Another way of claiming that there is a strong connection between Heads and Complements is to say that Heads *subcategorize for* (i.e. syntactically require the presence of) their Complements. We use so-called **subcategorization frames** to specify exactly which Complements a Head takes. Here's the subcategorization frame for *destroy*, *send*, etc.

destroy (verb)

[—, NP]

send (verb)

[—, NP NP]   e.g. He **sent** her some details of the plan.

send (verb)

[—, (NP) NP]   e.g. Martin didn't come to the party, but he **sent** his sister.

blush (verb)

[—, ø]   e.g. She **blushed**.

fact (noun)

[—, (that-clause)] e.g. She hates the **fact** that he is a genius.

appreciative (adjective)

[—, of-NP]   e.g. She is **appreciative** of classical music.

behind (preposition)

[—, NP]   e.g. The bike is **behind** the shed.

4 Complements and Adjuncts

(1) Complements and Adjuncts in NPs '06, 08, '09, '10, '14, '16

Take NPs as a prototypical example. Consider the difference in meaning between the two NPs below:

(1) the book of poems

(2) the book with a red cover

Although both these examples seem to have, on the surface, parallel structures (a determiner, followed by a noun, followed by a prepositional phrase), in reality, they have quite different structures. The PP in (1) is a complement and has the following tree:

(3)
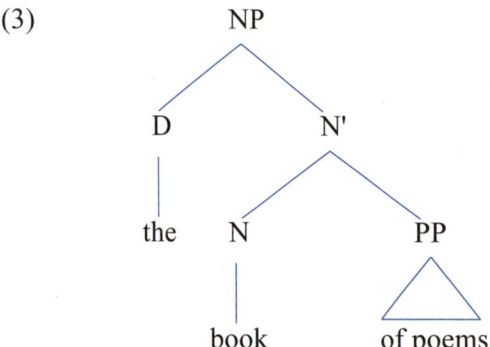

You'll note that the PP is a sister to N, so it is a complement. By contrast, the structure of (2) is:

(4)
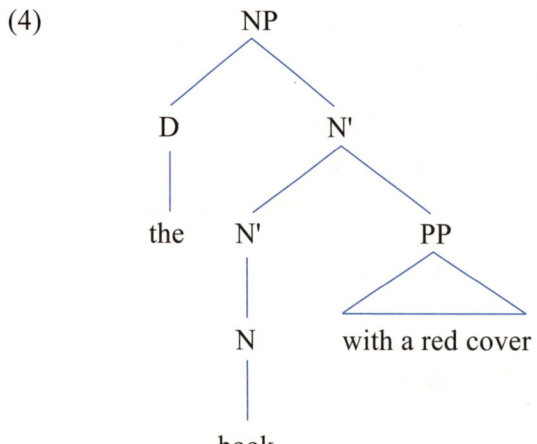

Here the PP *with a red cover* is a sister to N', so it is an adjunct. Consider first the meaning of our two NPs. In (1), the PP seems to complete (or complement) the meaning of the noun. It tells us what kind of book is being referred to. In (2), by contrast, the PP seems more optional and more loosely related to the NP. This is a highly subjective piece of evidence, but it corresponds to more syntactic and structural evidence too.

Let's look at some of the other behavioral distinctions between complements and adjuncts. Think carefully about the two rules that introduce complements and adjuncts.

1) Word order '06, '16

> **Word order**
> Complements will always be 'closer' to their head Noun than Adjuncts.

First observe that the complement PP will always be adjacent to the head. Or more particularly, it will always be closer to the head than an adjunct PP will be. This is seen in the following data:

(5)   the book   [of poems]   [with a red cover]
        head   *complement*   *adjunct*

(6)   *the book   [with a red cover]   [of poems]
        head   *adjunct*   *complement*

2) Coordination '08

> **Coordination**
> Two different types, a complement and an adjunct, cannot be coordinated.

Note that adjuncts and complements are constituents of different types. The definition of adjuncthood holds that adjuncts are sisters to X'. Since conjunction requires that you conjoin elements of the same bar level, you could not, for example, conjoin an adjunct with a complement. This would result in a contradiction: Something can't be both a sister to X' and X at the same time. Adjuncts can conjoin with other adjuncts (other sisters to X'), and complements can conjoin with other complements (other sisters to X), but complements cannot conjoin with adjuncts:

(7)   a. the book of poems with a red cover and with a blue spine
      b. the book of poems and of fiction from Blackwell
      c. *the book of poems and from Blackwell

3) *One*-substitution '09, '14

> ***One*-substitution**
> The proform *one* replaces N'-constituents.

There is one final difference between adjuncts and complements that we will examine here. Recall the test of *one*-replacement:

(8) ***One*-replacement**: Replace an N' node with ***one***.

This operation replaces an N' node with the word *one*. Look at the tree in (9):

(9)
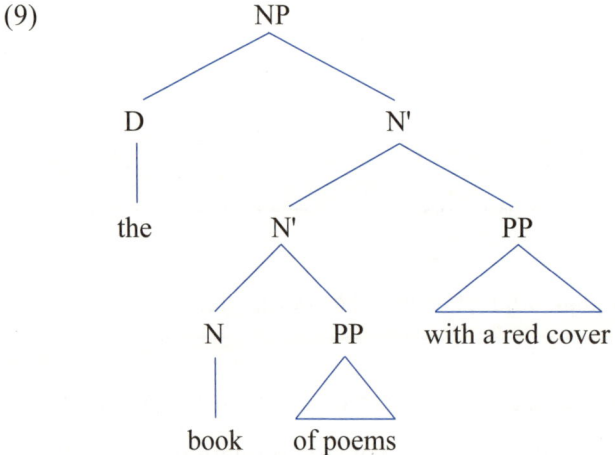

If you look closely at this tree, you'll see that two possibilities for *one*-replacement exist. We can either target the highest N' and get:

(10) the one

or we can target the lower N' and get:

(11) the one with a red cover

But we cannot target the N head; it is not an N'. This means that *one* followed by a complement is ill-formed:

(12) *the one of poems with a red cover

(2) Complements and Adjuncts in VPs

1) Word order

In VPs, the direct object of a verb is a complement of the verb. Prepositional and adverbial modifiers of verbs are adjuncts:

(13) I   loved   [the policeman]   [intensely]   [with all my heart].
     V   direct object   adverbial   PP phrase
                      complement   *adjunct*   *adjunct*

(14)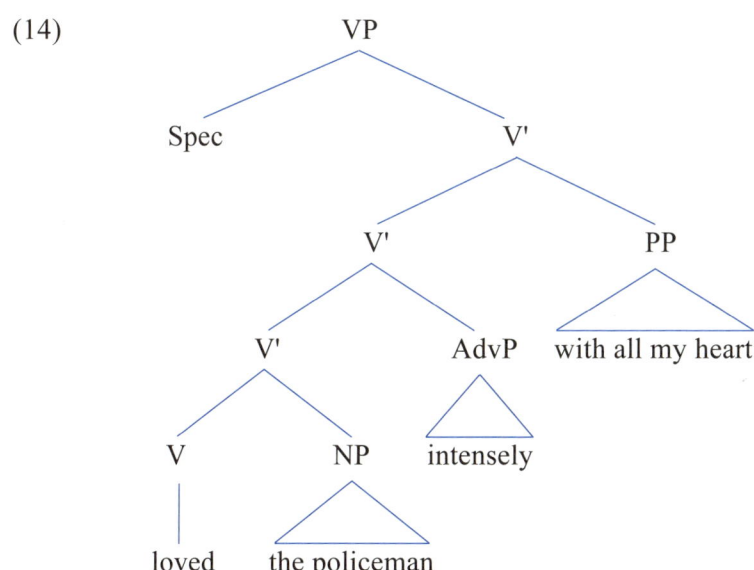

Direct objects must be adjacent to the verb, and there can only be one of them.

(15) a. *I loved intensely the policeman with all my heart.
　　 b. *I loved the policeman the baker intensely with all my heart.

2) *Do so*-substitution

***Do-so*-**replacement targets V'. Like *one*-replacement, this means that it can only apply before an adjunct and not before a complement:

(16) Mike loved the policeman intensely and

    a. Susan did so half-heartedly.

    b. *Susan did so the baker.

(3) Clausal Complements vs. Clausal Adjuncts '03

The use of *that* as both **a relative pronoun** and a pure **complementizer** can lead to confusion between appositive *that*-clauses and relative clauses:

(1) a. The suggestion that he might fail is disturbing.

    b. The suggestion that he made is disturbing.

In (1a) is a clause functioning as a complement of N (equivalent to a direct object of the verb *suggest*: Someone suggested that he might fail). The complementizer *that* has no function in its own clause, and the embedded clause is complete without *that* and can stand alone as a complete sentence **He might fail**. The *that*-clause can also function as an NP: **That he might fail is disturbing**. In (1b) is a clause functioning as a modifier of N' (or N). The relative *that* has the function of direct object in its own clause, and hence the embedded clause is not complete without the relative: *He made*. The embedded clause cannot function as an NP: ***That he made is disturbing**. Note that *which* can substitute for *that* in this case but not in the other: **The suggestion which he made is disturbing**, ***The suggestion which he might fail is disturbing**. The trees for the sentences are given below:

(2) (a)

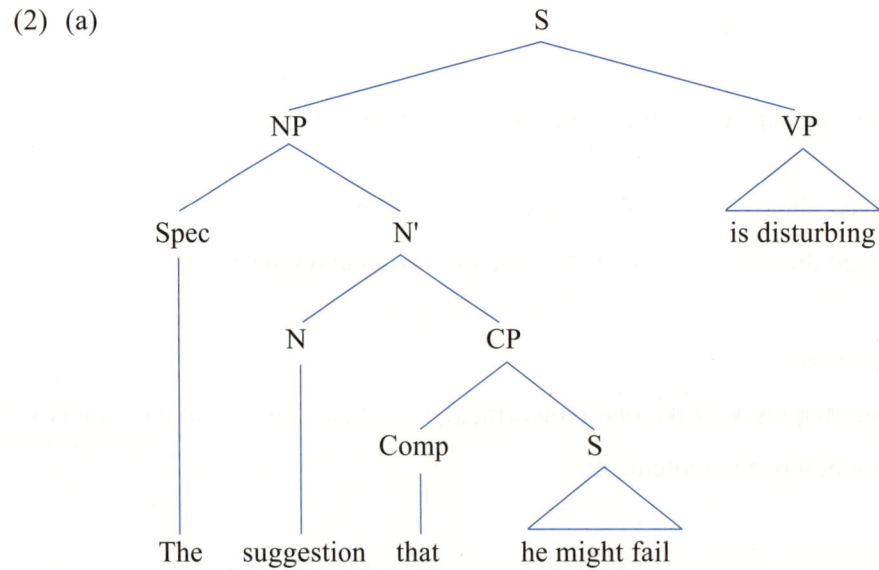

(b)

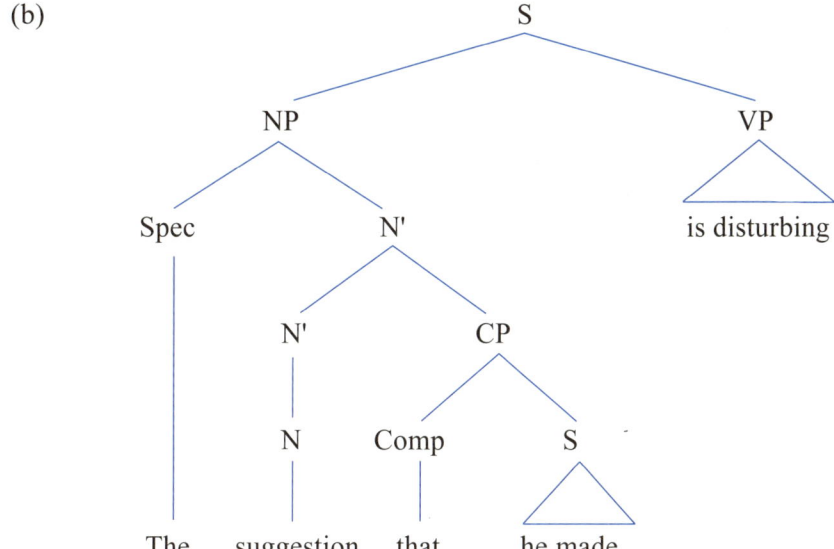

The surface similarity of these two types of clauses can lead to **ambiguity**:

(3) The idea that he proposed made her laugh.
   ① *that*-clause: his proposing made her laugh (that he proposed made her laugh)
   ② relative clause: his idea made her laugh (he proposed the idea)

(4) The fact that Bill forgot was verified.
   ① *that*-clause: Bill's forgetting was verified (that Bill forgot was verified)
   ② relative clause: the fact was verified (Bill forgot the fact)

03 Clauses

1 Raising and Control Constructions '06, '07, '09, '09 Mock, '12, '18, '19

◆ Raising and Control Predicates

Certain verbs select an infinitival VP as their complement. Compare the following pairs of examples:

(1) a. John <u>tries</u> to fix the computer.

    b. John <u>seems</u> to fix the computer.

(2) a. Mary <u>persuaded</u> John to fix the computer.

    b. Mary <u>expected</u> John to fix the computer.

At first glance, these pairs are structurally isomorphic in terms of complements: both *try* and *seem* select an infinitival VP, and *expect* and *persuade* select an NP and an infinitival VP. However, there are several significant differences which motivate two classes, known as **control** and **raising** verbs:

(3) a. Control verbs and adjectives: try, hope, eager, promise, persuade, etc.

    b. Raising verbs and adjectives: seem, appear, happen, likely, certain, believe, expect, etc.

Verbs like ***try*** are called 'control' or 'equi' verbs, where subject is understood to be 'equivalent' to the unexpressed subject of the infinitival VP. In linguistic terminology, the subject of the verb is said to 'control' the subject of the infinitival complement. Let us consider the 'deep structure' of (1a) representing unexpressed subject of the VP complement of ***tries***:

(4) John tries [(for) John to fix the computer].

As shown here, in this sentence it is John who does the action of fixing the computer. In the original transformational grammar approach, this deep structure would be proposed and then undergo a rule of 'Equivalent NP Deletion' in which the second NP *John* would be deleted, to produce the output sentence. This is why such verbs have the label of 'equi-verbs'.

Meanwhile, verbs like ***seem*** are called 'raising' verbs. Consider the deep structure of (1b):

(5) △ seems [John to fix the computer].

In order to derive the 'surface structure' (1b), the subject *John* needs to be raised to the matrix subject position marked by △. This is why verbs like ***seem*** are called 'raising' verbs.

This chapter discusses the similarities and differences of these two types of verb, and shows how we explain their respective properties in a systematic way.

◆ Raising and Control Predicates

Subject Raising (Seem class) S-to-S Raising	**Subject Control (Eager class)** ★ PRO는 항상 CP에만 나타난다.
seem [*appear*] *likely* [*tend*] ↔ *unlikely* *certain* [*sure*] *turn out* [*prove*], *happen* [*chance*] *be said* [*be known, be found, be supposed, be believed, be reported*] e.g. He is *likely/unlikely/certain* to pass the test. Edith *seems/appears/happens* to enjoy my company. He *is said* to be honest.	*eager* [*anxious, keen*], *try* *promise* [*agree, willing*] ↔ *refuse* [*reluctant*] *able* [*eligible, available, free, ready, welcome*] *plan, prefer, want* [*intend, hope, wish, long*] e.g. John is *eager* to please. He *tried* to fix the computer. I *promised* Howard to take two shirts for his father. I *want* to clean the house. (Want + to-infinitive) I *intend* to go to Australia next year.
Object Raising (Believe class) S-to-O Raising (= ECM verbs)	**Object Control (Persuade class)**
believe [*consider, feel, find, think, judge, acknowledge, report*] *expect* [*intend, mean, imagine*] *know* [*suppose, understand*] e.g. I *consider* Einstein to be a genius. John *believed* the stranger to be a policeman. The police *reported* the traffic to be heavy. I *expected* her to wait for me. I *intended* her to see the painting.	*persuade* [*convince*] *ask* [*beg, request*] *order* [*command, force, compel*] ↔ *forbid* *instruct* [*tell*], *remind* *encourage* [*invite, tempt*], *advise* [*urge*], *cause* e.g. I *convinced* her to change her mind. I *asked* her to clean the room.
※ tough movement: O(-to-S) Raising	**Want** class (Want + NP + to-infinitive)
tough [*hard, difficult, challenging*], *boring, annoying, impossible, dangerous* *easy* [*simple, convenient*], *fun* [*interesting*], *pleasant, wonderful* [*nice*], *safe* *a chore* [*a pain*], *a problem, a surprise* *a piece of cake* [*a snap, a cinch*], *a pleasure* [*a joy*] e.g. Bob is *hard* to convince. John is *easy* to please. *possible: *The doctor is possible to see.	*want* [*need, hope, wish, long, desire, yearn*] *love* [*like, prefer*] ↔ *hate* *plan* [*arrange*] e.g. She *wanted* me to help her. I *hope* for her to survive. She *wished* for him to get better. He *loved* her to sing to him. ※ want/long/prefer + (for) NP + to-infinitive She *longed for* him to visit her. I *prefer* very much *for* the boys to leave first. We *arranged for* him to leave at once.

2 Differences between Raising and Control Verbs

There are many differences between the two classes of verb, which we present here.

(1) Subject Raising and Control '06, '07, '09, '09 Mock, '12, '18, '19

The semantic role of the subject: One clear difference between raising and control verbs is the semantic role assigned to the subject. Let us compare the following examples:

(6) a. John tries to be honest.

b. John seems to be honest.

These might have paraphrases as follows:

(7) a. John makes efforts for himself to be honest.

b. It seems that John is honest.

As suggested by the paraphrase, the one who does the action of trying is John in (6a). How about (6b)? Is it John who is involved in the situation of 'seeming'? As represented in its paraphrase (7b), the situation that the verb *seem* describes is not about the individual John, but is rather about the proposition that John is honest. Due to this difference, we say that a control verb like *try* assigns a semantic role to its subject (the 'agent' role), whereas a raising verb *seem* does not assign any semantic role to its subject (this is what (5) is intended to represent).

Expletive subjects: Since the raising verb does not assign a semantic role to its subject, certain expressions which do not have a semantic role or any meaning may appear in the subject position. Such items include the expletives *it* or *there*:

(8) a. It tends to be warm in September.

b. It seems to bother Kim that they resigned.

The situation is markedly different with control verbs:

(9) a. *It/*There tries to be warm in September.

b. *It/*There hopes to bother Kim that they resigned.

Since control verbs like ***try*** and ***hope*** require their subject to have an agent role, an expletive ***it*** or ***there***, which takes no semantic role, cannot function as their subject.

We can observe the same contrast with respect to raising and control adjectives:

(10) a. It/*John is <u>easy</u> to please Maja.

   b. John/*It is <u>eager</u> to please Maja.

Since the raising adjective ***easy*** do not assign any semantic role to its subject, we can have ***it*** as its subject. On the other hand, the control adjective ***eager*** assigns a role and thus does not allow the expletive ***it*** as its subject.

Selectional Restrictions: <u>In raising constructions, it is not the raising verb or adjective, but the infinitival complement's predicate which determines the characteristic of the subject.</u> In raising constructions, the subject of the raising predicate is selected as the subject of the complement VP. Observe the following contrast:

(11) a. Stephen seemed [to be intelligent].

   b. It seems [to be easy to fool Ben].

   c. There is likely [to be a letter in the mailbox].

(12) a. *There seemed [to be intelligent].

   b. *John seems [to be easy to fool Ben].

   c. *John is likely [to be a letter in the mailbox].

For example, the VP *to be intelligent* requires an animate subject, and this is why (11a) is fine but (12a) is not. Meanwhile, the VP *to be easy to fool Ben* requires the expletive *it* as its subject. This is why *John* cannot be the subject in (12b). In (11c) and (12c), the VP [*to be a letter in the mailbox*] allows its subject to be *there* (cf *There is a letter in the mailbox*) but not *John*.

However, for control verbs, there is no direct selectional relation between the subject of the main verb and that of the infinitival VP. <u>It is the control verb or adjective itself which fully determines the properties of the subject</u>:

(13) a. Sandy tried [to eat oysters].

   b. *There tried [to be riots in Seoul].

   c. *It tried [to bother me that Chris lied].

Regardless of what the infinitival VP would require as its subject, a control predicate requires its subject to be able to bear the semantic role of agent. For example, in (13b) and (13c), the subject of the infinitival VP can be *there* and *it*, but these cannot function as the matrix subject—because the matrix verb tried requires its own subject, a 'trier'.

Meaning preservation: We have seen that the subject of a raising predicate is that of the infinitival VP complement, and it has no semantic role at all coming from the raising predicate. This implies that an idiom whose meaning is specially composed from its parts will still retain its meaning even if part of it appears as the subject of a raising verb.

(14) a. The cat seems to be out of the bag.

   in the sense of: 'The secret is out'.

   b. #The cat tries to be out of the bag.

In the raising example (14a), the meaning of the idiom *The cat is out of the bag* is retained. However, since the control verb **tries** assigns a semantic role to its subject *the cat*, 'the cat' must be the one doing the action of trying, and there is no idiomatic meaning.

This preservation of meaning also holds for examples like the following:

(15) a. The dentist is likely to examine Pat.

= b. Pat is likely to be examined by the dentist.

(16) a. The dentist is eager to examine Pat.

≠ b. Pat is eager to be examined by the dentist.

<u>Since the raising predicate **likely** does not assign a semantic role to its subject, (15a) and (15b) have more or less identical meanings</u>—the proposition is about the dentist examining Pat, in active or passive grammatical forms: the active subject is raised in (15a), and the passive subject in (15b).

However, the control predicate *eager* assigns a semantic role to its subject, and this forces (16a) and (16b) to differ semantically: in (16a), it is the dentist who is eager to examine Pat, whereas in (16b), it is Pat who is eager to be examined by the dentist. Intuitively, if one of the examples in (15) is true, so is the other, but this inference cannot be made in (16).

(2) Object Raising and Control '07, '09, '09 Mock, '18, '19

Similar contrasts are found between what are known as object raising and control predicates:

(17) a. Stephen believed Ben to be careful.

b. Stephen persuaded Ben to be careful.

Once again, these two verbs look alike in terms of syntax: they both combine with an NP and an infinitival VP complement. However, the two are different with respect to the properties of the object NP in relation to the rest of the structure. Observe the differences between *believe* and *persuade* in (18):

(18) a. Stephen believed it to be easy to please Maja.

b. *Stephen persuaded it to be easy to please Maja.

(19) a. Stephen believed there to be a fountain in the park.

b. *Stephen persuaded there to be a fountain in the park.

One thing we can see here is that unlike *believe*, *persuade* does not license an expletive object (just like *try* does not license an expletive subject). And in this respect, the verb *believe* is similar to seem in that it does not assign a semantic role (to its object). The differences show up again in the preservation of idiomatic meaning:

(20) a. Stephen believed the cat to be out of the bag.

    in the sense: 'Stephen believed that the secret was out'.

b. #Stephen persuaded the cat to be out of the bag.

While the idiomatic reading is retained with the raising verb *believed*, it is lost with the control verb *persuaded*.

Active-passive pairs show another contrast:

(21) a. The dentist was believed to have examined Pat.

= b. Pat was believed to have been examined by the dentist.

(22) a. The dentist was persuaded to examine Pat.

≠ b. Pat was persuaded to be examined by the dentist.

With the raising verb *believe*, there is no strong semantic difference in the examples in (21). However, in (22), there is a clear difference in who is persuaded. In (22a), it is the dentist, but in (22b), it is Pat who is persuaded. This is one more piece of evidence that *believe* is a raising verb whereas *persuade* is a control verb, with respect to the object.

◆ **Summary: Three Differences between Raising and Control Predicates**

	Raising Predicates	Control Predicates
① Expletive Elements (Dummy Elements)	○	×
② Meaning Preservation—Idiom Chunks	○	×
③ Meaning Preservation—Passivization	○	×

The reason for ①~③: A control verb like *try* assigns a semantic role to its subject (the 'agent' role), whereas a raising verb *seem* does not assign any semantic role to its subject.

3 Infinitival Complementation '07, '13

There are three types of verbs that can take an NP plus infinitive complementation, i.e. V + NP + to-infinitive construction:

Believe Verbs: *believe* [*consider*, *judge*, *acknowledge*], *expect* [*intend*, *imagine*, *mean*], *know* [*suppose*, *understand*]

e.g. I *consider* Einstein to be a genius. I *expected* her to wait for me.

Want Verbs: *want* [*need*, *hope*, *wish*, *desire*, *yearn*], *love* [*like*, *prefer*] ↔ *hate*, *plan* [*arrange*]

e.g. He *loved* her to sing to him.

Persuade Verbs: *persuade* [*convince*], *order* [*command*, *request*, *urge*, *force*, *compel*], *instruct* [*tell*], *encourage* [*invite, tempt*], *advise, remind, cause*

e.g. I *convinced* her to change her mind.

(1) *Believe* Verbs: Subject-to-Object Raising

(1) Ed believes the story to be false.

① Dummy Elements and Idiom Chunks

Dummy elements are lexical elements without semantic content, i.e. they are meaningless. English has two such elements, namely nonreferential *it* and existential *there*. Dummy *it* and *there* (also called *expletive* or *pleonastic* elements) always occur in Subject position.

Idioms containing Subject idiom chunks are exemplified as follows:

(2) The coast is clear.
(3) The fat is in the fire.

In these examples *the coast* and *the fat* are Subject idiom chunks. These NPs cannot be replaced by different NPs without the particular meanings associated with the full expressions being lost.

Dummy elements and Subject idiom chunks can be used to show that the NP in *believe* + NP + to-infinitive structures like (1) cannot be analyzed as a Direct Object. In this connection consider the data below:

(4) Ed believes *it* always to be raining in London.
(5) Ed believes *there* to be a traitor in the company.

These sentences pose problems for frameworks in which the NP in *believe* + NP + to-infinitive structures is analyzed as a Direct Object. The reason is that dummy elements *must* occur in Subject position. The fact that dummy *it* and *there* can appear in the postverbal NP slot of *believe* is evidence that the postverbal NP is the subject of a subordinate clause (the to-infinitive clause). We therefore analyze the postverbal NPs as Subjects of a subordinate clause. Thus, in (1) *believe* takes a clausal DO (Direct Object, or complement), *the story to be false*.

Likewise, the second test is to use idioms as in (2) and (3). Both idioms have idiomatic interpretations only when their Subject idiom chunks occur in the subject position.

  (6) Ed believes the coast to be clear.
  (7) Ed believes the fat to be in the fire.

The fact that the idioms in (6) and (7) retain their idiomatic meanings demonstrates that the postverbal NPs, i.e., ***the coast*** and ***the fat*** function as the subject of the subordinate clauses ***the coast to be clear*** and ***the fat to be in the fire***.

② **Passivization**

  (8) Ed believes the jury to have given the wrong verdict.
  (9) Ed believes the wrong verdict to have been given by the jury. [postverbal passivization]

With regard to (8) and (9), the generalization we can now make is that if we can passivize the postverbal portion in any verb + NP + to-infinitive construction without a resulting change in meaning, then the postverbal NP is not a Direct Object, but the Subject of a subordinate clause.

 Matrix passivization is also possible for ***believe***-type verbs because the postverbal NP becomes the object of the verb ***believe*** through the process of **Subject-to-Object Raising**. For example, we can passivize (8) and get the following synonymous sentence:

  (10) The jury was believed to have given the wrong verdict by Ed. [matrix passivization]

(2) *Want* Verbs

① **Dummy Elements and Idiom Chunks**

  (11) Kate wanted *it* to rain on Ralph's birthday.
  (12) Ralph wanted *there* to be a ceasefire between him and Kate.

In these sentences the dummy elements *it* and *there* appear in postverbal position. We know that they cannot be Direct Objects, because dummy elements *must* occur in Subject position. The same conclusion can be drawn from sentences that contain idiom chunks:

(13) Kate wants ***the coast*** to be clear, in order for her to escape from Ralph.

(14) Kate doesn't want ***the fat*** to be in the fire, because of some stupid action of Ralph's.

<u>Both idioms can have idiomatic readings only when their Subject idiom chunks occur in the subject position.</u> In (13) and (14) the two idioms preserve their idiomatic interpretations. Thus, the postverbal NPs after ***want*** are the subjects of the to-infinitive clauses.

② **Passivization**

(15) Kate wanted Janet to poison Ralph.

(16) Kate wanted Ralph to be poisoned by Janet. [postverbal passivization]

The active sentence and its postverbal passive version are synonymous. This fact supports the argument that the verb ***want*** takes a clausal complement, NP + to-infinitive, and the postverbal NP is the subject of the following to-infinitive.

The similarity between ***believe*** and ***want*** is that both verbs take a postverbal clausal complement. The difference is that in the case of ***believe***, but not in the case of ***want***, the main clause can also be passivized:

(17) Ed believes the jury to have given the wrong verdict. (=(8))

(18) The jury was believed to have given the wrong verdict by Ed. (=(10)) [matrix passivization]

(19) Kate wanted Janet to poison Ralph. (=(15))

(20) *Janet was wanted to poison Ralph by Kate. [matrix passivization]

(3) *Persuade* Verbs: Object Control

① **Dummy Elements and Idiom Chunks**

Now, if the postverbal NP in the ***persuade*** + NP + to-infinitive construction is indeed a Direct Object, we would not expect it to be possible for this position to be occupied by dummy elements, as these can only occur in Subject position. This expectation is borne out:

(21) *Ed persuaded ***it*** to be hot in the room.

(22) *Ed persuaded ***there*** to be a party.

Idiom chunks also cannot occupy the position following ***persuade***:

(23) *Ed persuaded the coast to be clear.
(24) *Ed persuaded the fat to be in the fire.

This is what we would expect if the NP slot after ***persuade*** is a Direct Object position: given the fact that ***the coast*** and ***the fat*** are Subject idiom chunks, they cannot appear in Direct Object position. (cf ***Persuade*** require [+animate] NP in its postverbal NP complement.)

② **Passivization**

(25) Ed persuaded Brian to interview Melanie.
(26) Ed persuaded Melanie to be interviewed by Brian. [postverbal passivization]

If we can passivize the postverbal portion in a verb + NP + to-infinitive construction without a change in meaning, then the postverbal NP is *not* a Direct Object, but the Subject of a subordinate clause. Clearly, (25) and its passivized version (26) do not mean the same, and we therefore conclude that the NP in the ***persuade*** + NP + to-infinitive construction functions as a DO. ***Persuade*** is a three-place predicate, and apart from a Subject and DO we have a to-infinitive clause which functions as Complement. The implied Subject of this Complement clause has the same referent as the DO of the matrix clause. In a labelled bracketing we can indicate this implied Subject using the symbol 'Ø'.

(27) Ed persuaded Brian$_i$ [Ø$_i$ to interview Melanie]

Persuade is called an **Object Control** predicate, and the sentence (27) an object control construction.

◆ **Summary 1—Structure**

- ***Believe* class**: V + [$_{CLAUSE}$ NP + to-infinitive]

  Verb + DO clause in the form of an NP + to-infinitive. The NP can be fronted under passivization (thanks to **Subject-to-Object Raising**).

- ***Want* class**: V + [$_{CLAUSE}$ NP + to-infinitive]

  Verb + DO clause in the form of an NP + to-infinitive. The NP cannot be fronted under passivization.

- ***Persuade* class**: V + [NP$_i$] + [PRO$_i$ to-infinitive]

  Verb + DO NP + second Complement in the form of a to-infinitive clause with an implied Subject that is coreferential with the matrix clause DO (**Object Control**). The NP can be fronted under passivization.

◆ **Summary 2—Passivization, Dummy Elements & Idiom Chunks**

	Believe class	*Want* class	*Persuade* class
postverbal passivization	○	○	meaning preservation ✕
matrix passivization	○	✕	○
dummy *it*, *there* in postverbal NP slot idiomatic meaning preservation	○	○	✕

4 Complementizers *that, for, whether, if* '05

Complementizers can be classified into types on the basis of two different criteria: (i) syntactic (whether they are used in interrogative or noninterrogative Clauses), and (ii) morphological (whether they serve to introduce finite or nonfinite Clauses). So, for example, we might classify *that* as a noninterrogative finite Complementizer, since it only introduces finite Clauses, not infinitives:

(1) a. I am anxious [*that* you should arrive on time]
    b. *I am anxious [*that* you to arrive on time]

Conversely, we might classify *for* as a noninterrogative infinitive Complementizer, since it can introduce infinitive Clauses, but not finite Clauses:

(2) a. I am anxious [*for* you to arrive on time]
    b. *I am anxious [*for* you should arrive on time]

By contrast, **whether** is an interrogative Complementizer which can introduce finite and nonfinite Clauses alike; whereas *if* is an interrogative Complementizer which can only introduce finite Complement Clauses:

(3) a. I don't know [**whether**/*if* I should agree]
    b. I don't know [**whether**/**if* to agree]

If we were to use the feature [±WH] to indicate whether a Complementizer is interrogative or not, and the feature [±FINITE] to indicate whether a Complementizer can introduce a finite or nonfinite Clause (or both), then we could analyze each of the four Complementizers discussed above as having the structure (4) below:

(4) that   = [−WH, +FINITE]
    for   = [−WH, −FINITE]
    whether   = [+WH, ±FINITE]
    if   = [+WH, +FINITE]

We might further assume that the constituent C can be expanded into a feature complex by a feature rule such as (5) below:

(5) C → [±WH, ±FINITE]

5 Complementizers *whether* vs. *if* '05

If is more restricted syntactically than **whether**. It must occur as complementation of verbs and adjectives, in consequence of which it is excluded from certain contexts:

① ***If*** cannot introduce a subject clause unless the clause is extraposed:

Whether she likes the present ⎫
*If she likes the present ⎭ is not clear to me.

It's not clear to me { *whether* / *if* } *she likes the present*.

② *If* cannot introduce <u>a subject complement clause</u>:

My main problem right now is ***whether I should ask for another loan***.
*My main problem right now is ***if I should ask for another loan***.

③ The ***if***-clause cannot be <u>the complement of a preposition</u>:

It all depends on ***whether they will support us***.
*It all depends on ***if they will support us***.

④ The ***if***-clause cannot be <u>an appositive</u>:

You have yet to answer my question, ***whether I can count on your vote***.
*You have yet to answer my question, ***if I can count on your vote***.

⑤ ***If*** cannot introduce <u>a to-infinitive clause</u>:

I don't know ***whether to see my doctor today***.
*I don't know ***if to see my doctor today***.

⑥ ***If*** cannot be followed directly by <u>or not</u>:

He didn't say ***whether or not he'll be staying here***.
*He didn't say ***if or not he'll be staying here***.

But ***or not*** can be postposed:

He didn't say ***if he'll be staying here or not***.

04 Ambiguity '07, '11, '15, '18, '20

1 Syntactic Ambiguity '07, '11, '20

Syntactic ambiguity means ambiguity in which the variant readings of a sentence involve identical lexical units; the ambiguity is thus necessarily a matter merely of the way the elements are grouped together.

(1) old men and women

(2) French silk underwear

For instance, the meaning of *old men and women* differs according to whether *old* goes with *men* only:

(old men) and women

or with *men and women*:

old (men and women)

Likewise, *French silk underwear* may be underwear made of French silk ((*French silk*) *underwear*) or French underwear made of silk (*French* (*silk underwear*)). Such cases are characteristically very insensitive to the semantic properties of the constituent lexical items: *porcelain egg container*.

More examples which show phrases can be syntactically (or structurally) ambiguous are provided below:

(3) an American history teacher
   (Reading 1: a teacher of American history
   Reading 2: an American teacher of history)

Possessive expressions often result in structurally ambiguous sentences:

(4) a. The hatred of the killer
   (Reading 1: Someone hates the killer.
   Reading 2: The killer hates someone.)
   b. The shooting of the hunters was terrible.
   (Reading 1: For someone to shoot the hunters was terrible.
   Reading 2: The hunters' shooting somebody was terrible.)

Sentences can be syntactically (or structurally) ambiguous.

(5) Flying planes can be dangerous '11
(6) Visiting relatives can be boring.

One interpretation of (5) is "For someone to fly planes can be dangerous." The other is "Planes that are flying can be dangerous." Similarly, one reading of (6) is "For someone to visit relatives can be boring." The other is "Relatives who are visiting can be boring."

2 Lexical Ambiguity

Lexical ambiguity arises from **homonymy** or **polysemy**.

(7) He reached the **bank**. (① financial institution ② a riverside)
(8) The minister conducted a **service**. (① act of worship ② first shot in tennis)
(9) The captain corrected the **list**. (① inventory ② tilt)
(10) She bought a **pen**. (① handwriting instrument using ink ② cage)
(11) She loved the **plane**. (① airplane ② flat surface)
(12) What is his **position**? (① title ② location)
(13) Mary believed the boy was **lying**. (① speak falsely
    ② stay in a horizontal position)

3 Lexico-Syntactic Ambiguity '15

Lexico-syntactic ambiguity refers to the ambiguity through both the ascription of multiple meanings to a single word and the assignment of different syntactic structures to a single string of words in a sentence. For example,

(14) The children saw her duck.

The sentence (14) is ambiguous. It can be understood either in the sense that the children saw her bird or as the manner that the children saw her lower her head. The ambiguity is **lexical**, because the two readings are associated with two different lexical meanings of the noun *duck* and the verb *duck*, and it is **syntactic** in the sense that the two interpretations are associated with two different grammatical structures.

| Exercise 1 | The following English sentences are all *structurally* ambiguous. Provide a paraphrase (a sentence with roughly the same meaning) for each of the possible meanings. |

(a) John said Mary went to the store quickly.
(b) I discovered an old English poem.
(c) The boy saw the man with a telescope.
(d) Enraged cow injures farmer with ax
(e) Hospitals are sued by seven foot doctors (Lexico-syntactic ambiguity)
(f) Dealers will hear car talk after noon

Sentences (d), (e), and (f) are ambiguous newspaper headlines.

Answers

(a) ① John said quickly Mary went to the store.
　　② John said Mary went quickly to the store.
(b) ① I discovered a poem written in old English.
　　② I discovered an old poem written in modern English.
(c) ① The boy saw the man who possessed a telescope.
　　　(*with a telescope* modifies the NP *the man*.)
　　② The boy saw the man by using a telescope.
　　　(*with a telescope* modifies the VP *saw the man*.)
(d) ① An enraged cow injures a farmer possessing an ax.
　　　(*with an ax* modifies the NP *a farmer*.)
　　② An enraged cow injures a farmer by using an ax.
　　　(*with an ax* modifies the VP *injures a farmer*.)
(e) ① Hospitals are sued by seven-foot-tall doctors.
　　　(*seven foot doctors* = adv + adj + N, a noun phrase)
　　② Hospitals are sued by seven doctors specializing in treating the foot.
　　　(*foot doctor* = compound noun)
(f) ① Dealers will hear a car speech after noon. (*car talk* = N + N, compound noun)
　　② Dealers will hear car make a noise after noon. (*hear* + O + OC)

> **Exercise 2** The following English sentences are all ambiguous. First, write two possible interpretations for each sentence. Then, decide what kind of ambiguity the sentence has, i.e., lexical ambiguity, structural ambiguity or lexico-syntactic ambiguity.

(1) I don't seem to have a chair.

(2) He reached the bank.

(3) He gave her dog biscuits.

(4) The old dogs and cats were hungry.

(5) The tourists objected to the guide that they couldn't hear.

(6) The chicken is too hot to eat.

(7) We saw her duck.

(8) Mary saw John's nose ring '15

Answers

(1) Reading 1: I don't seem to have a chair to sit on.

Reading 2: I don't seem to have a chairperson to talk to.

The sentence has **lexical** ambiguity.

(2) Reading 1: He arrived at a financial institution.

Reading 2: He arrived at a riverside.

The sentence has **lexical** ambiguity.

(3) Reading 1: He gave a woman's dog some biscuits.

Reading 2: He gave a woman biscuits intended for dogs.

The sentence has **structural** ambiguity.

(4) Interpretation 1: The old dogs and old cats were hungry.

Interpretation 2: The old dogs and young or old cats were hungry.

The sentence has **structural** ambiguity.

(5) Reading 1: The tourists objected to the guide whose voice was hard to hear.

([objected to] [the guide that they couldn't hear]) that: a relative

Reading 2: The tourists protested to the guide that they couldn't hear the guide.

([objected] [to the guide] [that they couldn't hear]) that: noun cl.

The sentence has **structural** ambiguity.

(6) Reading 1: The chicken is too hot for anybody to eat the chicken.

Reading 2: The chicken is too hot (for it) to eat anything.

The sentence has **structural** ambiguity.

(7) Reading 1: We looked at a duck that belonged to her.

Reading 2: We looked at her quickly squat down to avoid something.

The sentence has **lexico-syntactic** ambiguity.

(The ambiguity is **lexical**, because the two readings are associated with two different lexical meanings of the noun *duck* and the verb *duck*, and it is **syntactic** in the sense that the two interpretations are associated with two different grammatical structures.)

(8) Reading 1: Mary saw John's nose make a sound like a bell.

Reading 2: Mary saw John's nose-piercing jewelry.

The sentence has **lexico-syntactic** ambiguity.

The sentence (8) is both lexically and structurally ambiguous. One source of the ambiguity is that 'ring' can be analyzed as two homonyms 'ring' (jewelry, noun) and 'ring' (make a bell-like sound, verb). The other source of the ambiguity is the two differing structures of the verb 'saw' which can take a direct object or a direct object and object complement (bare infinitive). Thus, the sentence has two readings: ① Mary saw John's nose make a sound like a bell. ② Mary saw John's nose-piercing jewelry.

05 Constituency Tests '01, '06, '09, '14, '18, '19

Constituents are strings of one or more words that syntactically and semantically behave as a unit.

1 Movement

Movement Test: If we can move a particular string of words in a sentence from one position to another, then it behaves as a constituent.

◆ **Leftward Movement**

(1) Topicalization (= Preposing) '01

    (1) Nobody liked [$_{NP}$ the books about New York that she bought].

    (2) [$_{NP}$ The books about New York that she bought] nobody liked —.

    (3) *[$_{NP}$ The books about New York] nobody liked — that she bought.

    (4) Wendy: Is Elly always so nervous?

        Al: [$_{AP}$ Neurotic] I would say she is —, not nervous.

    (5) Kate: Does Greg really keep his pets in his attic?

        Len: [$_{PP}$ In his attic] he keeps his plants —, not his pets.

    (6) Nicky promised to write an essay, and [$_{VP}$ write an essay] he will —.

We turn now to a more detailed discussion of VP-Topicalization, better known as VP-Preposing. VP-Preposing is a special type of Topicalization.

(2) VP-Preposing '19

    (7) Ralph says that he will clean his room, and [clean his room] he **will** —

    (8) Sally says that she will return my book, and [return my book] she **will** —

Notice that VP-Preposing can only apply if the sentence in question contains an auxiliary verb, such as *will* in the examples we have looked at, or *did* in (9):

(9) Sally said that she returned my book, and [return my book] she **did** —

The following is impossible:

(10) *Sally said that she returned my book, and [returned my book] she —

(3) *Though*-Movement

The next type of movement is Though-Movement, which is a kind of Topicalization:

(11) a. Though students are fare dodgers, they're not thieves.
  b. [Fare dodgers] though students are — , they're not thieves.
(12) a. Though Ken usually is quite happy, today he is sad.
  b. [Quite happy] though Ken usually is — , today he is sad.
(13) a. Though she works very hard all day, at night she's lazy.
  b. [Very hard] though she works — all day, at night she's lazy.
(14) a. Though she is in debt, she's very generous.
  b. [In debt] though she is — , she's very generous.
(15) a. Though he ate the mushrooms, he hasn't been sick.
  b. [Eat the mushrooms] though he did — , he hasn't been sick.

As you can see from (11)–(15), in each case a string of words has moved to a clause-initial position: an NP in (11), an AP in (12), an AdvP in (13), a PP in (14), and a VP in (15).

◆ Rightward Movement

Both kinds of the Rightward Movement described below are motivated by **End-weight Principle**.

(1) Heavy-NP-Shift

(16) We brought — into the country *six boxes of excellent French wine*.

(17) She sold — at the market *the prints that she had made*.

Because Direct Objects typically occur immediately to the right of the verb that subcategorizes for them, it is reasonable to assume that in (16) and (17) the italicized NPs have moved to the right from the position indicated by the dash. These movements are triggered by the relative 'heaviness' of the NPs in question, caused by the PP *of excellent French wine* in (16) and by the relative clause *that she had made* in (17). For this reason this type of movement is called Heavy-NP-Shift (HNPS).

Both Heavy-NP-Shift and Extraposition from NP, kinds of movements, can be used as a constituency test.

(2) Extraposition from NP '19

Consider the following sentences:

(18) Six women — appeared *with yellow hats*.
(19) We employed two people — last week *from European Union countries*.
(20) The dogs — escaped *that were chained to the house*.

In (18) the PP *with yellow hats* has been extraposed out of the Subject NP, whereas in (19) the PP *from European Union countries* is moved out of a Direct Object NP. In (20) a relative clause has been displaced from the Subject NP. We call this kind of movement ***Extraposition from NP*** (ENP). ENP seems to be more acceptable if the Verb Phrase is relatively light; for example, if it contains an intransitive verb or a raising verb (*seem*, *appear*, *become*, etc.). The following sentence, which contains a transitive verb, seems to be much less good:

(21) *Three men — noisily left the theatre *who were drunk*.

2 Substitution

Substitution Test: A particular string of words is a constituent if it can be substituted by a suitable proform.

(1) Proform Substitution

(22) ***My father*** admires ***my mother***. ⇒ ***He*** admires ***her***.

(23) I like ***those funny people who eat with their hands and sing at the dinner table***. ⇒ I like ***them***.

Other phrase types, and even clauses, can be replaced by proforms too, as the following sentences demonstrate:

(24) They say that Wayne is ***very unhappy*** and ***so*** he is.

(25) Our neighbors will go on holiday ***on Sunday***, and we will leave ***then*** too.

(26) Tim sat ***on the couch*** and stayed ***there***.

(27) Janet drove her car ***too fast***, and Sam rode his bike ***likewise***.

(28) He believes ***that politics is a dirty game***. We all believe ***that***.

(29) He said ***that the operation will be successful***. I certainly hope ***so***.

(2) *One*-Substitution '09, '14

So far we have seen that proforms in the form of personal pronouns (***he***, ***she***, ***it***, etc.) can replace full NPs. English also possesses a word that can replace less than a full NP, and this is the proform ***one***. Consider (30):

(30) Mark is a dedicated teacher of language, but Paul is an indifferent one.

(31)

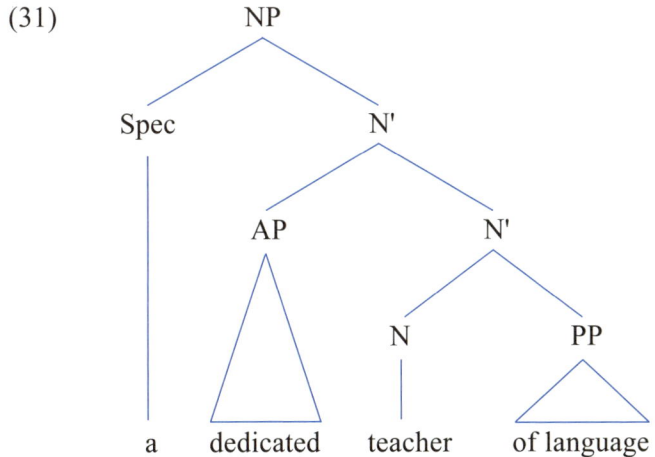

(32)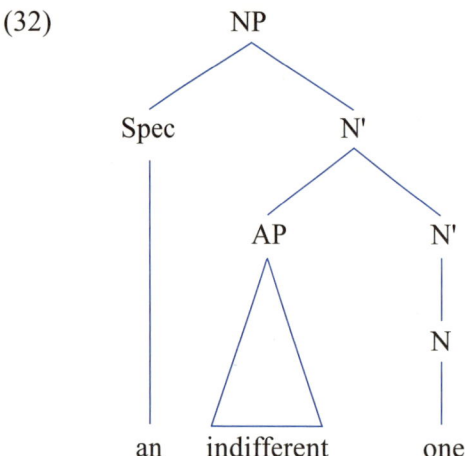

One-Substitution: The proform *one* replaces N'-constituents.
(ⓒf (Personal) pronouns (*he*, *she*, *it*, *them*, etc.) replace full NPs.)

(33) Ben likes the Italian student of English, but not the Spanish one.
(34) *Ben likes the Italian student of English, but not the Spanish one of literature.

Can *one* replace **student** here? The answer is 'no', because the proform *one* cannot replaces N-constituents (i.e., Heads).

Ambiguity may arise when there are more than one N'-node. Consider the following NP:

(35) a clever Italian student of English

The tree for (35) contains two AP modifiers (*clever* and *Italian*), and hence two N'-nodes:

(36)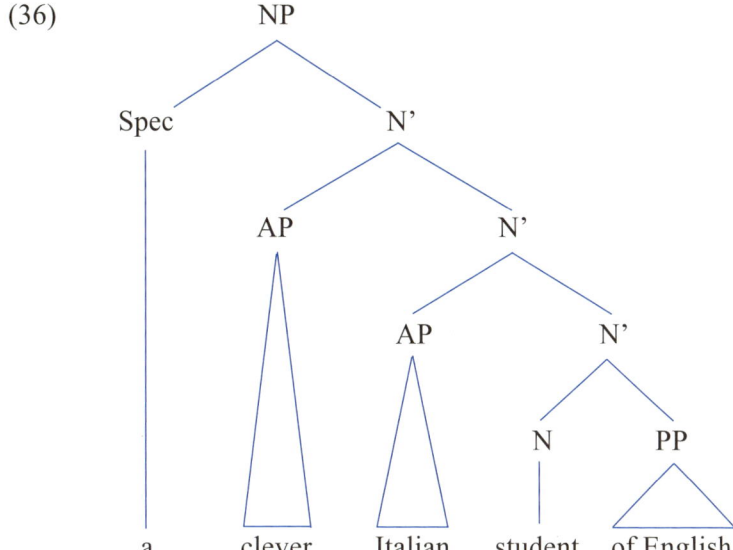

Now consider the following sentence. Explain why this sentence is **ambiguous**, and provide its two readings (interpretations):

(37) Marco is certainly a clever Italian student of English, but Paolo is an absolutely brilliant one.

One can replace the italicized strings in (38) and (39):

Marco is certainly a clever Italian student of English, . . .
(38) . . . but Paolo is an absolutely brilliant *Italian student of English*.
(39) . . . but Paolo is an absolutely brilliant *student of English*.

These sentences show that (37) can receive more than one interpretation, depending on which N' *one* replaces. It can replace either ***Italian student of English***, in which case both Marco and Paolo are students of English of Italian extraction, or it can replace only ***student of English***, in which case all we know about Paolo is that he studies English.

(3) *Do so*-Substitution

(40) Dawn cleaned the windows diligently.

(41)

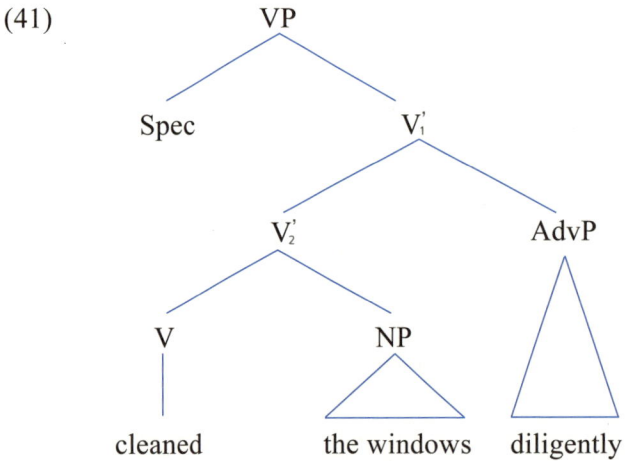

(42) Dawn cleaned the windows diligently, and Sean *did so* too.

(43) Dawn cleaned the windows diligently, but Sean *did so* lazily.

Do so-Substitution: *Do so* replaces V'-constituents.

Here are some more examples:

(44) Barry hired a big Jaguar, and Milly *did so* too.

(45) Lenny sent Will a postcard, and Gemma *did so* too.

Do so can never replace less than a V'. The following sentences are out (i.e., ungrammatical):

(46) *Barry hired a big Jaguar, and Milly *did so* a Volkswagen.

(47) *Lenny sent Will a postcard, and Gemma *did so* a present.

3 Coordination

(1) Ordinary Coordination '18, '21

Coordination Test: Only constituents can be coordinated.

(48) Frank *washed* and *ironed* his shirts yesterday. (coordinated main verbs)

(49) Frank *washed his shirts* and *polished his shoes* yesterday. (coordinated lower V-bars)

(50) Frank *washed his shirts yesterday* and *polished his shoes last week*. (coordinated higher V-bars)

(51) Anna loudly *announced the election victory* and *gave an interview to the press*. (coordinated lower V-bars)

(52) Anna *loudly* and *cheerfully* announced the election victory. (coordinated AdvPs)

(53) Anna *loudly announced the election victory* and *cheerfully gave an interview to the press*. (coordinated higher V-bars)

(2) Right Node Raising

Right Node Raising (RNR) Test: Only constituents can undergo RNR.

(54) Frank washed —, and Dick ironed —, *the shirts*.

(55) Frank will —, but Dick won't —, *wash the shirts*.

(56) Frank will —, but Dick won't —, *iron the shirts tomorrow*.

4 Cleft and Pseudocleft Sentences '21

Cleft and Pseudocleft: Only constituents can occur in the focus position of a Cleft or Pseudocleft.

(57) Michael loudly announced the election victory.   (Regular sentence)

(58) It was *Michael* who loudly announced the election victory.   (cleft)

(59) It was *the election victory* that Michael loudly announced.   (cleft)

(60) It was *loudly* that Michael announced the election victory.   (cleft)

(61) What Michael loudly announced was *the election victory*.   (pseudocleft)

(62) What Michael did loudly was *announce the election victory*.   (pseudocleft)

(63) What Michael did was *loudly announce the election victory*. (pseudocleft)

5 (Adverb) Insertion

Insertion Test:

VP-adverbs can only be attached to a VP-node.

S-adverbs (parenthetical elements) can only be attached to an S-node.

① VP-adverbs (manner adverbs): *completely* [*entirely*], *carefully* [*meticulously*], *passionately*, *quickly*

② S-adverbs (evaluation or comment adverbs): *certainly* [*definitely*, *clearly*, *obviously*], *however*, *probably* [*possibly*], *frankly*, *fortunately*, *surprisingly*, *naturally*

(64) I myself won't be going on holiday this summer. Pam, *however*, will take two weeks off in August.

(65) Pam will, *however*, take two weeks off in August.

(66) *However*, Pam will take two weeks off in August.

(67) Pam will take two weeks off in August, *however*.

(68) *Pam will take, *however*, two weeks off in August.

(68) is clearly ungrammatical. The reason for this is that a parenthetical element intervenes between the main verb and its Direct Object. These are not S-constituents, but constituents of VP.

6 The Constituent Response Test

Constituent Response Test: Only constituents can serve as responses to open interrogatives.

(69) Dick: Where did you buy this bread?

Frances: **In the supermarket**.

(70) Who rudely interrupted the speaker? **Ray**.
　　 How did Ray interrupt the speaker? **Rudely**.
　　 Who did Ray (rudely) interrupt? **The speaker**.
　　 What did Ray do rudely? **Interrupt the speaker**.
　　 What did Ray do? **Rudely interrupt the speaker**.

06 Syntactic Argumentation

1 Phrasal Verbs vs. Prepositional Verbs '00

We can apply the various constituency tests described above to prepositional verbs and phrasal verbs. These tests illuminate the differences between the two.

◆ **Differences between Phrasal Verbs and Prepositional Verbs**

(1) a. Peter looked at the road. (prepositional verb)
　　 b. Peter looked up the new words. (phrasal verb)

The differences are both syntactic and phonological. The final difference (stress pattern) is phonological.

(1) Movement

(2) After deliberating for minutes with his eyes closed, and at the road Peter would look.
(3) *The teacher encouraged his students to consult the dictionary frequently, and up the new words Peter certainly would look.

The string at the road can be moved, indicating that it is a constituent. On the other hand, up the new words cannot be preposed because it is not a constituent.

(2) Coordination

(4) a. Peter would look at the road and at the building.

b. *Peter would look <u>up the new words</u> and <u>up the train times</u>.

In (4a), both PPs, <u>at the road</u> and <u>at the building</u>, are constituents and can be conjoined. In contrast, in (4b), both <u>up the new words</u> and <u>up the train times</u> are nonconstituents and hence cannot be coordinated.

(3) Shared Constituent Coordination Test '00

　　(5) a. Peter would look—and Mary would stare—*at the road*.
　　　　b. *Peter would look—and Mary would also look—*up the new words*.

The string in (5a), <u>at the road</u> is a constituent because it can become a shared constituent. The string in (5b) <u>up the new words</u> is not a constituent because it fails the Shared Constituent Test.

(4) Sentence Fragment

　　(6) A: Did he look at the road?
　　　　B: No, <u>at the building</u>.

　　(7) A: Would he look up the new words?
　　　　B: *No, <u>up the train times</u>.

The string in (6), <u>at the building</u> is a constituent because it can serve as responses to open interrogatives. The test shows that the string in (7) <u>up the train times</u> is not a constituent because it fails the Constituent Response Test.

(5) (VP-Adverb) Insertion '00

　　(8) a. Peter would look *carefully* at the road.
　　　　b. *Peter would look *diligently* up the new words.

Adverbs can be inserted between *look* and *at* in (8a) while they can't between *look* and *up* in (8b).

(6) Gapping [V-Deletion]

(9) a. Peter would look at the road and Mary ~~would look~~ at the building.

b. *Peter would look up the new words, and Mary ~~would look~~ up the train times.

c. Peter would look up the new words, and Mary ~~would look up~~ the train times.

The gapping (or V-deletion) can leave a PP constituent, <u>at the building</u>, as in (9a). The string in (9b), <u>up the train times</u> cannot be left without the verb. However, we can gap the whole expression *look up* along with *would* as in (9c).

(7) Clefting

(10) a. It was <u>at the road</u> that Peter looked.

b. *It was <u>up the new words</u> that Peter looked.

The string <u>at the road</u> can appear in the focus position of a cleft sentence while <u>up the new words</u> can't.

(8) Word Order '00

(11) a. Jack and Jill looked at the road.   Jack and Jill looked at *it*.

b. *Jack and Jill looked the road at.   *Jack and Jill looked *it* at.

c. ***At the road** looked Jack and Jill.

d. Jack and Jill looked up the new word.   *Jack and Jill looked up *it*.

e. Jack and Jill looked the new word up.   Jack and Jill looked *it* up.

f. ***Up the new word** looked Jack and Jill.

In the case of a prepositional verb, the preposition must occur before its object, whether a full NP object or a pronoun object. On the other hand, in the case of a phrasal verb, the particle must follow a pronoun object.

(9) Stress Pattern '00

(12) a. Peter lóoked <u>at the road</u>.

b. Peter <u>looked úp</u> the new word.

The verb *looked* in the prepositional verb gets the main stress whereas the particle *up* is stressed in the phrasal verb.

2 Binding Theory '09 Mock, '13, '15, '17, '18

The interpretation of **reflexive pronouns** and **pronominals** (or (personal) pronouns) can be determined by their antecedents in the same sentence.

(1) a. [s Clare knew that [s Alexis trusted ***her***]].
 b. [s Clare knew that [s Alexis trusted ***herself***]].

Notice that ***her*** can refer to either Clare or someone not mentioned in the sentence, but that ***herself*** refers only to Alexis.

The contrast illustrated in (1) reflects the fact that the interpretation of reflexive pronouns, but not ordinary pronominals, is subject to the following principle.

(2) A reflexive pronoun must have an antecedent in the smallest S containing it.

The sentence in (1b) presents an interesting case in that there are two Ss, with ***Clare*** in the larger one and ***Alexis*** and ***herself*** in the smaller one. However, only the NP ***Alexis*** can serve as antecedent since only it occurs in the smallest S containing the reflexive pronoun.

(1) Anaphors (Reflexives & Reciprocals) '09 Mock, '13, '15, '17, '18

(3) The boy's teacher admired himself.

The sentence (3) has the following tree structure.

(4)

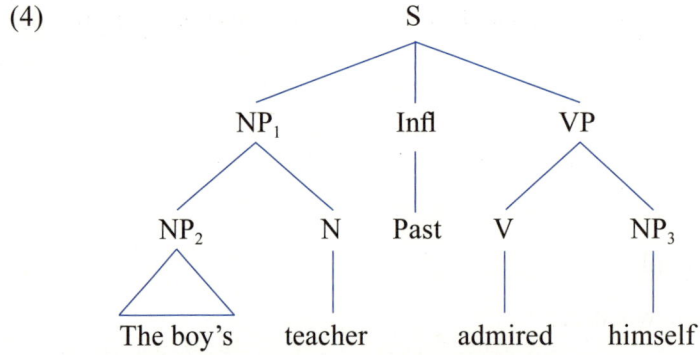

Although there are two NPs in the same S as *himself* (*the boy* and *the boy's teacher*), only one (*the boy's teacher*) can serve as antecedent for the reflexive pronoun. Thus, the person who was admired in (3) must have been *the boy's teacher*, not *the boy*.

The principle needed to ensure this interpretation makes use of the notion **c-command**. We can now formulate the constraint on the interpretation of reflexives, called **Principle A**, as follows.

> **Principle A:**
>
> A reflexive pronoun must have an antecedent that **c-commands** it in the smallest [same] clause.

When using Principle A, the key step involves determining whether a potential antecedent c-commands the reflexive pronoun. Compare in this regard the status of the NPs *the boy* and *the boy's teacher* in (4).

Since NP_1 (*the boy's teacher*) c-commands NP_3 (*himself*), NP_1 can serve as antecedent of NP_3. On the other hand, because NP_2 (*the boy*) doesn't c-command NP_3 (*himself*), NP_2 cannot function as antecedent of NP_3.

(2) Pronominals [(Personal) Pronouns]

(5) The boy's teacher admired him.

In contrast to (3), *him* in (5) can refer to *the boy*, but not to *the boy's teacher*—the opposite of what we observed for *himself*. We can account for this fact with the relevant constraint on the interpretation of pronominals, called **Principle B**, as follows.

> **Principle B:**
>
> A pronominal must not have an antecedent that **c-commands** it in the smallest [same] clause.

(6)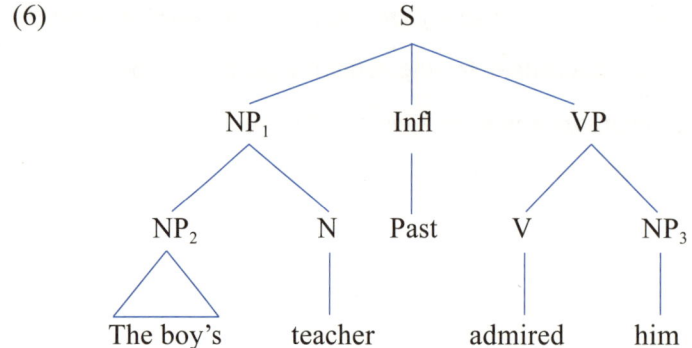

In this structure, since NP₁ (*the boy's teacher*) c-commands NP₃ (*him*), Principle B prevents NP₁ from serving as antecedent of NP₃. In contrast, because NP₂ (*the boy*) does not c-command NP₃ (*him*), nothing prevents the interpretation in which *him* and *the boy* refer the same person.

◆ **Summary:**

The Binding Principles

(1) **Principle A** '09 Mock, '13, '15, '17, '18

An anaphor must have an antecedent that **c-commands** it in the smallest [same] clause.

(2) **Principle B**

A pronominal must not have an antecedent that **c-commands** it in the smallest [same] clause.

◆ **Principle A consists of two constraints:**

The Binding Constraint (BC)

A reflexive or a reciprocal must be bound by its antecedent.

The Locality Constraint (LC)

A reflexive or a reciprocal must find its antecedent within the local binding domain.

= in the smallest **clause**

3 Case Theory '07, '08, '10

(1) Case Filter and Adjacency Requirement

Case Filter

Every overt NP must be assigned abstract case by case assigners (transitive verbs, prepositions, prepositional complementizer *for*, and finite tense).

*NP, if NP has phonetic content and has no Case.
(A caseless NP results in an ungrammatical sentence.)

Adjacency Requirement

An NP can receive Case only if it is adjacent to the Case-assigner.

(2) NOMINATIVE and ACCUSATIVE case

◆ **Summary**

ACCUSATIVE case is assigned by a governing transitive verb or preposition.
NOMINATIVE case is assigned by finite tense.
(Note: The theory on the assignment of genitive case is murky, so we don't discuss it here.)

Let us first look at the complements of transitive verbs and prepositions. Transitive verbs and prepositions assign ACCUSATIVE case to the NP they govern. They case-mark an NP which they govern. Thus in (1) the transitive verb and the preposition will case-mark the complement NPs.

(1) a. She killed *him*.

b. She moved towards *him*.

(2) a. *He* attacked *him*.

b. That *he* attacked *him* is surprising.

c. For *him* to attack *him* would be surprising.

Subjects of finite clauses have NOMINATIVE case (cf (2a)). Let us try to link the assignment of NOMINATIVE case to a governing head just as we have linked the assignment of ACCUSATIVE case to V or to P. One important element in the discussion is the contrast between the subjects of finite clauses and those of infinitivals: subjects of finite clauses are NOMINATIVE, subjects of infinitivals are ACCUSATIVE (cf (2c)). The distinction between finite and non-finite clauses can be drawn in terms of the feature composition of the head of the clause, INFL or I. In finite clauses INFL is [+Tense, +AGR]; in non-finite clauses INFL is [−Tense, −AGR]. This suggests that the assignment of NOMINATIVE case can be associated with finite INFL. We leave it open at this point whether it is Tense or AGR or a combination of Tense and AGR which is responsible for the NOMINATIVE case.

Consider the following examples:

(3) a. I know [IP John to be the best candidate].
    b. I don't know [CP whether [IP — to go to the party]].
    c. *I don't know [CP whether [IP John to go to the party]] '08

Know takes an IP complement and case-marks **John**. In (3b), the presence of **whether** indicates that we have an infinitival clause of the type CP. In this example, there is no overt subject in the infinitival clause, thus the case filter does not come into play with respect to subject of the lower clause. In (3c) **know** again takes a clausal CP complement (witness the presence of **whether**). In this example the infinitival clause contains an overt NP subject **John**. The sentence is ungrammatical because it violates the case filter. Infinitival **to** is assumed to be unable to assign case. The potential case assigner **know** is separated from the relevant NP by the maximal projection CP, which is a barrier.

Consider the following examples:

(4) a. Poirot speaks [NP English] fluently.
    b. *Poirot speaks fluently [NP English].
    c. Poirot sincerely believes [IP English to be important].
    d. *Poirot believes sincerely [IP English to be important].
    e. Poirot believes sincerely [CP that English is important].

In (4a) the verb *speak* takes an NP complement *English* and VP further includes an adjunct *fluently*. The NP *Poirot* is case-marked by the finite INFL; the NP *English* is case-marked by the transitive verb. In (4b) the constituents of the sentence are not altered and yet the sentence is ungrammatical. The only contrast with (4a) is that the V *speak* and the complement NP *English* are no longer next to each other or **adjacent**.

A similar pattern is found in (4c) and (4d). In both sentences *believe* takes an IP complement. In (4c) the verb *believe* case-marks the subject NP of the lower clause (*English*) and the sentence is grammatical, while in (4d) the non-adjacency of the verb and the NP to which it should assign structural case leads to ungrammaticality.

By the **adjacency requirement** case assigners must not be separated from the NPs which they case-mark by intervening material and hence (4b) and (4d) are ungrammatical. In (4b) the verb *speak* would not be able to case-mark the NP *English* because there is intervening material; the NP *English* will violate the case filter (including adjacency requirement). In (4d) the verb *believe* must case-mark the subject of the non-finite clause, hence ought not be separated from it; again the NP *English* violates the case filter.

The adjacency requirement has nothing to say about (4e). On the one hand, a finite clause does not need to be case-marked. The case filter applies to NPs, not to clauses. On the other hand, the subject of the finite clause, the NP *English*, will satisfy the case filter because it receives NOMINATIVE from the finite I.

In the examples (5) the interaction of the **case filter** and the **adjacency requirement** on case assignment will again account for the judgements given. We leave the reader to work out these examples.

(5) a. I prefer [the boys to leave first].

b. *I prefer very much [the boys to leave first].

c. I prefer very much [for the boys to leave first].

d. I prefer very much [that the boys should leave first].

(3) Adjectives and Nouns

Nouns and adjectives are not case assigners in English:

(6) a. Poirot envies Miss Marple.

b. *Poirot is envious Miss Marple.

c. Poirot is envious of Miss Marple.

d. *Poirot's envy Miss Marple.

e. Poirot's envy of Miss Marple.

In (6a) *envy*, the verb, is used; in (6b) and (6c) we find the related adjective *envious*; in (6d) and (6e) the noun *envy*.

Let us consider how the case filter above applies to these examples. In (6a) case assignment is straightforward: **Poirot** is assigned NOMINATIVE by the finite inflection and **Miss Marple** is assigned ACCUSATIVE by the transitive verb *envy*.

(6b) is ungrammatical. If we compare it with the grammatical (6a) the only difference is that we have replaced the verb *envy* by the adjective *envious*. Apparently (6b) can be rescued by the insertion of the preposition *of* as seen in (6c). How can we account for these data?

We shall try to explain the ungrammaticality of (6b), without *of*, and the grammaticality of (6c), with *of*, also in terms of the case filter. If adjectives like *envious* cannot case-mark their complement, then (6b) is ruled out by the case filter since the NP **Miss Marple** will not be assigned case.

We also posit that English has a default procedure to rescue sentences like (6b) which consists of inserting the preposition *of* in front of the NP. We refer to this procedure by the term *of*-**insertion**. Like any other preposition, *of* can assign ACCUSATIVE case and thus will avoid a case filter violation: in (6c) **Miss Marple** is case-marked by *of*.

Let us turn to (6d) and (6e). First of all we see that these NPs contain a GENITIVE NP, **Poirot's**, in front of their head N. We shall not discuss GENITIVE assignment in the pre-nominal position. Let us assume that there is an element POSS in the specifier position of NPs which is able to assign GENITIVE to the NP in that position.

We turn to the post-nominal complement of *envy*, the NP **Miss Marple**. Analogously to (6b) and (6c), we shall try to account for the ungrammaticality of (6d) and the grammaticality of (6e) in terms of case theory. If nouns fail to assign case to their complements (6d) violates the case filter. *Of*-insertion in (6e) enables the complement NP to receive case.

Grammar 01-02 mind map

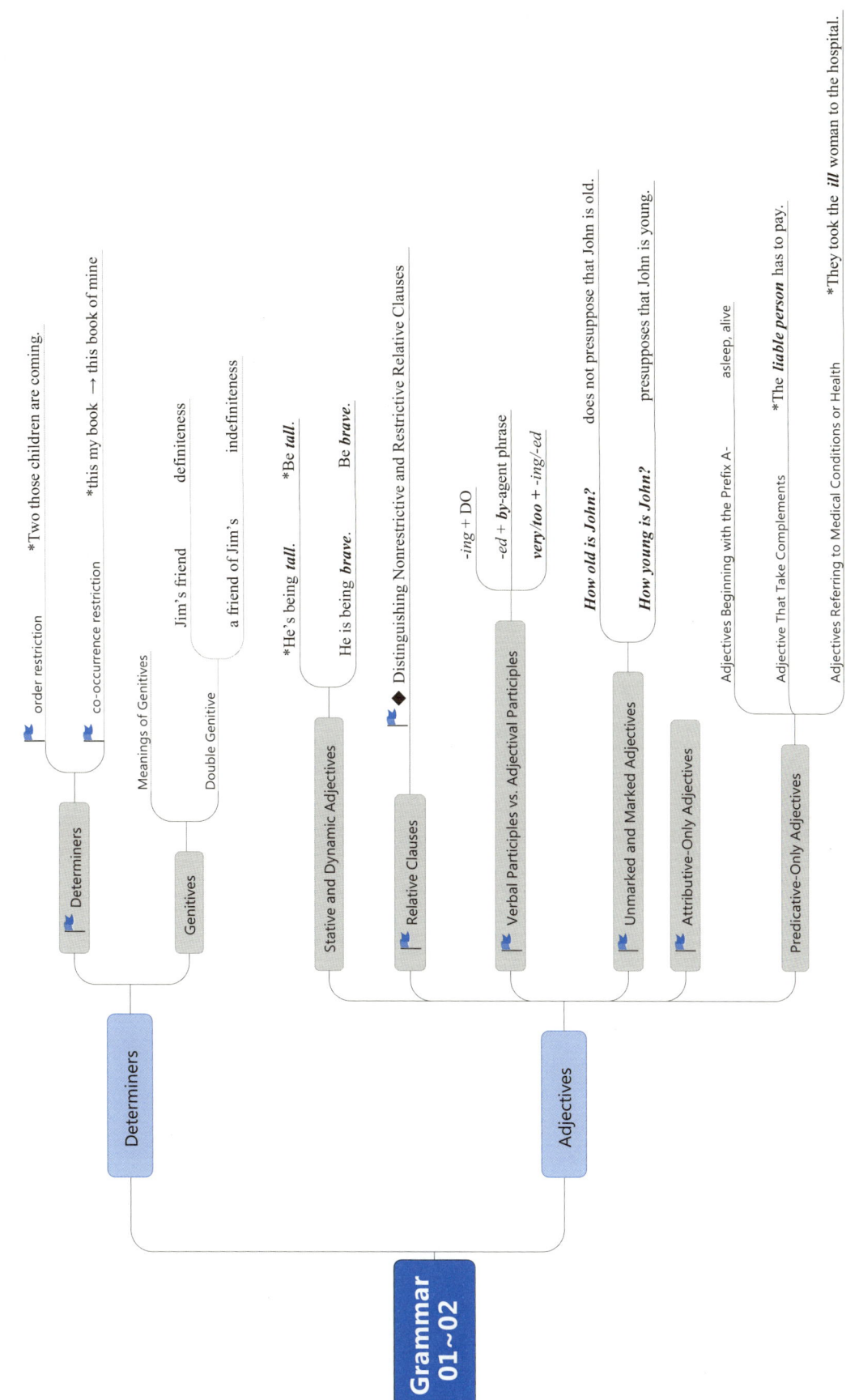

Grammar 03-04 mind map

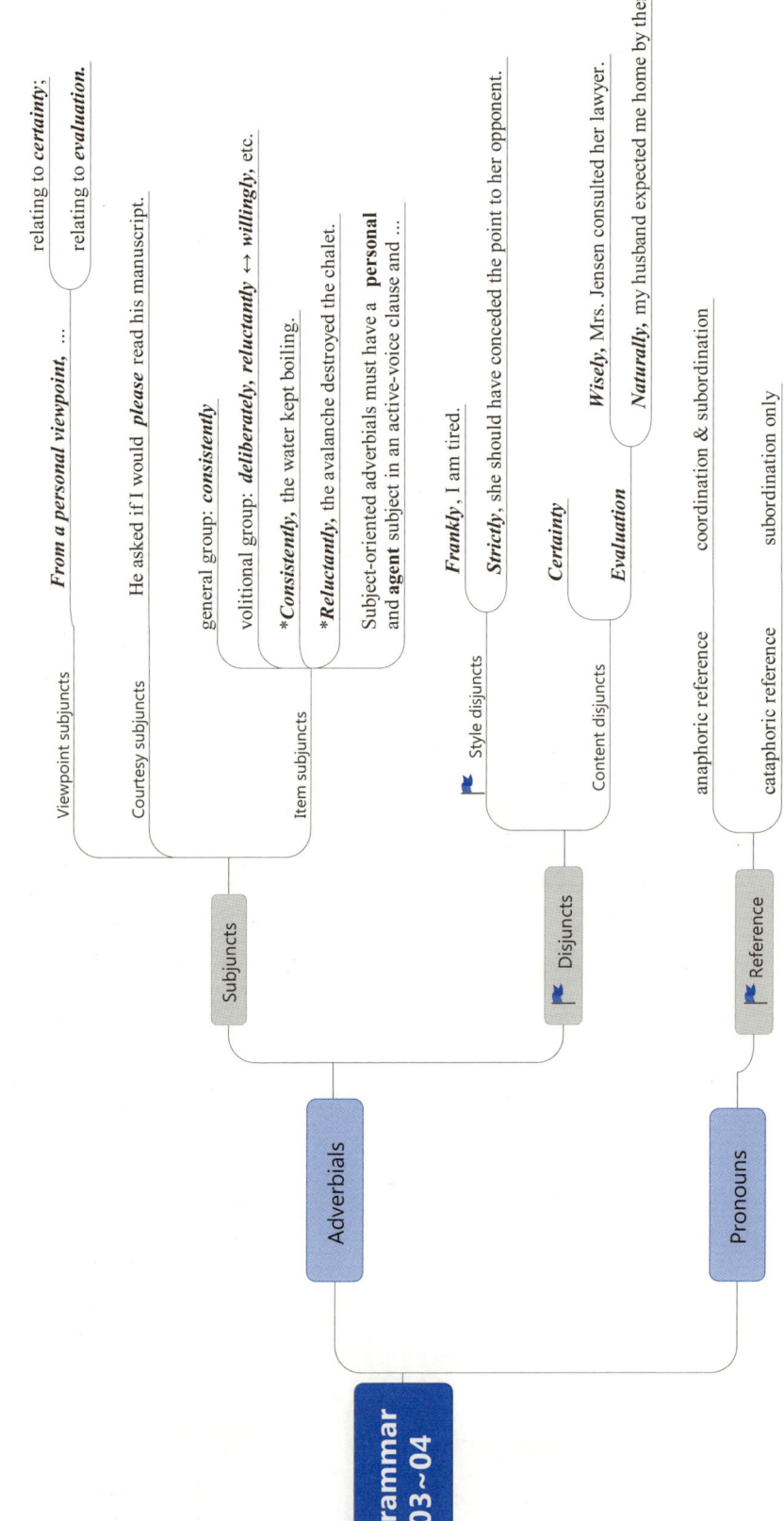

Grammar 05 mind map

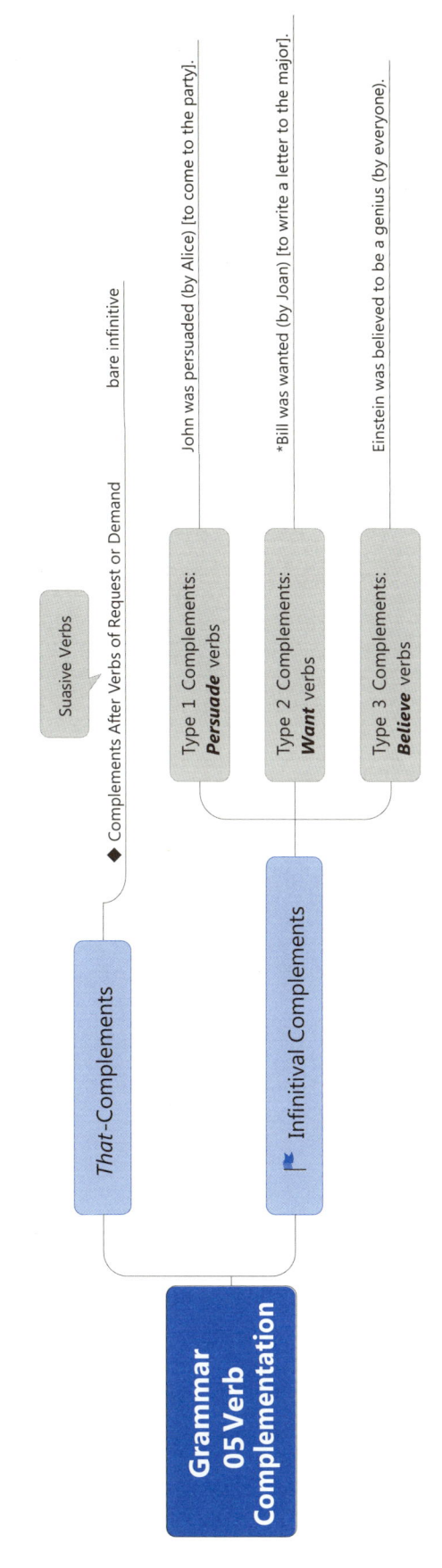

Grammar 06-1 mind map

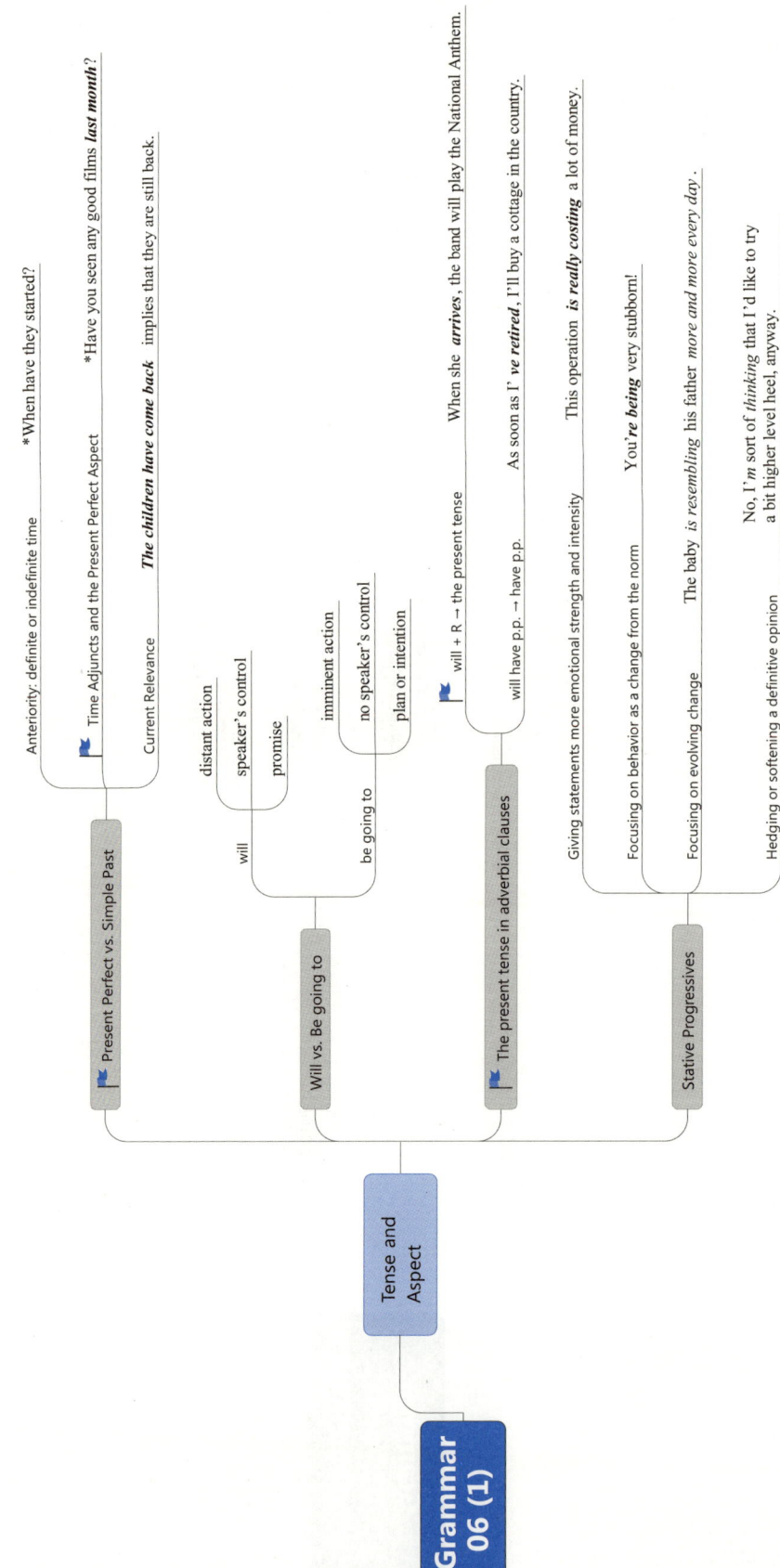

Grammar 06-2 mind map

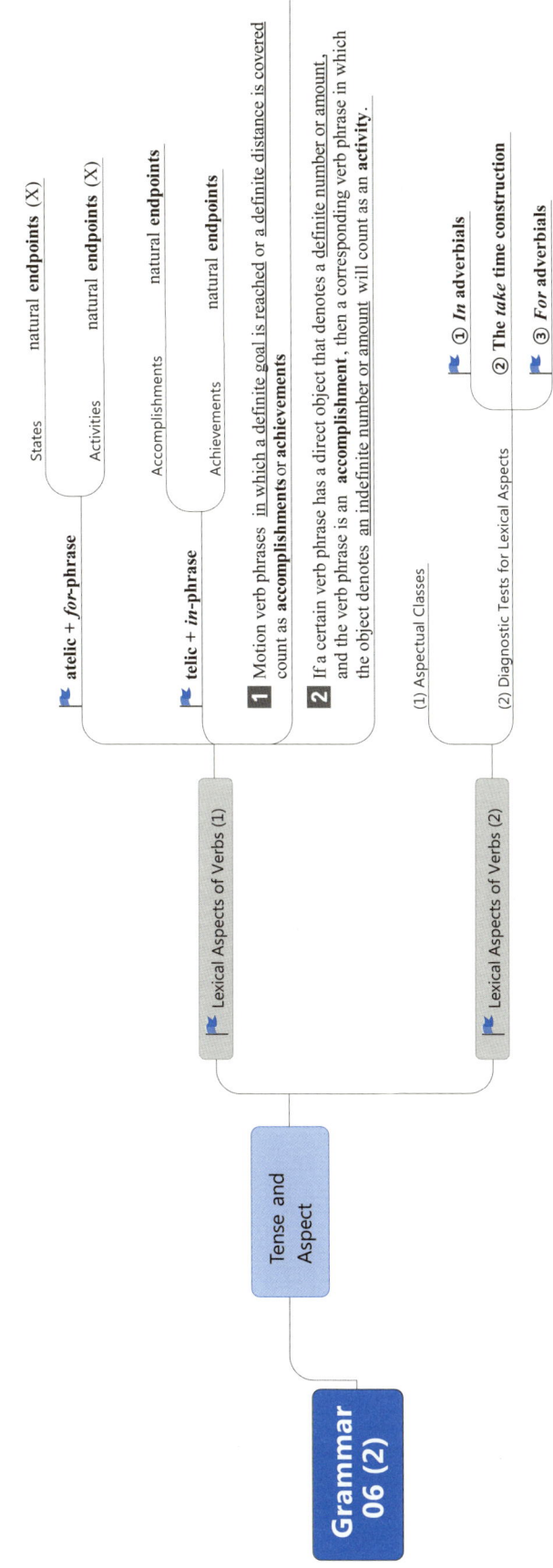

Grammar 07 mind map

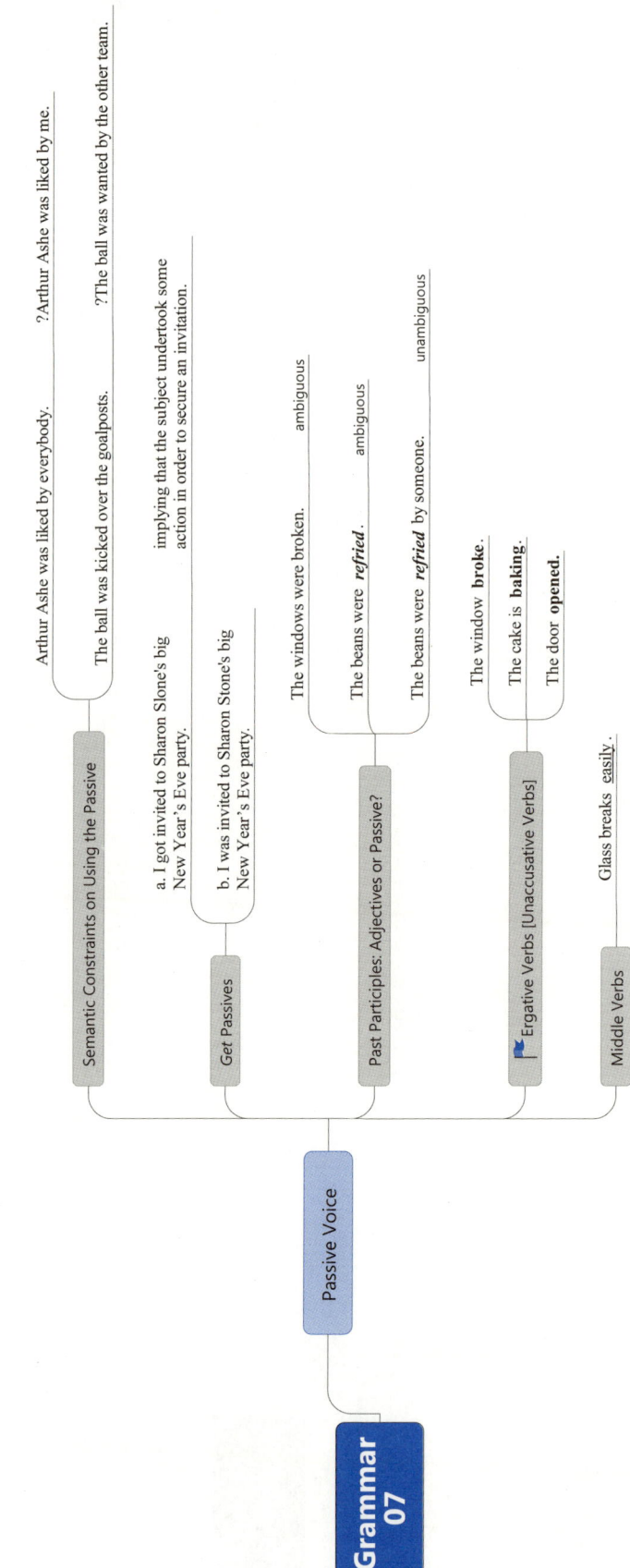

Grammar 08 mind map

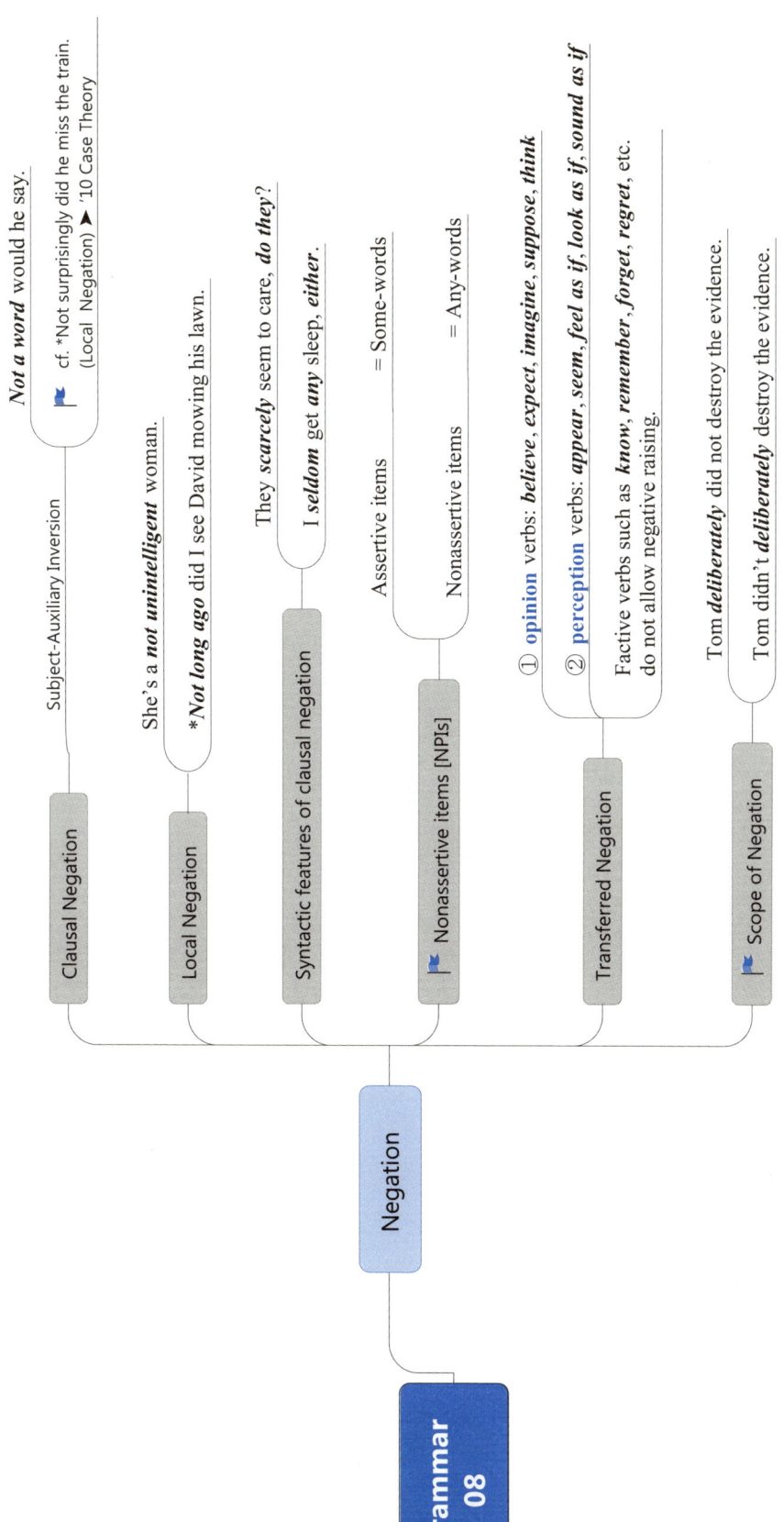

Grammar 09-10 mind map

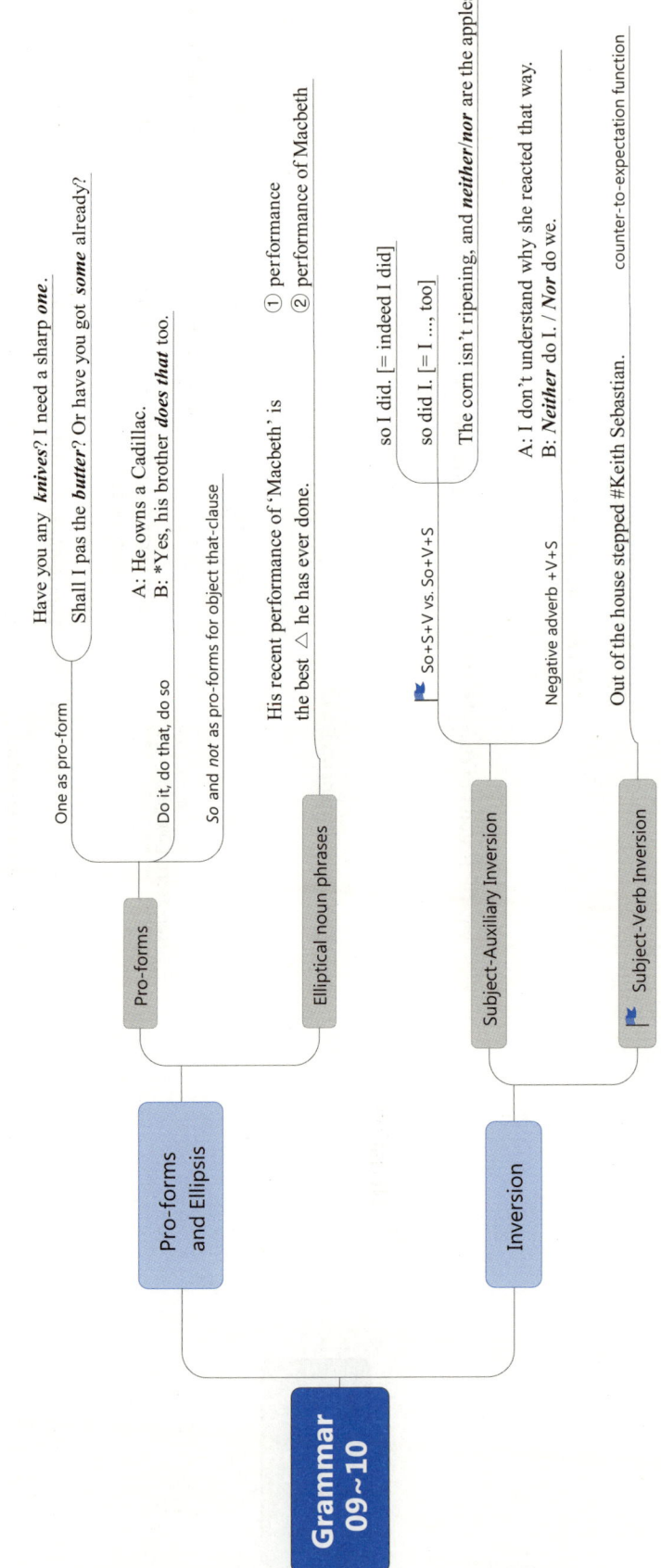

Grammar 11-12 mind map

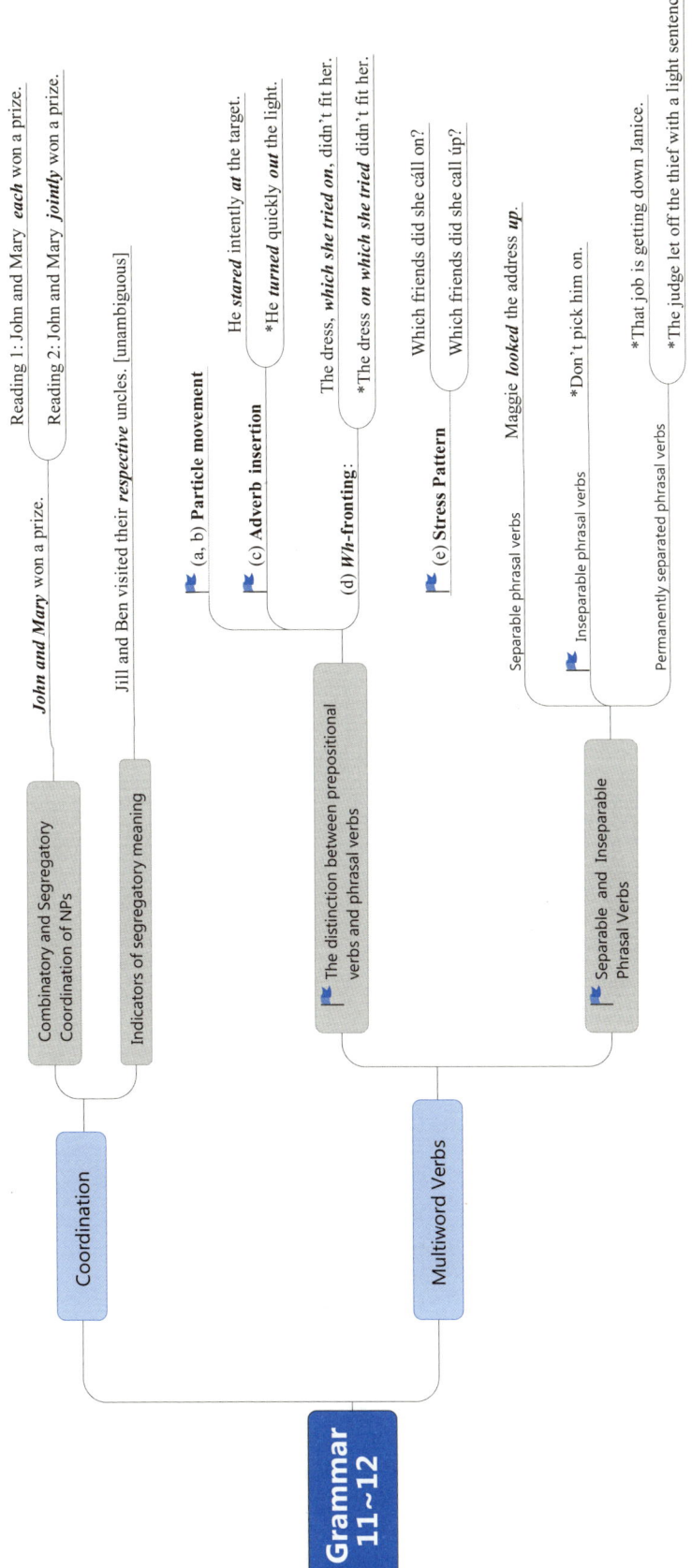

Grammar 13 mind map

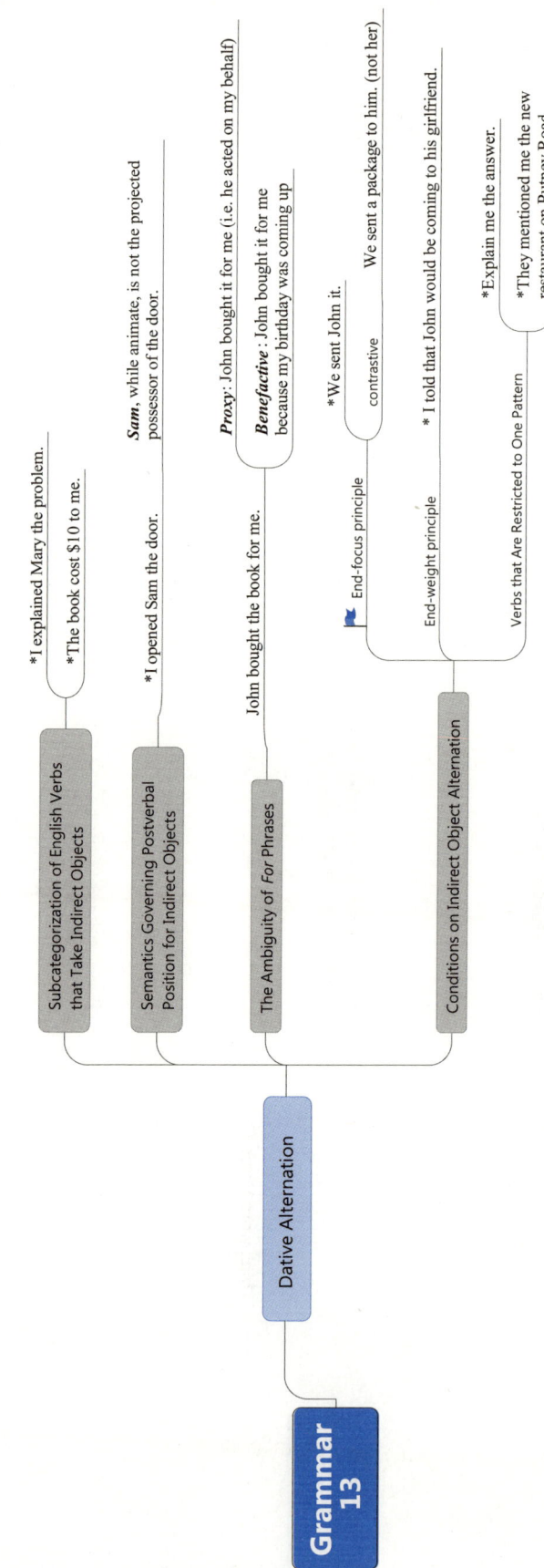

Grammar 14 mind map

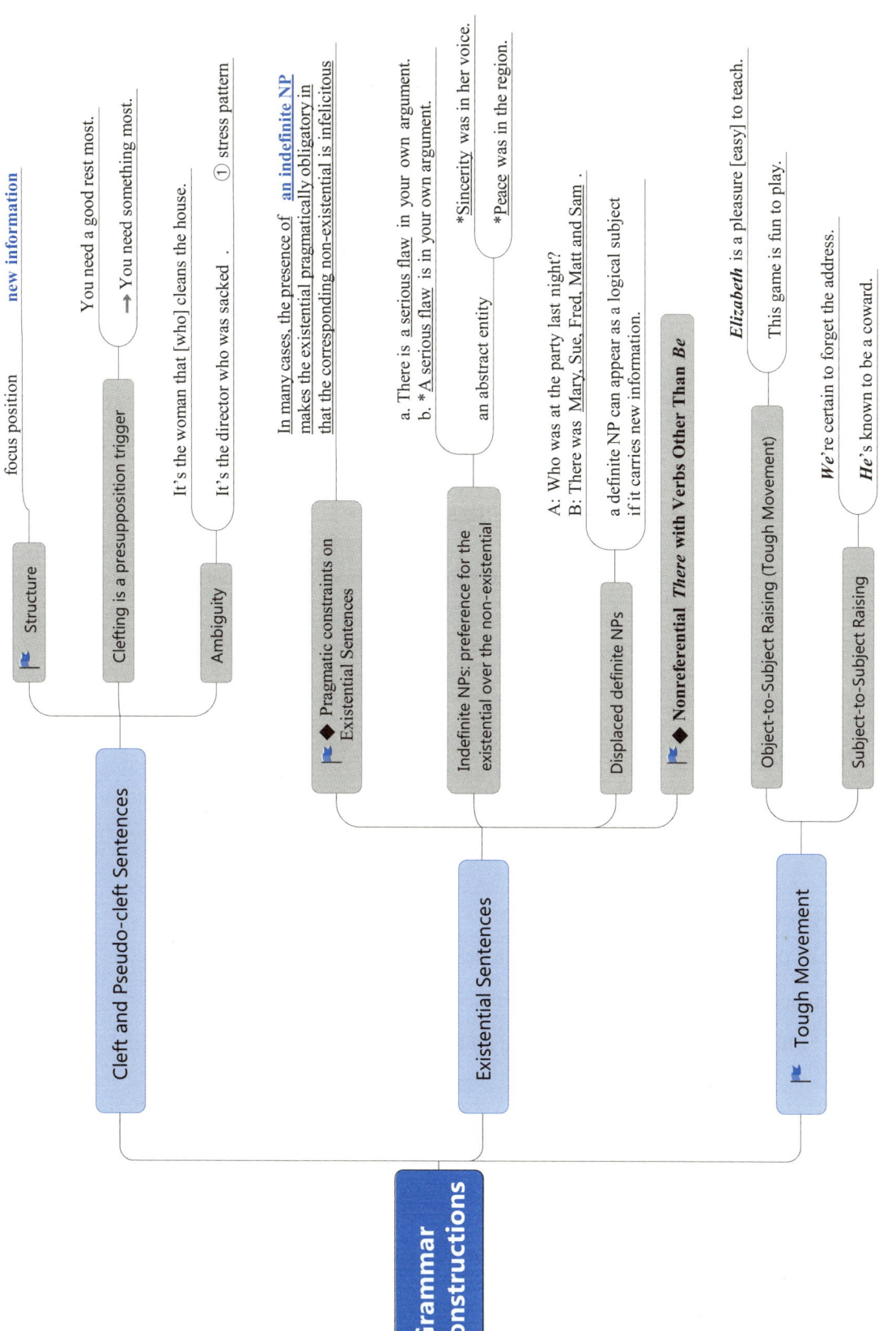

Chapter 04 Grammar

01 Determiners

1 Determiners '00

pre-determiners	central determiners	post-determiners
all, both, half **Multipliers**: double, twice, etc.	**Articles**: the, a, an **Possessives**: my, your, her, their **Demonstratives**: this [these], that [those] **Quantifiers**: some, any, no, every, each, etc. ***wh*-determiners**: which, whose, whichever, whatever, etc.	**Ordinals**: first, second, fourth, etc. **Cardinals**: seven, ninety **Quantifiers**: many, few, plenty of, a lot of, etc.

(1) order restriction

When multiple determiners from different categories appear before a head noun, they must follow the order.

(1) pre-determiner + central determiner + Noun:

all the students, all their bills, both the girls

twice the length, three times her salary

*I like the all three boys. → I like all the three boys. '00

*Two those children are coming. → Those two children are coming.

*The both sisters wanted to go. → Both the sisters wanted to go.

(2) co-occurrence restriction

More than one member of the pre-determiners or the central determiners cannot co-occur before a head noun.

(2) *this my book → this book of mine

2 Genitives

(1) Meanings of Genitives

The meanings expressed by the genitive can conveniently be shown through paraphrase; at the same time, we can compare the analogous use of the *of*-construction.

① Possessive genitive

Mrs. Johnson's coat.   Mrs. Johnson owns this coat.

The ship's funnel   The ship has a funnel.

② Genitive of attribute

The victim's outstanding courage.   The victim was very courageous.

③ Partitive genitive

The heart's two ventricles.   The heart contains two ventricles.

④ Subjective genitive

The parents' consent.   The parents consented.

⑤ Objective genitive

The prisoner's release.   Someone released the prisoner.

⑥ Genitive of origin

Mother's letter.   The letter is from Mother.

England's cheeses.   The cheeses were produced in England.

⑦ Descriptive genitive

Children's shoes.   The shoes are designed for children.

A *doctor's* degree.   The degree is a doctorate.

(2) Double Genitive

An *of*-construction can be combined with a genitive to produce a construction known as the POST-GENITIVE (or 'double genitive'). In this construction, the independent genitive acts as prepositional complement following *of*:

some friends *of Jim's* ['some of Jim's friends']

that irritating habit *of her father's*

an invention *of Gutenberg's*

several pupils *of his*

But the independent genitive is not in this case elliptical. Rather, the post-genitive contrasts in terms of indefiniteness or unfamiliarity with the normal determinative genitive. Whereas [1] and [2] presuppose definiteness, the presupposition in [1a] and [2a] is one of indefiniteness:

[1] Jim's friend   [1a] a friend of Jim's
[2] Joseph Haydn's pupil [2a] a pupil of Joseph Haydn's

02 Adjectives

1 Stative and Dynamic Adjectives

Adjectives are characteristically stative. Many adjectives, however, can be seen as dynamic. In particular, most adjectives that are susceptible to subjective measurement are capable of being dynamic. Stative and dynamic adjectives differ syntactically in a number of ways. For example, a stative adjective such as *tall* cannot be used with the progressive aspect or with the imperative:

*He's being *tall*.   *Be *tall*.

On the other hand, we can use silly as a **dynamic adjective**.

He was being *silly*.
He is being *brave*.   Be *brave*.

Adjectives that can be used dynamically include ***brave, calm, cheerful, conceited, cruel, foolish, friendly, funny, good, greedy, helpful, jealous, naughty, noisy,*** and ***tidy***.

◆ **Summary**

Stative Adjectives	cannot be used with progressive aspect or with the imperative	e.g. *tall*
Dynamic Adjectives	can be used with progressive aspect or with the imperative	e.g. *silly*, *brave*, *funny*, etc.

2 Relative Clauses

◆ Restrictive vs. Nonrestrictive Relative Clauses '13 Essay

A *restrictive relative clause* is one that serves to restrict the reference of the noun phrase modified. In (1), the restrictive relative clause **who lives in Canada** restricts **my sister** by specifying the sister in Canada. The sentence implies that the speaker has more than one sister, but only one sister in Canada is a biologist. It could be an answer to the question **Which of your sisters is a biologist?** The information added by the relative clause identifies the sister.

(1) My sister *who lives in Canada* is a biologist.

Sentence (2) contains a nonrestrictive relative clause, indicated as such by the commas around it. A *nonrestrictive relative clause* adds information about the noun modified. The noun's reference is already clear; the clause does not restrict it. Thus, in (2) the relative clause is just an added comment to the main clause content *my sister is a biologist*. The relative clause in essence says "Oh, by the way, she lives in Canada." There is no implication that the speaker has other sisters.

(2) My sister, *who lives in Canada*, is a biologist.

◆ Distinguishing Nonrestrictive and Restrictive Relative Clauses

Several form criteria distinguish nonrestrictive relative clauses from their restrictive counterparts:

(1) Punctuation

Nonrestrictive relative clauses have commas around them, as in (3a). Restrictive relative clauses must not be separated by commas, as shown in (3b).

(3) a. My sister, who lives in Canada, is a biologist.

b. My sister who lives in Canada is a biologist.

(2) Modification of a proper nouns

Nonrestrictive relative clauses can modify proper nouns, as in (4a); restrictive relatives, as in (4b), cannot.

(4) a. John, who is a linguist, was not impressed by Professor Fish's arguments.

b. *John who is a linguist was not impressed by Professor Fish's arguments.

(3) Modification of *any*, *every*, *no*, etc.

Nonrestrictive relative clauses may not modify **any**, **every**, or **no** + noun or indefinite pronouns such as **anyone**, **everyone**, or **no one**, as shown by (5a); restrictive relatives may, as shown in (5b).

(5) a. *Any man, who goes back on his word, is no friend of mine.

b. Any man who goes back on his word is no friend of mine.

(4) *That* as relative pronoun

Nonrestrictive relative clauses may not be introduced by **that**, as shown by (6a); restrictive relatives may, as in (6b).

(6) a. *The plan, that we discussed yesterday, will be adopted.

b. The plan that we discussed yesterday will be adopted.

(5) Stacking

Nonrestrictive relative clauses cannot be stacked. Stacking results in ungrammatical sentences like (7a). Restrictive relatives can be stacked, as in (7b).

(7) a. *They gave the job to Rob, who is very qualified, who starts next month.

b. I really like that car that you have that your wife is always zipping around town in.

(6) Sentence modification

Nonrestrictive relative clauses may modify an entire sentence, that is, a preceding independent clause, as in (8a). Restrictive relatives like (8b) may only modify noun phrases.

(8) a. Professor Fish gave everyone an A, which was just fine with Alice.
   b. *Professor Fish gave everyone an A which was just fine with Alice.

	restrictive relative clauses	nonrestrictive relative clauses
function	<u>identify</u> the entity by narrowing down the set	<u>add</u> information

3 Verbal Participles vs. Adjectival Participles [20]

Often the difference between the adjective and the participle is not clear-cut. The verbal force of the participle is explicit for the *-ing* form when <u>a direct object</u> is present. Hence, the following *-ing* forms are participles that constitute a verb phrase with the preceding auxiliary:

Her views were ***alarming*** her audience.
You are ***frightening*** the children.
They are ***insulting*** us.

Similarly, the verbal force is explicit for the *-ed* form when <u>a ***by***-agent phrase</u> with a personal agent is present, indicating the correspondence to the active form of the sentence:

The man was ***offended*** by the policeman.
He is ***appreciated*** by his students.
She was ***misunderstood*** by her parents.

<u>For both participle forms, premodification by the intensifier ***very/too*** is an explicit indication that the forms have achieved adjective status</u>:

Her views were very ***alarming***.

You are very *frightening*.

The man was very *offended*.

John was too *startled* to move.

We might therefore expect that the presence of *very/too* together with an explicit indicator of verbal force would produce an unacceptable sentence. This is certainly so for the *-ing* participle form:

*His views were very *alarming* his audience.

*John was too *startled* to move by his boss.

◆ **Distinguishing Verbal Participles from Adjectival Participles**

Verbal Participle	Adjectival Participle
-ing + DO	very/too + -ing/-ed
-ed + by-agent phrase	

4 Unmarked and Marked Adjectives '99, '07

We use the adjective *old* in measure expression (*x years old*) when we refer to a person's age, regardless of the age:

Mr. Jespersen is 75 years *old*.

His granddaughter is two years *old*.

In the scale of measurement, *old* indicates the upper range (*He is old*) but it is also the unmarked term for the whole range, so that *She is two years old* is equivalent to *Her age is two years*. The measure adjectives used in this way are the following, with the marked term in parentheses:

deep (shallow)	high (low)	long (short)	old (young)	heavy (light)
wide (narrow)	tall (short)	thick (thin)	big (small)	bright (dim)
large (little)	strong (weak)	fat (thin)		

The unmarked terms are also used in *how*-questions and again, they do not assume the upper range. *How old is she?* is equivalent to *What is her age?* Other adjectives are also used in the same way in *how*-questions, e.g.:

How heavy is your computer?
How accurate is that clock?

Some adverbs are also used as an unmarked term in *how*-questions, e.g.:

How much does it cost?
How far did you drive today?

If we use the marked term, as in *How young is John?*, we are asking a question that presupposes that the relevant norm is towards the lower end of the scale, i.e. that John is young, whereas the unmarked term in *How old is John?* does not presuppose that John is old.

◆ Summary

Unmarked Adjectives	Usually used in how-questions & answers e.g. How old is John?	No presupposition
Marked Adjectives	Sometimes used in how-questions & answers e.g. How young is John?	Presupposition (John is young.)

5 Attributive-Only Adjectives '19

A number of adjectives, including *drunken*, *erstwhile*, *eventual*, *future*, *mere*, *principal*, and *utter*, can appear only as modifiers of head nouns; that is, they can appear only in the attributive position, as shown in (1).

(1) a. At last night's party, he saw one of his *former* wives.

b. *At last night's party, he saw one of his wives who is *former*.

c. She thought that he was an *utter* fool.

d. *In terms of being a fool, he was *utter*.

(1) Adjectives of Degree

Adjectives of degree describe the degree of the property expressed by the head noun. For instance, in the sentence **The show was an utter disaster**, the adjective utter describes the degree of the disaster. The degree expressed by such an adjective is usually absolute, as shown in (2).

(2) a. an *absolute* hero
 b. a *complete* ballplayer
 c. a *total* moron
 d. *sheer* nonsense

(2) Quantifying Adjectives

Quantifying adjectives indicate the amount, quantity, or frequency of the head noun.

(3) a. the *only* way
 b. the *entire* crew
 c. an *occasional* cloud
 d. the *usual* suspects

(3) Adjectives of Time and Location

Adjectives of time and location place a head noun within a particular time frame or location.

(4) a. a *future* appointment
 b. an *old* friend
 c. his *former* girlfriend
 d. a *previous* version
 e. her *left* arm
 f. the *northeastern* provinces

(4) Associative Adjectives

Associative adjectives do not express literal properties of a head noun but instead describe it in terms of some entity that is associated with it. For instance. the phrase *nuclear physicist* certainly does not imply that the physicist is somehow nuclear. Instead, the adjective describes the area of science in which the physicist works. Similarly, in the phrase *criminal attorney*, the adjective does not express a property of the attorney but instead describes an entity with which the attorney is associated.

(5) a. a *mathematical* journal
　　b. *urban* planning
　　c. a *gothic* novelist
　　d. a *public* official
　　e. a *moral* dilemma

6 Predicative-Only Adjectives

Most adjective can be used as both **attributive adjectives** and **predicative adjectives**, as in (1).

(1) a. He gave an *interesting* talk.　*attributive*
　　b. His talk was *interesting*.　　　*predicative*

Attributive adjectives modify the head noun in an NP and occur before that head noun. In contrast, **predicative adjectives** appear after a verb.

　Predicative-only adjectives can occur only in the predicative position. They are divided into three groups.

(1) Adjectives Beginning with the Prefix *A-*

The first group of predicate-only adjectives is formed with the prefix *a-* and includes adjectives such as *afloat*, *afraid*, *aghast*, *alive*, *asleep*, and *awake*. These cannot occur attributively, as (2b) and (2d) illustrate.

(2) a. The young girl was *asleep*, so she did not hear the storm outside.
　　b. *The *asleep* girl did not hear the storm outside.
　　c. The rescue squad finally discovered a man who was still *alive*.
　　d. *The rescue squad happy to discover an *alive* man.

(2) Adjective That Take Complements

The second group of predicate-only adjectives is made up of adjectives that take complements that are either infinitives (e.g., **able to run**, **liable to sue**) or prepositional phrases (e.g., **devoid of fear**, **fraught with tension**), as shown in (3).

 (3) a. She is **liable to make a scene**. *infinitive*
   b. *The **liable person** has to pay.
   c. He is **devoid of any humor**. *prepositional phrase*
   d. *He was a **devoid comic**.

(3) Adjectives Referring to Medical Conditions or Health

Finally, there is a small group of adjectives that refer to medical conditions or health (i.e., **faint**, **ill**, **poorly**, **unwell**, **well**, etc.) that can appear only in the predicative position, as shown in (4). The adjective **ill** can appear attributively if it is modified (e.g., **a mentally ill patient**).

 (4) a. He feels **faint**.
   b. *They revived the **faint** patient.
   c. My mother is **ill**.
   d. *They took the **ill** woman to the hospital.

03 Adverbials

1 Subjuncts

<u>Subjuncts have a subordinate and parenthetic role</u> in comparison with adjuncts. There are two main types. Those with *narrow orientation* are chiefly related to the predication or to a particular part of that predication. Those with *wide orientation* relate more to the sentence as a whole.

◆ **Wide orientation**

(1) Viewpoint subjuncts

The subjuncts which express a viewpoint are characteristically placed at *I*.

Architecturally, the plans represent a magnificent conception.
From a personal viewpoint, he is likely to do well in this post.
Looked at politically, the proposal seems dangerous.
Weatherwise, the outlook is dismal.

(2) Courtesy subjuncts

A small number of adverbs in *–ly*, along with *please*, serve to convey a formulaic tone of politeness to a sentence. They normally occur at *M*:

You are *cordially* invited to take your places.
He asked if I would *please* read his manuscript.
She *kindly* offered me her seat.

◆ Narrow orientation

(3) Item subjuncts

General GROUP

The commonest item to be associated with subjuncts is the *subject* of a clause, with the subjunct operating in the semantic area of *manner* but distinguished from the corresponding manner adjunct by being placed at *I* or *M*:

She has *consistently* opposed the lawyer's arguments.

This does not mean that her own argument have been conducted consistently but that she has been consistent in always opposing the lawyer's.

VOLITIONAL GROUP

Many subject-oriented adverbials express **volition**:

deliberately [*(un)intentionally*, *without intention*, *on purpose*, *purposely*, *willfully*], *reluctantly* [*with reluctance*] ↔ *voluntarily*, *(un)willingly*; for example:

Intentionally, they said nothing to him about the fire.

With great reluctance, he rose to speak.

Subject subjuncts cannot co-occur with a nonpersonal subject in an intransitive or active-voice clause:

**Consistently, the water kept boiling.

**Reluctantly, the avalanche destroyed the chalet.

However, in the passive form it is the agent (whether present or not) that must not be nonpersonal:

The chalet was *reluctantly* destroyed { (by the developers). / *(by the avalanche). }

The lawyer's objections were *consistently* overruled.

Passive sentences with personal subject and agent leave an adverbial equivocal:

John was *willingly* sent to friends for the summer (by his mother).
[either 'John was willing' or 'his mother was willing']

Contrast:

The parcel of valuables was *willingly* sent to the charity organizers.
[only 'the sender was willing']

◆ Summary

Item subjuncts (= Subject-oriented adverbials)	
GENERAL GROUP: *consistently* VOLITIONAL GROUP: *deliberately*, *reluctantly* ↔ *willingly*, etc.	Subject-oriented adverbials must have a **personal** and **agent** subject in an active-voice clause and the agent after by-phrase must be **personal** in a passive-voice clause.

2 Disjuncts

(1) Style disjuncts '12 Choice

Style disjuncts convey the speaker's comment on the style and form of what is being said and define in some way the conditions under which 'authority' is being assumed for the statement. Thus where (1) is stated as an unsupported fact, (2) is conditioned by a **style disjunct**:

(1) Mr. Forster neglects his children.
(2) *From my personal observation*, Mr. Forster neglects his children.

Many style disjuncts can be seen as abbreviated clauses in which the adverbial would have the role of manner adjunct:

Frankly, I am tired.
(cf "I tell you *frankly* that I am tired'.)

Sometimes the disjunct has full clausal form:

If I may say so without giving you offence, I think your writing is rather immature.

More often, a clausal disjunct is nonfinite, as in **to be frank**, **putting it bluntly**, **considered candidly**.

The semantic roles of disjuncts fall under two main heads:

(a) **Manner** and **modality**, thus involving items such as *crudely*, *frankly*, *honestly*, *truthfully*:

(To put it) briefly, there is nothing I can do to help.
You can, *in all honesty*, expect no further payments.

(b) **Respect**, thus involving items such as *generally*, *literally*, *personally*, *strictly*:

Strictly (in terms of the rules), she should have conceded the point to her opponent.

I would not, *(speaking) personally*, have taken offence at the remark.

From what he said, the other driver was in the wrong.

(2) Content disjuncts

Content disjuncts make an observation on the actual content of an utterance and on its truth conditions.

To the disgust of his neighbors, Mr. Forster neglects his children.

Comment on the content of the utterance (Content Disjuncts) may be of two kinds:

(a) relating to *certainty*;
(b) relating to *evaluation*.

Both can be expressed by a wide range of adverb phrases, by prepositional phrases and — especially those in (a) — by clauses.

(a) *Certainty*. These disjuncts comment on the truth value of what is said, firmly endorsing it, expressing doubt, or posing contingencies such as conditions or reasons. For example, beside the statement 'The play was written by Francis Beaumont', we may have:

The play was $\begin{Bmatrix} \textit{undoubtedly} \\ \textit{apparently} \\ \textit{perhaps} \end{Bmatrix}$ written by Francis Beaumont

(b) *Evaluation*. These disjuncts express an attitude to an utterance by way of evaluation. Some express a judgment on the utterance as a whole, including its subject:

Wisely, Mrs. Jensen consulted her lawyer.
('Mrs. Jensen was wise in consulting her lawyer.')

So also **correctly, cunningly, foolishly [stupidly], justly [rightly]**, etc. Other evaluation disjuncts carry no implication of a comment on the subject:

> *Naturally*, my husband expected me home by then.
> ('It was natural for my husband to expect me back by then'
> — *not* 'My husband was natural …')

So also *curiously* [*strangely*], *funnily (enough)*, *unexpectedly*, *predictably*, *understandably*, *disturbingly*, *regrettably* [*To my regret*], *fortunately* [*luckily*], *pleasingly* [*happily*], *sadly*, *amusingly*, *hopefully*, *significantly*.

04 Pronouns

1 Reference '05, '20

Reference is classified into two types: **anaphoric reference** and **cataphoric reference**.

anaphoric reference: antecedent ← pronoun
cataphoric reference: pronoun → antecedent

Anaphoric reference is possible in both coordination and subordination.

When <u>the doctor</u> had examined the patient, *she* picked up the telephone (subordination)

There is <u>an excellent museum</u> here and everyone should visit *it*. (coordination)

Cataphoric reference is possible only in subordination. Contrast the grammaticality of the following examples:

When *she* had examined the patient, <u>the doctor</u> picked up the telephone. (subordination)

*She examined the patient and then <u>the doctor</u> picked up the telephone. (coordination)

◆ Summary

Anaphora	
anaphoric reference: antecedent ← pronoun	coordination & subordination
cataphoric reference: pronoun → antecedent	subordination only

05 Verb Complementation

1 *That*-Complements

◆ **Complements After Verbs of Request or Demand**

A subset of verbs that we can call ***verbs of request or demand*** — for example, ***ask***, ***demand***, ***insist***, ***recommend***, and ***stipulate*** — must be followed by a that complement containing a bare infinitive, as shown in (1).

(1) We ***recommend*** that she **accept** his offer.

Suasive verbs	*that*-complement
insist	
ask [require, request], demand	
order, command	**that** S (should) + **R**
recommend [suggest, propose, move, urge], prefer	
agree, decide	

2 Infinitival Complements '07, '13

Many verbs take ***to*** clauses beginning with infinitives as complements. Complements of the three types differ in whether they have an overt subject and if not, what that subject is understood as being. More specifically, they differ with regard to three questions:

- Is there an NP following the main clause verb?
- If so, is this NP the object of the main clause verb?
- What is the subject of the infinitive complement?

(1) Type 1 Complements: *Persuade* verbs

A large number of verbs, such as ***advise***, ***authorize***, ***cause***, ***compel***, ***convince***, ***order***, ***persuade***, and ***tell*** are transitive, and there, must have an NP object, as shown in (1).

(1) Alice persuaded John to come to the party.

We can confirm that **John** is the object of **persuade** through passivization, which moves **John** into subject position in the main clause. The result is shown in (2).

(2) John was persuaded (by Alice) [to come to the party].

Since **John** is the object of **persuade**, the infinitive complement in (1) has no overt subject. However, **John** is understood as being its subject. The diagram in (3) reflects our intuition that the missing subject of the complement is identical to the object of the main clause (parentheses indicate an understood subject).

(3) Alice persuaded **John** [(**John**) to come to the party].

In short, we can characterize sentences with **persuade** verbs as having the following pattern: NP_1 V NP_2 [*to* V], with NP_2 understood as the complement subject.

In terms of their meaning, **persuade** and the other verbs that take this complement type have been called **influence**, or **manipulative**, **verbs** because their object is usually influenced by the main clause subject to carry out the action expressed in the complement.

(2) Type 2 Complements: *Want* verbs

Another group of verbs that include **want** [*need, hope, wish, desire, yearn*], **love** [*like, prefer*] ↔ **hate**, and **plan** [*arrange*] can occur without a following NP (except the verb **arrange**), as shown in (4).

(4) Joan **wanted** to write a letter to the mayor.   (Subject control)

These verbs can also have a following NP, as shown in (5).

(5) Joan **wanted** Bill to write a letter to the mayor.

What is the NP following the verb? Notice that if we ask the question **What did Joan want?**, we get the answer **for Bill to write a letter to the mayor**. Thus, the NP **Bill** is not itself the object of **want** but is instead the subject of the infinitive complement, as shown in the bracketing in (6).

(6) Joan wanted [Bill to write a letter to the mayor].

Passivization supports this conclusion. The only way to apply the passive rule to (5) is within the infinitive complement, so that the complement object, *a letter*, is moved into subject position, as is shown in (7a). If **Bill** were the object of *want*, the passive in (7b) would be grammatical, but it clearly is not.

(7) a. Joan wanted [a letter to be written to the mayor (by Bill)].
    b. *Bill was wanted (by Joan) [to write a letter to the major].

In the case of some *want* verbs (including *arrange*, *like*, *love*, *plan*, and *prefer*), the complementizer *for* can appear at the beginning of the complement, as illustrated in (8).

(8) a. We will arrange *for* your group to have access to the conference room.
    b. I won't plan (*for*) you to be back in time to go with us.
    c. I will arrange (*for*) us to be away while they do the cleaning.

One *want* verb is somewhat of an exception to the pattern discussed — namely, *promise*. When *promise* occurs without a following NP, it clearly is like the other *want* verbs.

(9) Bill *promised* to write a letter to the mayor.

Like many other *want* verbs, *promise* can also be followed by an NP.

(10) Bill *promised* Joan to write a letter to the mayor.

The NP after *promise* (i.e., *Joan*) is clearly the object of *promise*, and the subject of the complement is missing but is understood as identical to the main clause subject (**Bill**).

(3) Type 3 Complements: *Believe* verbs

A number of verbs, including *acknowledge, believe, consider, expect,* and *judge*, have an infinitival complement that contains *be* plus an NP or an adjective, as shown in (11). With these verbs, as in (11), there is always an NP.

(11) Everyone believed Einstein to be a genius/brilliant.

The NP that follows the verb is the subject of the complement, not the object of the verb. This is expressed in the bracketing in (12).

(12) Everyone believed [Einstein to be a genius].

In other words, what everyone believed was not Einstein but the proposition that Einstein was a genius. With these verbs, the pattern is thus NP_1 V [NP_2 *to be* NP/adj].

Notice, however, sentence (13), a passive version of (12). Although **Einstein** is the subject of the infinitive complement in (12) rather than the object of **believe**, passivization can move it to subject position.

(13) Einstein was believed to be a genius (by everyone).

To account for sentence such as (13), grammarians have proposed a rule called **subject-to-object raising**. The operation of this rule is shown in (14); once **Einstein** has become the object, passivization can operate on it, producing (13).

(14) Everyone believed Einstein [_____ to be a genius]. **subject-to-object raising**

◆ Summary

	Infinitival Complements	postverbal NP
ditransitive verb	persuade + [NP] + [to-inf] 　　　　　　O　　　O	the object of the main clause verb
monotransitive verb	want　+ [NP + to-inf] 　　　　　　O	the subject of the infinitive complement
monotransitive verb	believe + [NP + to-inf] 　　　　　　O	both

06 Tense and Aspect

1 Present Perfect vs. Simple Past '99

The Present Perfect is a subtle retrospective tense-aspect which views states or events as occurring in a time-frame leading up to speech time. Expressed by *have* + past participle, the *have* element is present, the participle is past. The event is psychologically connected to the present as in the following example:

speech time

His marriage *has broken down* and he *has gone* to live in another part of England

These and other features contrast with those of the Past tense:

Figure 1. The Present Perfect and the Past tense.

Present Perfect	Simple Past
① Its time-frame is the extended **now**, a period of time which extends up to speech time.	Its time-frame is the **past**, which is viewed as a separate time-frame from that of the present.
② The event occurs at some **indefinite** and **unspecified time** within the extended now. The Perfect is **non-deictic** — it doesn't 'point' to a specific time but relates to a relevant time.	The event is located at a **specific** and **definite time** in the past. The Past tense is **deictic** — it points to a specific time in the past.
③ The event has '**current relevance**', that is, it is viewed as **psychologically connected** to the moment of speaking.	The event is seen as **psychologically disconnected** from the moment of speaking.

(1) Anteriority: definite or indefinite time '99

Within the extended now, the Present Perfect is used in English when the speaker wishes to refer, not to a definite moment of occurrence of the event, but simply to the **anteriority** of the event. This is in marked contrast with the definite time use of the Past tense. Compare:

They *have left* for New York.

They *left* for New York an hour ago.

Similarly, the Present Perfect is not normally used in main clauses with interrogative adverbs, which imply definite time and require the Past tense.

We can say	Have they started?	Have they finished? (Present Perfect)
Or	When did they start?	At what time did they finish? (Past tense)
But not	*When have they started?	*At what time have they finished?

Furthermore, the Present Perfect operates in a time-frame that is still open, blocking examples such as **1a** and **2a**. By contrast the **b** examples are grammatical, as are **3** and **4**:

1a *James Joyce *has been born* in Dublin.

1b James Joyce *was born* in Dublin.

2a *He *has lived* in Ireland until 1904.

2b He *lived* in Ireland until 1904.

3   Michael *has lived* in Ireland all his life (implying that he still lives there).

4   Generations of writers *have been influenced* by Joyce (and are still influenced).

In **1a** and **2a** the Perfect is blocked because Joyce's life-span is over. In **3** this is not the case. In **4** the plural subject 'generations of writers' allows for a time-frame that is open. The perspective of the 'extended now' time-frame in contrast with that of the Past tense can be seen in many sentences.

(2) Time Adjuncts and the Present Perfect Aspect

The Present Perfect aspect is frequently accompanied by time Adjuncts that refer to a period of time that is still open at the moment of speaking, e.g. ***this week, this month, this year***, etc. Adjuncts which refer to a period of past time that is now over (e.g. ***last month, last year, yesterday, ago***) are incompatible with the Perfect. Compare:

Have you seen any good films ***this month***?

*Have you seen any good films ***last month***?

A period of time expressed by an adjunct such as ***in July*** is either open or closed depending on the speaker's vantage-point. If closed, the verb is in the Past tense:

Temperatures have reached an all-time high *in July*. (July is not yet over)

Temperatures reached an all-time high *in July*. (July is over)

Figure 2. Adjuncts of indefinite time and adjuncts of definite time.

Adjuncts of indefinite or unspecified time used with the Perfect, such as:	Adjuncts of definite or specific time used with Past Tense, such as:
sometimes, often, always, ever, at times twice, three times in the last ten years lately, recently, now, to date, so far	yesterday last week, last year, last month, last June an hour ago, two years ago in 1066 at 4 o'clock, at Christmas, at Easter

(3) Current Relevance

By 'current relevance' we mean that the event referred to by means of the Present Perfect is psychologically connected to speech time, and has some (implicit) relevance to it.

The notion of **current relevance** is essential: ***The children have come back*** implies that they are still back, whereas ***The children came back*** has no such implication. It would not be normal to say *****The children have come back a moment ago*** (since an adjunct such as 'a moment ago' visualizes a definite point of time in the past, whereas the Perfect does not).

2 Will vs. Be going to

◆ neutral vs. future fulfillment of a present intention/cause

Will with the infinitive has the connotation of colorless, **neutral future.**

He ***will be*** here in half an hour.

Will you ***need*** any help?

No doubt I***'ll see*** you next week.

The general meaning of the construction of ***be going to*** with the infinitive is 'future fulfillment of the present'. We can further distinguish two specific meanings. The first, ① 'future fulfillment of a present intention', is chiefly associated with personal subjects and agentive verbs:

When *are* you *going to get* married?

Randy and Joyce *are going to get* married in October.

Martha *is going to lend* us her camera.

I*'m going to complain* if things don't improve.

The other meaning, ② 'future result of a present cause', is found with both personal and nonpersonal subjects:

It*'s going to rain* today.   She*'s going to have* a baby.

There*'s going to be* trouble.   You*'re going to get* soaked.

◆ Speaker's control & distant action vs. no speaker's control & imminent action

Secondly, *be going to* is closely tied to action already begun in the present or immediately imminent, given evidence available in the present but over which the speaker has no control (or has lost control). Thus English speakers say things like:

"Help! I'm going to fall."

"Look, it's gonna rain soon."

The equivalents with *will* would sound strange in such statements. The form *will* occurs in conditions and other statements where future outcome is contingent on some other result, is more distant, or involves speaker control:

"If you put your pawn there, he'll win the game."

"Go to the cafe at 9 P.M., and I'll meet you there."

In the immediately preceding example, *will* (*'ll*) conveys a sense of promise or commitment in the statement, but use of *be going to* would convey a plan or intention instead.

◆ **Summary**

will	be going to
neutral	future fulfillment of a present intention/cause
distant action speaker's control promise	imminent action no speaker's control plan or intention

3 The present tense in adverbial clauses '18

(1) will + R → the present tense '18

The simple present is commonly used in preference to the auxiliary *will* or *shall* in certain types of adverbial clauses to express future meaning:

> When she **arrives**, the band will play the National Anthem.
> While I **am** away, the children will look after the house.
> Next time I'll do as he **says**.
> The harder you **exercise**, the better you'll feel.
> Even if tomorrow's match **is** cancelled, Lancashire will still be at the top of the league.
> Whether or not they **win** this battle, they won't win the war.
> Whatever they **say**, I won't play.

The subordinators chiefly involved belong to the temporal, conditional, and conditional–concessive categories.

(2) will have pp → have pp

The present perfect is common in temporal and conditional clauses when the clauses refer to a sequence of future events:

> When they **'ve scored** their next goal, we'll go home.
> As soon as I **'ve retired**, I'll buy a cottage in the country.
> After they **have left**, we can smoke.

If I've **written** the paper before Monday, I'll call you.

4 Stative Progressives

> ◆ **Stative(State) Verbs**
>
> States of 'being' and 'having': be, contain, depend, have, resemble.
>
> Intellectual states: believe, know, realize, think, understand.
>
> States of emotion or attitude: disagree, dislike, like, want, wish.
>
> States of perception: feel, hear, see, smell, taste.
>
> States of bodily sensation: ache, feel sick, hurt, itch, tickle.

State verbs rarely appear in the progressive aspect. However, there are some exceptions to this. For a number of reasons, a native speaker may use stative verbs in the present progressive. Some of the reasons for using these stative progressives are as follows:

(1) Giving statements more emotional strength and intensity

The action becomes more emotional, intense, and vivid if a stative verb appears in the present progressive instead of the simple present. Thus, (1a), with the present progressive, expresses much more emotion than the more usual (1b), with the simple present. The presence of modifiers such as **really**, **always**, **constantly**, and **dreadfully**, common in these constructions, contributes to the effect.

(1) a. This operation *is really costing* a lot of money.

   b. This operation costs a lot of money.

(2) Focusing on behavior as a change from the norm

Progressive statives sometimes occur with a following predicative adjective — that is, in sentences of the type NP + *is/are* verb + *ing* + adjective. This use of stative progressives expresses the idea that the behavior of the subject is not his or her usual behavior. Compare (2a) to (2b), its equivalent in the simple present; only (2a) conveys the notion of a change from the norm.

(2) a. You're *being* very stubborn!

   (Implication: What's the matter with you? You don't usually behave this way.)

   b. You're very stubborn!

   (Implication: No one can get along with you.)

(3) Focusing on evolving change

Stative **appearance verbs** such as **appear**, **resemble**, and **seem**, and stative **cognitive verbs** such as **believe**, **know**, **mean**, and **understand** occur in the progressive aspect when the speaker wishes to express the idea of evolving process. Sentences (3a), (3b), and (3c) have stative appearance verbs, and (3d) has a stative cognitive verb. Here the direction of the process is often indicated by expressions such as **more and more**, **worse and worse**, **faster and faster**, and so on.

(3) a. The baby *is resembling* his father *more and more* every day.

   b. He's *looking worse and worse* by the minute.

   c. That example *is sounding less and less acceptable* with each repetition.

   d. I'*m understanding more and more* about the English tense-aspect system.

(4) Hedging or softening a definitive opinion

Cognitive stative verbs, such as **doubt**, **remember**, and **think**, in the progressive aspect allow the speaker to hedge, or soften, what would otherwise seem a more definitive stance. In (4a), the speaker uses a progressive stative in an effort to avoid offending the person addressed while still expressing a degree of skepticism about what she has heard. In (4b), a speaker feeling pressured by a somewhat aggressive shoe salesperson wanted to politely reject his suggestion that she choose the pair of shoes that she had just tried on.

(4) a. Mind you, I'*m* not *doubting* your word, but I did get a different version of what happened from Peter.

   b. No, I'*m* sort of *thinking* that I'd like to try a bit higher level heel, anyway.

5 Lexical Aspects of Verbs (1)

◆ Four Basic Aspectual Classes

This section will introduce four major aspectual classes. Intuitive descriptions and a few examples will be given here. Then in the natural course of studying the rules in which these classes play a role, we will develop some experimental tests that will help us to determine what class a given verb phrase belongs to.

(1) States

The first aspectual class is the class of *states*. Examples of sentences that report states are given in (1).

(1) a. Roger had a rash.
　　b. Karen felt happy.
　　c. Jonah owned a horse.
　　d. Fred's grandfather weighed two hundred pounds.
　　e. This tree is dead.
　　f. Thor has a tumor on his toe.
　　g. Nora liked the book.

States characteristically are interpreted as being more or less uniform throughout an interval; consequently, they do not have natural **endpoints**. In addition, they generally do not involve any action on the part of their subject.

(2) Activities

The aspectual class consisting of *activity* sentences is one whose members, at first glance, look very much like states. Here are some examples:

(2) a. Karen talked to Martha.
　　b. Jonah pestered the cat.
　　c. Mavis snored.
　　d. Martin wandered around.

As their name implies, activities are in general more "active" than states. However, they are similar to states in not having any natural **endpoints**. For instance, there is no point at which an episode of "talking to Martha" would necessarily come to a conclusion, as "pestering the cat" would have to.

(3) Accomplishments

The next aspectual class of verb phrases is generally referred to by the term *accomplishment*. In contrast with states and activities, accomplishments have natural **endpoints**. We have already seen two examples of accomplishment verb phrases: *write a sonnet* and *eat a peach*. Other accomplishment verb phrases occur in the following sentences:

(3) a. Ron peeled the carrot.
   b. Jody repaired the toaster.
   c. Dorothy built a house.
   d. Heifetz performed the Third Partita.
   e. Georgia wrote a sonnet.
   f. A man traveled from Jerusalem to Jericho.

The definable endpoints here are the point at which the carrot is completely peeled, the point at which the toaster works again, the point at which the house is finished, and so on.

(4) Achievements

The final aspectual class of verb phrases consists of *achievements*. Verb phrases of this class are like accomplishment verb phrases in having a clear natural **endpoint**. Yet, as we will see more clearly below, they differ from accomplishments in attaching much greater importance to the endpoint than to any earlier point. Several examples are given in (4).

(4) a. Linda finished her dissertation.
   b. Joel arrived at the meeting.
   c. Fred's goldfish died.
   d. Carol got to Boston.

atelic + *for*-phrase		telic + *in*-phrase	
States	**Activities**	**Accomplishments**	**Achievements**
have	run	paint (a picture)	recognize (something)
contain	walk	make (a chair)	realize (something)
seem	swim	build (a house)	lose (something)
want	live	write (a novel)	find (something)
like	study	grow up	win the race

◆ **Rules in Which the Aspectual Classes Play a Role**

< Rules concerning Aspectual Adverbial Phrases >

Two kinds of adverbial phrases are commonly used to indicate the duration of a state or event. One kind is headed by *in*, the other by *for*.

As a preliminary matter, we need to observe that phrases such as ***in four minutes*** can be used in two distinct ways, only one of which is relevant in what follows. These phrases can indicate how long a certain event goes on, or they can indicate how long it is before a certain state or event begins. Both readings are possible in the following **ambiguous** sentence:

(5) Roger Bannister will run a mile in four minutes.

On one reading, the sentence means that the task of running a mile will require four minutes from start to finish. On the other reading, the sentence means that the running of the mile is scheduled to begin four minutes after utterance time. The former interpretation is aspectual in nature, having to do with the time internal to the event itself, whereas the latter interpretation is relational, having to do with the time of the event relative to another time. In what follows, we will be interested exclusively in the aspectual interpretation.

We turn now to the matter of primary concern. ***In*** phrases are most acceptable in situations in which natural endpoints exist (accomplishments and achievements).

(6) a. Ron peeled the carrot ***in three minutes***/ ***?for three minutes***. (accomplishment)
  b. Linda finished her thesis ***in three months***/ ***?for three months***. (achievement)

By contrast, ***for*** phrases are most natural in situations in which such endpoints do not exist (states and activities).

(7) a. Ron had a rash *for three days*/ *?in three days*. (state)

　　b. Karen talked to Martha *for thirty minutes*/ *?in thirty minutes*. (activity)

The above discussion affords a practical dividend that merits special attention: the differing hospitality to *for* phrases and *in* phrases provides an effective means for distinguishing between states and activities on one hand, and accomplishments and achievements on the other. For instance, suppose that we want to determine the class membership of the two sentences in (8).

(8) a. Simon treated Roger's rash.

　　b. Simon healed Roger's rash.

When we add aspectual adverbials of these two kinds to the two sentences, we get a clear result.

(9) a. Simon ***treated Roger's rash*** for three weeks (*in three weeks).

　　b. Simon ***healed Roger's rash*** in three weeks (*for three weeks).

We conclude from this experiment that treating Roger's rash is a state or an activity, whereas healing Roger's rash is an accomplishment or an achievement. (Tests described later will show that the former is an activity rather than a state, and that the latter is an accomplishment rather than an achievement.)

Applied to a variety of verb phrases, this test yields some surprises. In particular, we find many examples in which two nonstate verb phrases are headed by the same verb but nevertheless have to be placed in different classes. One group of examples is given in (10) and (11).

(10) a. Brenda ***drove to San Francisco*** in an hour (*for an hour).

　　 b. Brenda ***drove toward San Francisco*** for an hour (*in an hour).

(11) a. Gordon ***rowed two miles*** in an hour (*for an hour).

　　 b. Gordon ***rowed*** for an hour (*in an hour).

The contrast between (10a) and (10b) derives from the fact that in the former but not in the latter, a specific goal is attained. Similarly, (11a) asserts that a definite distance was covered, whereas (11b) does not. These examples, then, can be accounted for by the following rule:

(12) Generalization: Motion verb phrases <u>in which a definite goal is reached or a definite distance is covered</u> count as **accomplishments** or **achievements**, whereas motion verb phrases in which neither of these conditions hold count as **activities**.

The examples in (13)–(16) illustrate another contrast between accomplishments and activities.

(13) a. Freddy *ate a pancake* in two minutes (*for two minutes).

　　b. Freddy *ate pancakes* for two hours (*in two hours).

(14) a. Linda *drank a glass of beer* in thirty seconds (*for thirty seconds).

　　b. Linda *drank beer* for thirty minutes (*in thirty minutes).

(15) a. Frances *read a story* in thirty minutes (*for thirty minutes).

　　b. Frances *read stories* for three hours (*in three hours).

(16) a. Grant *wrote a poem* in three weeks (*for three weeks).

　　b. Grant *wrote poetry* for three months (*in three months).

In each of these pairs of examples, the first sentence involves some definite unit or amount of something, whereas the second does not. These examples can be accounted for by the following rule:

(17) Generalization: If a certain verb phrase has a direct object that denotes <u>a definite number or amount</u>, and the verb phrase is an **accomplishment**, then a corresponding verb phrase in which the object denotes <u>an indefinite number or amount</u> will count as an **activity**.

◆ Summary (Lexical Aspects of Verbs)

Verb Type	Telic Aspects	phrase test for telicity	Telicity
Stative	States	+ *for*-phrase	atelic (natural endpoint ✗)
Dynamic	Activities		
Dynamic	Accomplishments	+ *in*-phrase	telic (natural endpoint ◯)
Dynamic	Achievements		

◆ Expressing More Than One Type of Action

It is possible for some verbs to express more than one type of meaning. There are two reasons for this. First, some verbs can be seen as belonging to two semantic classes. For example, *know*, *see*, and *understand*, are basically **stative verbs**, since they denote conditions that do not change — for example, *I see poorly* = *I have poor vision*. However, they can also express a dynamic event that occurs instantaneously — for example, *I see a parking spot over there*. In this case, they are **achievement verbs**.

Second, certain verbs will express a different meaning when constituents are added to the sentence they appear in. **Activity verbs**, for example, can express **accomplishments**. Thus, *run* is an activity verb in the sentence *He ran*, but if the prepositional phrase *to the post office* is added (i.e., *He ran to the post office*), it expresses an accomplishment. Only some prepositional phrases will have this effect. The sentence *He ran through/in the post office* is still an activity. The addition of an object NP after an activity verb like *sing* creates the context for an accomplishment. *He sang* is an activity, but *He sang a song* is an accomplishment. The grammatical features of the noun — count or noncount, singular or plural — can also play a role. With noncount nouns and plural count nouns (e.g., *They sang folk music/songs*), we are dealing with an activity. With singular or plural count nouns preceded by articles or numbers (e.g., *They sang a song/two songs*), we have an accomplishment.

6 Lexical Aspects of Verbs (2) '11 Essay, '16

(1) Aspectual Classes

① **States** are atelic. States are durative — they occupy time, and can be said to last for minutes, weeks, years and centuries. States are static — nothing 'happens' in a state.

② **Processes** or **activities** are atelic and durative, like states, but unlike states, processes are dynamic.

③ **Accomplishments** consists of a process or activity with forward movement, leading up to a specified finishing point — that is, a culmination.

④ **Achievements** are telic and dynamic.

States	Activities [Processes]
(1) a. Brigitte is taller than Danny. b. The light is on. c. Clive knows my brother. d. Coal and coke are different. e. The cat is asleep. f. Your umbrella is in the hall.	(2) a. John walked in the garden. b. The leaves fluttered in the wind. c. Clive pushed a supermarket trolley. d. They chatted. e. The guests swam in the river. f. The visitors played cards.
Accomplishments	**Achievements**
(3) a. John built a house. b. Marcia ate an apple. c. Jones ran a mile. d. We did the dishes. e. The new mayor made a speech. f. Raffaele painted a triptych.	(4) a. Clive realized that Deirdre was gone. b. They reached the summit. c. Jones spotted the car on the road. d. Leo discovered a hoard of rare LPs in the attic.

A canonical achievement is the onset of a state. In the examples in (4), ***realize*** expresses the onset of knowledge of a particular fact; ***reach*** expresses the onset of being at a location; ***spot*** expresses the first moment of seeing the car, and ***discover*** expresses the onset of knowing that the LPs are there. Given that an achievement is an event boundary rather than a 'full' event, it is non-durative.

(2) Diagnostic Tests for Lexical Aspects '11 Essay, '16

The most frequently used test for telicity is modification of the event duration by an adverbial of the form *in ten minutes* or *for ten minutes*, in a sentence in the simple past tense. Telic predicates take *in* adverbials; atelic predicates take *for* adverbials.

① *In* **adverbials**

 (5) **accomplishment**

  a. He can eat a meat pie in 60 seconds.

  b. They built the barn in two days.

  c. Jones walked to town in 45 minutes.

 (6) **achievement**

  a. He recognized her in a minute or so.

  b. Jones noticed the marks on the wallpaper in five minutes at most.

  c. Jones lost his keys in three days.

 (7) **state**

  a. #The couple were happy in two years.

  b. #The room was sunny in an hour.

  c. #Jones knew him well in five years.

 (8) **process**

  a. #They walked in the park in half an hour.

  b. #People waiting to buy tickets chatted in half an hour.

  c. #Jones pushed a supermarket trolley in 90 seconds.

It is essential with *in* adverbial test to use simple past tense sentences, as *in* adverbials with future tense can modify any class of predicate, with the 'delay before event begins' reading. This is illustrated in (9)–(12). With the accomplishments in (11) the adverbial is ambiguous between expressing the actual duration of the event and the time to pass before the event begins.

(9) **state**

　　a. They will be happy in a year.

　　b. The room will be sunny in an hour.

　　c. Jones will know him in five years.

(10) **process**

　　a. We will walk in the park in an hour.

　　b. They'll chat in a few minutes.

　　c. Jones will push the supermarket trolley in 90 seconds.

(11) **accomplishment**

　　a. He'll eat a meat pie in an hour.

　　b. They'll build the barn in two weeks.

　　c. Jones will walk to town in 45 minutes.

(12) **achievement**

　　a. He will recognize her in a minute.

　　b. Jones will notice the marks on the wallpaper in five minutes.

　　c. Jones will lose his keys in three days.

② **The *take* time construction**

(13) **accomplishment**

　　a. It took 60 seconds for him to eat the pie.

　　b. It took two days for them to build the barn.

　　c. It took 45 minutes for Jones to walk to town.

(14) **achievement**

　　a. It took a minute for him to recognize her.

　　b. It took five minutes for Jones to notice the marks on the wallpaper.

　　c. It took three days for Jones to lose his keys.

(15) **state**

   a. It took two years for the couple to be happy.

   b. It took an hour for the room to be sunny.

   c. It took five years for Jones to know him well.

(16) **process**

   a. #It took half an hour for them to walk in the park.

   b. #It took half an hour for people waiting to buy tickets to chat.

   c. #It took 90 seconds for Jones to push a supermarket trolley.

③ *For* **adverbials**

(17) **state**

   a. They were happy for forty years.

   b. The room was sunny for most of the day.

   c. Jones believed in UFOs for several years.

(18) **process**

   a. The cast rehearsed for three weeks.

   b. They strolled about for several hours.

   c. The choir sang for half an hour.

(19) **accomplishment**

   a. #He ate the meat pie for half an hour.

   b. #They built the barn for two days.

   c. #Harry swam the length of the pool for nine seconds.

   achievement

   d. #They reached the summit for half an hour.

07 Passive Voice

1 Semantic Constraints on Using the Passive

The passive requires a transitive verb. This is not to say, however, that every passive sentence with a transitive verb is acceptable. The acceptability of passive sentences is influenced by several factors:

① The more definite the subject is, the more acceptable the sentence in passive form is:

> This poem was written by Henry Wadsworth Longfellow.
> ?Poems were written by Henry Wadsworth Longfellow.

② With stative verbs, the more indefinite the object in the **by** phrase is, the more likely it is to be acceptable in its passive form.

> Arthur Ashe was liked by everybody.
> ?Arthur Ashe was liked by me.
> The movie has been seen by everyone in town.
> ?The movie has been seen by Jim.

③ The more the verb denotes a physical action, as opposed to a state, the more acceptable its use in a passive sentence is:

> The ball was kicked over the goalposts.
> ?The ball was wanted by the other team.

Notice, though, that if factors ① and ② are honored, then a stative verb like **want** can more easily be used in the passive voice.

> This old jalopy of mine must be wanted by somebody!

Presumably the first two observations, ① and ②, can be accounted for by recognizing that the **information status** of constituents appearing in initial position and in predicate position in

English sentences is different. The subject NP is typically more definite than any predicate NP because it represents **given information** — what the predicate is about.

2 *Get* Passives

Get passives are generally considered more informal than *be* passives and occur mostly in spoken English. They are frequently used to talk about events that affect the subject in an adverse way, like the event in (1):

(1) a. John got mauled by a vicious dog.

　　b. My car got stolen.

　　c. Susan got fired.

However, *get* passives can also express events that have no adverse implication, as in (2a), (2b), and (2c), as well as actions that benefit the subject, as in (2d).

(2) a. Fred got examined by a specialist.

　　b. The mail gets delivered every day.

　　c. My letter to the editor got published in the Sunday Times.

　　d. Janice got promoted last week.

◆ Constraints on *Get* Passives

Get passives cannot occur with verbs that describe cognition (e.g. *comprehend*, *know*, *understand*, etc.). Compare (3a) with (3b).

(3) a. His solution to the problem was *known/understood* by everyone.

　　b. *His solution to the problem got *known/understood* by everyone.

In most cases, *get* passives have the same meaning as passive sentences formed with *be*. For example, the two sentences in (4) have the same meaning.

(4) a. Our house got broken into last year.

　　b. Our house was broken into last year.

However, **get** passives with human subjects can sometimes imply that the subject is responsible in some way for the action expressed in the sentence. Compare (5a) to (5b).

(5) a. I got invited to Sharon Stone's big New Year's Eve party.
 b. I was invited to Sharon Stone's big New Year's Eve party.

Sentence (5a) with **get**, but not (5b) with **be**, may be interpreted as implying that the subject undertook some action in order to secure an invitation. If a speaker intends to indicate willful self-involvement on the part of the subject, he or she may insert a particular adverbial expression such as ***deliberately*** or ***on purpose***, as in (6).

(6) a. John deliberately got fired from his job.
 b. Sally got arrested on purpose.

3 Past Participles: Adjectives or Passive?

Most of the time the distinction between a past participle functioning as a passive verb and one serving as an adjective will be obvious. However, the distinction is not always clear-cut:

The windows were broken.

In the **ambiguous** sentence above, the past participle **broken** could be regarded as either adjectival or passive.

Reading 1: The house was a mess. The paintwork was peeling and the windows were broken. (participle is adjectival)
Reading 2: The windows were broken by the force of the explosion. (participle is passive)

In the first interpretation, the past participle is descriptive, or stative, and thus adjectival. In the second, the past participle is dynamic and thus passive. However, adjectives can sometimes be dynamic. Thus, in the end, in cases of ambiguity, the only distinguishing sentence-level feature we are left with is the use of **by** with a noun phrase to mark an agent in the passive voice, if there is one:

The beans were *refried*. $\begin{cases} \text{by someone (passive)} \\ \text{present state of the beans (adjective)} \end{cases}$

4 Ergative Verbs [Unaccusative Verbs] '10 Essay, '17

> **Two types of intransitive verbs:**
>
> (1) An angel jumped on the hill.   (*jump*: unergative verb)
>   **Agent**
>
> (2) An angel appeared [*t*] on the hill.   (*appear*: ergative verb = unaccusative verb)
>   **Theme**
>   NP movement
>
> Although both of the above sentences are intransitive, they are not of the same kind. They have different syntactic and semantic properties. In (1), the subject originates in the specifier position external to the V-bar constituent, receiving an **Agent** role. Verbs like *jump* are known as <u>unergative</u> verbs. However, in (2), the superficial subject originates in the **complement** position within the immediate V-bar projection of the verb, receiving a **Theme** role. Then it moves to subject position. Verbs like *appear* are known as <u>unaccusative</u> verbs.

There is a "middle voice," intermediate between active and passive voices. The middle voice allows the subject of a sentence to be nonagentive, as in the passive voice, but the morphology of the verb to be in the active voice.

(1) Her high C **shattered** the glass. (active voice)
(2) The glass **was shattered** by her high C. (passive voice)
(3) The glass **shattered**. (middle voice)

English uses special verbs to express spontaneous occurrences. Such verbs, which allow the object of a transitive clause to be a subject of an intransitive clause without changing voice, are called **ergative**, or **change-of-state**, **verbs**. Ergative verbs take either agents or undergoers of the action as subjects.

Verb	Active voice	Middle voice (Ergative Verbs)
shatter	Her high C **shattered** the glass.	The glass **shattered**.
open	Paul **opened** the door.	The door **opened**.
roll	Peter **rolled** the ball.	The ball **rolled**.
boil	Pat **boiled** the water.	The water **boiled**.
ring	I **rang** the bell.	The bell **rang**.
burn	I've **burned** the toast.	The toast has **burned**.
break	A stone **broke** the window.	The window **broke**.
burst	She **burst** the balloon.	The balloon **burst**.
close	He **closed** his eyes.	His eyes **closed**.
cook	I'm **cooking** the rice.	The rice is **cooking**.
fade	The sun **has faded** the carpet.	The carpet **has faded**.
freeze	The low temperature **has frozen** the milk.	The milk **has frozen**.
melt	The heat **has melted** the ice.	The ice **has melted**.
run	Tim **is running** the bathwater.	The bathwater **is running**.
stretch	I **stretched** the elastic.	The elastic **stretched**.
tighten	He **tightened** the rope.	The rope **tightened**.
wave	Someone **waved** a flag.	A flag **waved**.
change	John **has changed** the program.	The program **has changed**.
drop	He **dropped** the book.	The book **dropped**.
move	Mary **moved** the glass.	The glass **moved**.
shut	He **shut** the window.	The window **shut**.
stand	**Stand** the lamp here!	The lamp **stands** here.
start	He **started** the car.	The car **started**.
turn	Someone **turned** the doorknob.	The doorknob **turned**.

Many ergative verbs suggest **changes of state**:

start [*begin*] ↔ *stop* [*end*, *finish*], *open* ↔ *close*, *condense* [*decrease*] ↔ *increase* [*spread*], *bend*, *break* [*tear*], *burst*, *change* [*develop*, *improve*], *cool*, *drop* [*sink*], *dry* [*evaporate*], *grow* [*age*], *melt*, *empty*, *slow*, and others.

There are three other categories of ergative verbs:

- Verbs of cooking (*cook*, *fry*, *bake* [*roast*], *boil* [*simmer*], *defrost* [*melt*], etc.):

    I'm baking a cake.

    The cake is baking.

    The cake is being baked by her friends.

- Verbs of physical <u>movement</u> (***move***, ***rock*** [***shake***], ***spin***, ***swing***, ***turn***, etc.):

    The boy spun the top.

    The top spun.

    The top was spun by the boy.

- Verbs that involve <u>vehicles</u> (***drive*** [***run***, ***fly***, ***sail***] ↔ ***park***, ***reverse*** [***back***], ***crash***, etc.):

    She drove the car.

    The car drives well.

    The car was driven all the way to Tallahassee.

Rutherford tells us that ESL/EFL students, for whom the idea of ergative verb is new, sometimes object to such sentences as

(4) The window broke.

The students argue that windows can't break themselves, and thus they feel obliged to use the passive or express an agent.

(5) The window was broken.
(6) Someone broke the window.

While such sentences are not wrong, of course, the active voice sentence with a nonagentive subject is perfectly permissible in English with ergative verbs. The difference between the two options is that <u>the passive sentence suggests the existence of an agent, even if the agent is not explicit. The verb used ergatively does not permit an agent. This can be shown by the addition of a **by** phrase</u>.

(7) The window was broken. (passive)   The window broke. (ergative)

    The window was broken by the gang. *The window broke by the gang.

5 Middle Verbs

A further type of Affected Subject occurs with certain processes (***break***, ***read***, ***translate***, ***wash***, ***tan***, ***fasten***, ***lock***) which are intrinsically transitive, but in this construction are construed as intransitive, with an Affected subject.

Glass breaks easily. (cf The glass broke.)
This case doesn't shut/close/lock/fasten properly.
Colloquial language translates badly. (cf Colloquial language is translated badly.)
Some synthetic fibers won't wash. Usually they dry-clean.
Fair skin doesn't tan quickly, it turns red.

Middle Constructions differ from other intransitives in the following ways:

- They express a general property or propensity of the entity to undergo (or not undergo) the process in question. Compare *glass breaks easily* with *the glass broke*, which refers to a specific event.
- Middle Constructions tend to occur in the present tense.
- The verb is accompanied by negation, or a modal (often ***will***/***won't***), or an adverb such as ***easily***, ***well***, any of which specify the propensity or otherwise of the thing to undergo the process.
- A cause is implied but an Agent can't be added in a ***by***-phrase.
- There is no corresponding transitive construction, either active or passive, that exactly expresses the same meaning as these intransitives. To say, for instance, ***colloquial language is translated badly*** is to make a statement about translators' supposed lack of skill, rather than about a property of colloquial language.

Passive counterparts (***be***-passive and ***get***-passive), like copular counterparts, are not identical in meaning to the structures discussed here, but demonstrate some of the many ways of conceptualizing an event.

Ed broke the glass.   active
The glass was broken (by Ed).   *be*-passive

The glass got broken.   *get*-passive
The glass was already broken. copular (state)
The glass broke.   Ergative Construction
Glass breaks easily.   Middle Construction

◆ **Summary**

Ergative verbs	**Middle verbs**
① Report an **event**.	Describe a **generic property** of the subject.
② Can be used in past tense. 　Can be used with 'yesterday'.	Used in the **present tense**. Cannot be used with 'yesterday'.
③ Cannot be used with a manner adverb.	A **negation**, or a **modal**, or an **adverbial** (manner adverb, e.g. *easily*) is required.
④ **Do not imply an agent**. 　(spontaneous occurrences)	Have an **implicit**, **non-specific agent**, i.e., anybody.
⑤ an Agent can't be added in a *by*-phrase.	the same

08 Negation

1 Clausal Negation

Clausal negation is two subtypes: verbal and non-verbal negation. We sometimes have a choice between the two:

< Verbal Negation >	< Non-verbal Negation >
An honest man would *not* lie.	*No* honest man would lie.
That was *not* an accident.	That was *no* accident.
He would*n't* say a word.	He would say *not* a word.

(1) Subject-Auxiliary Inversion

The negative element may often be moved from its usual position to initial position, in which case there is inversion of subject and operator.

Not a word would he say.

Never will I make that mistake again.

ⓒ ***Not surprisingly** did he miss the train. (Local Negation) '10 Case Theory

2 Local Negation

Local negation negates a word or phrase, without making the clause negative.

She's a *not unintelligent* woman. ['She's a fairly intelligent woman']

I saw Dave *not long ago*. ['fairly recently']

If moved to initial position, these do not cause **subject-auxiliary inversion**.

Not long ago I saw David mowing his lawn. (Local Negation, not clausal negation)

ⓒ **Not long ago* did I see David mowing his lawn.

3 Syntactic features of clausal negation

Negative clauses differ syntactically from positive clauses:

(i) They can typically be followed by positive tag questions:

They aren't ready, *are* they?

[cf They are ready, *aren't* they?]

(ii) They can be followed by negative tag clauses, with additive meaning:

They aren't ready, and *neither* are you.

(iii) They can be followed by negative agreement responses:

A: He doesn't know Russian.   B: No, he *doesn't*.

(iv) They can be followed by nonassertive items:

He won't notice *any* change in you, *either*.

◆ Semi-negative words

Several words are negative in meaning but not in form. They are called semi-negative words. They include:

seldom, *rarely*

scarcely, *hardly*, *barely*

few, *little* (in contrast to the positive *a few* and *a little*)

They can effect clausal negation, inducing the characteristic syntactic features of clause negation.

They *scarcely* seem to care, *do they*?   (positive tag question)

I *hardly* have any friends, and *neither* do you. (additive)

A: Crime *rarely* pays. B: No, it *doesn't*.   (negative agreement)

I *seldom* get *any* sleep, *either*.   (nonassertive item)

Few members have *ever* attended the annual general meeting. (nonassertive item)

When positioned initially, the adverbs normally cause subject-operator inversion (Subject-Auxiliary Inversion):

Little did I expect such enthusiasm.

Scarcely ever had Britain suffered so much criticism.

4 Nonassertive items [NPIs]

Clause negation is frequently followed by one or more nonassertive items.

Assertive items = Some-words	Nonassertive items = Any-words
We've had *some* lunch. I was speaking to *somebody*. They'll finish it *somehow*. He *sometimes* visits us. He's *still* at school. Her mother's coming, *too*. I like her *a great deal*.	We haven't had *any* lunch. I wasn't speaking to *anybody*. They won't finish it *at all*. He doesn't *ever* visit us. He's not at school *any longer*. '95 Her mother's not coming, *either*. I don't like her *much*.

5 Transferred Negation

TRANSFERRED NEGATION is the transfer of the negative from a subordinate clause, where semantically it belongs, to the matrix clause. *I don't think it's a good idea* is an example of transferred negation, since it can be understood as virtually synonymous with *I think it isn't a good idea*.

The matrix verbs that allow transferred negation are classified into two types:

① **opinion** verbs: *believe, expect, imagine, suppose, think*

I don't believe I've met you before.

['I believe I haven't met you before']

She didn't imagine that we would say anything.

['She imagined that we wouldn't say anything']

He didn't expect to win.

['He expected not to win']

② **perception** verbs: ***appear***, ***seem***, ***feel as if***, ***look as if***, ***sound as if***

It doesn't seem that we can get our money back.

['It seems that we can't get our money back']

The baby doesn't appear to be awake.

['The baby appears not to be awake']

It doesn't look as if it's going to rain.

['It looks as if it isn't going to rain']

Note that negative raising is not possible with sentences in which the main clause verb is not one of the types mentioned above. With other types of main clause verbs, moving ***not*** from the complement into the main clause changes the meaning of the sentence, as shown in (1).

(1) a. We forgot that she doesn't like him.

b. We didn't forget that she likes him.

Factive verbs such as ***know***, ***remember***, ***forget***, ***regret***, etc. do not allow negative raising. In other words, the two versions of the sentence are not synonymous.

6 Scope of Negation [10]

The scope of the negation normally extends from the negative item itself to the end of the clause, but it need not include an end-placed adverbial. In a clause with the clause negator ***not*** or a negative word such as ***never*** or ***hardly*** in the same position after the operator, adverbials occurring before the negative normally lie outside the scope. There is thus a contrast between: (The scope of negation is marked by the underlines.)

(1) She definitely didn't speak to him.

   (= It's definite that she didn't speak to him.)

(2) She didn't definitely speak to him.

   (= It's not definite that she spoke to him.)

If an assertive form is used in the adjunct, the adjunct must lie outside the scope; contrast (3) with (4) below:

(3) I didn't listen to some of the speakers.

   (= There were some of the speakers that I didn't listen to.)

(4) I didn't listen to any of the speakers.

   (= There were not any speakers that I listened to.)

With adverbs like **deliberately** [*intentionally*, *knowingly*, *willfully*, *on purpose*, *purposefully*], and **expressly** [*definitely*, *clearly*], the scope of negation is different, depending on whether the adverb is before *not*, as in (5), or after it, as in (6). The position of the adverb causes (5) and (6) to have different meanings.

(5) Tom **deliberately** did not destroy the evidence.
(6) Tom didn't **deliberately** destroy the evidence.

The meaning of (5) is "*Tom acted deliberately in not destroying the evidence.*" Here, Tom did not destroy the evidence.

The meaning of (6) is "*Tom did not act deliberately in destroying the evidence.*" In this case, Tom did destroy the evidence, but not on purpose.

09 Pro-forms and Ellipsis

1 Pro-forms

(1) *One* as pro-form [98]

There are two pro-forms *one*: one has the plural *some*, and the other has plural *ones*. Both substitute for phrases with count noun as heads.

(i) *One*/*some* is a substitute for an indefinite noun phrase.

A: Can you give me a few nails? I need *one*.

B: I'll get you *some* soon.

Compare:

I need *a nail*/*one*.   I need *some nails*/*some*.

(ii) *One* and *ones* are substitutes for a NOMINAL EXPRESSION, a noun phrase head with or without one or more modifiers (not the whole noun phrase).

Have you any *knives*? I need a sharp *one*.

I wish I'd bought a few *jars of honey*. Did you notice the *ones* they were selling?

One as a pro-form for a nominal expression must have an overt determiner. The equivalent pro-form for noncount nouns is *some*.

Shall I pass the *butter*? Or have you got *some* already?

◆ Summary — Proforms

	sg.	pl.
Count Nouns	one	ones / some
Noncount Nouns	some	

(2) Do it, do that, do so

The transitive main verb *do* also combines with the pronouns *it* and *that* to form a unit that functions as a pro-form for the predicate or predication:

> Is Connie still trying to light the stove? She should have **done it** by now.
> Are you trying to light the stove with a match? I wouldn't **do that**.

In general, *do* in these two combinations (***do it*** and ***do that***) has dynamic and agentive reference; i.e. it refers to an action that is performed or intentionally initiated by the referent of the subject. It is hence abnormal for ***do it*** and ***do that*** to substitute for predicates or predications that are stative or denote involuntary processes:

> A: They think he's mad.
> B: *We **do it** too.
> A: He owns a Cadillac.
> B: *Yes, his brother **does that** too.

With regard to ***do so***, some speakers, particularly in AmE, treat *do* in *do so* as dynamic and agentive.

(3) *So* and *not* as pro-forms for object *that*-clause

So and its negative equivalent *not* can be pro-forms for a *that*-clause functioning as direct object:

> A: Will Oxford win the next boat race?
> B: I hope ***so***.   [= that Oxford will win ...]
> B: I hope ***not***. [= that Oxford will not win ...]

This use of ***not*** is restricted mainly to verbs of belief or assumption, whereas the corresponding use of *so* is frequently found also in some verbs of saying such as ***say*** and ***tell***. Verbs that commonly allow both *so* and *not* include:

believe	guess	imagine	reckon	suspect
expect hope	presume	suppose	think	

2 Elliptical noun phrases

Except in coordination, elliptical noun phrases result from final ellipsis. This means that heads and postmodifiers tend to be ellipted:

My own camera, like *Peter's* △, is Japanese.

He had to admit that *Sarah's drawings* were as good as *his own* △.

The first expedition to the Antarctic was quickly followed by *another two* △.

Tomorrow's meeting will have to be *our first* and *out last* △.

Although Helen is *the oldest girl in the class*, Julies is *the tallest* △.

In other cases one or more modifiers, as well as the head, may be ellipted:

[1] His recent performance of 'Macbeth' is the best △ he has ever done.

[2] That new thick plastic rope that they sell is stronger than any other △.

The sentences [1] and [2] are **ambiguous**.

The possible ellipted phrases in [1]:

① performance ② performance of Macbeth

The possible ellipted phrases in [2]:

① rope ② plastic rope ③ thick plastic rope ④ new thick plastic rope

10 Inversion

1 Subject-Auxiliary Inversion

(1) So+S+V vs. So+V+S '95 Choice, '13 Choice

◆ **So+S+V**

Initial *so* can be pro-predication in a construction consisting of *so* followed by the subject and the verb (So+S+V).

> You asked me to leave, and so I did. [= indeed I did]
> A: It's starting to snow.   B: So it is!
> A: You've spilled coffee on your dress. B: Oh dear, so I have.

◆ **So+V+S**

So in the construction So+V+S means *too* or *also*.

> You asked him to leave, and so did I. [= I asked him to leave, too]
> The corn is ripening, and so are the apples.
> You've spilled coffee on the table, and so have I.

In negative sentences, ***neither*** and ***nor*** are used instead of ***so***.

> The corn isn't ripening, and *neither/nor* are the apples. [= the apples aren't, either]

(2) Negative adverb +V+S

Negative adverbs: ***never, seldom, rarely, not often, only, not only, neither, nor***, etc. Sentences beginning with one of these adverbs trigger subject-aux inversion:

> (1) a. ***Never*** have I witnessed such a stunning upset.
>   b. ***Seldom*** will you see a performance as good as that.
>   c. ***Only*** with a bank loan will we be able to buy the car.

(2) a. ***Not only*** am I unhappy with his behavior, but I frankly just don't understand it.

　　b. A: I don't understand why she reacted that way.

　　　B: $\begin{cases} \textbf{\textit{Neither}} \text{ do I.} \\ \textbf{\textit{Nor}} \text{ do we.} \end{cases}$

2 Subject-Verb Inversion '09 Mock, '21

◆ Use of Marked Word Order

What is the motivation for fronting adverbials of direction or position in sentences where subject-verb inversion also occurs?

　　Into the house ran John.

　　In the garden stands an elm tree.

A pilot study by Gary suggests that the speaker/writer has selected the subject NP — now in final position — to surprise the listener/reader, create suspense, and specifically to go counter to the expectations of the listener/reader. For example, using texts such as the following, Gary claims that the **counter-to-expectation function** of the (b) version of the text-final sentence carries a special presupposition of **counterexpectancy** and that this contrasts with the **neutral**, **noninverted** (a) version, which has no special presuppositions:

　　Keith Sebastian had given me detailed instructions on how to find his house; he was to meet me there with the money. I drove up the driveway and got out of my car. Just as the car door closed, I heard the main door to the house open.

　　a. $\begin{cases} \text{Keith Sebastian} \\ \text{Dan Carlyle} \\ \text{The Sheriff} \end{cases}$ stepped out of the house.

　　b. Out of the house stepped $\begin{cases} \text{\#Keith Sebastian} \\ \text{Dan Carlyle} \\ \text{the Sheriff} \end{cases}$

(*Note*: # = not acceptable given the discourse context)

In the (b) version, *Keith Sebastian* is not acceptable as the postposed subject, according to Gary, because there is no counterexpectancy; that is, the reader would normally expect *Keith Sebastian* to be the subject just as he is in the first option of the (a) version, but given the use of the (b) construction, which signals counterexpectancy, the reader is invited to be surprised when someone else is the postposed subject.

11 Coordination

1 Combinatory and Segregatory Coordination of NPs

Phrases linked by **and** may express COMBINATORY or SEGREGATORY meaning. The distinction is clearest with noun phrases. When the coordination is segregatory, we can paraphrase it by clause coordination:

John and Mary know the answer.
= John knows the answer, and Mary knows the answer.

When it is combinatory we cannot do so, because the conjoins function in combination with respect to the rest of the clause:

John and Mary make a pleasant couple.
≠ *John makes a pleasant couple, and Mary makes a pleasant couple.

Many conjoint noun phrases are in fact **ambiguous** between the two interpretations:

John and Mary won a prize.

Reading 1: John and Mary *each* won a prize.   [SEGREGATORY meaning]
Reading 2: John and Mary *jointly* won a prize. [COMBINATORY meaning]

Further examples of combinatory meaning:

(1) **John and Mary** played as partners in tennis against **Susan and Bill**.
(2) **Peter and Bob** separated (from each other).
(3) **Paula and her brother** look alike.
(4) **Mary and Paul** are just good friends.
(5) **John and Peter** have different tastes (from each other).
(6) **Mary and Susan** are colleagues (of each other).
(7) **Law and order** is a primary concern of the new administration.

2 Indicators of segregatory meaning

Certain markers explicitly indicate that the coordination is segregatory:

| both (… and) | neither … nor | respectively |
| each | respective | apiece <rather rare> |

While **John and Mary won a prize** is ambiguous, we are left in no doubt that two prizes were won in:

John and Mary have *each* won a prize.
John and Mary have won a prize *each*.
Both John and Mary have won a prize.
John and Mary have ***both*** won a prize.

Similarly, whereas **John and Mary didn't win a prize** is ambiguous, **Neither John nor Mary won a prize** is unambiguously segregatory.

The adjective ***respective*** premodifies a plural noun phrase to indicate segregatory interpretation. For example,

Jill and Ben visited their ***respective*** uncles. [unambiguous]
= Jill visited her uncle or uncles and Ben visited his uncle or uncles.

Jill and Ben visited their uncles.　　　[ambiguous]

Reading 1: Jill visited her uncle or uncles and Ben visited his uncle or uncles.

Reading 2: Jill and Ben visited persons who were uncles to both.

12 Multiword Verbs

1 The Distinction between Prepositional Verbs and Phrasal Verbs '10, '11

Type I prepositional verbs resemble transitive phrasal verbs superficially, but the differences are both syntactic and phonological. The contrast is exemplified for the prepositional verb *call on* ('visit') and the phrasal verb *call up* ('summon').

(a) **Particle movement**: The particle of a prepositional verb <u>must precede</u> the prepositional object, but the particle of a phrasal verb can generally <u>precede or follow</u> the direct object:

　　She *called on* her friends.　　　She *called up* her friends.
　　~*She *called* her friends *on*.　　~She *called* her friends *up*.

(b) **Particle movement**: When the object is a personal pronoun, the pronoun <u>follows</u> the particle of a prepositional verb but <u>precedes</u> the particle of a phrasal verb:

　　She *called on* them.　　　She *called* them *up*.
　　~*She *called* them *on*.　　~*She *called up* them.

(c) **Adverb insertion**: <u>A VP-adverb</u> can often be <u>inserted</u> between verb and particle in prepositional verbs, but not in phrasal verbs:

　　She *called* angrily *on* her friends.
　　~*She *called* angrily *up* her friends.

　　He *stared* intently *at* the target.
　　*He *turned* quickly *out* the light.

(d) **Wh-fronting**: The particle of the phrasal verb cannot precede a relative pronoun or **wh-interrogative**:

the friends *on* whom she *called*
~*On* which friends did she *call*?
*the friends *up* whom she *called*
~**Up* which friends did she *call*?

The person *who he depends on the most* is his brother.
= The person *on whom he depends the most* is his brother.
The dress, *which she tried on*, didn't fit her.
*The dress *on which she tried* didn't fit her.

Who were you shouting at?
= At whom were you shouting?
What are you looking up?
= *Up what are you looking?

(e) **Stress Pattern**: The particle of a phrasal verb is normally stressed, and in final position normally bears the nuclear tone, whereas the particle of a prepositional verb is normally unstressed.

Which friends did she CÁLL on?
~Which friends did she call ÚP?

2 Separable and Inseparable Phrasal Verbs '11 Choice

Transitive phrasal verbs fall into three categories, depending on where the object NP can occur in relation to the verb and the particle.

(1) Separable phrasal verbs

In (1a), we see the transitive phrasal verb *looked up* followed by the direct object NP *the address*. This sentence could, however, be rewritten as in (1b).

(1) a. Maggie *looked up* the address.

b. Maggie *looked* the address *up*.

Sentence (1b) illustrates that *look up* is a *separable transitive phrasal verb*. It is classified as such because its parts may be "separated" by an object; that is, the direct object may appear between the verb *looked* and the particle *up*.

Separable transitive phrasal verbs occur frequently in conversation, fiction, and news reports. They appear less frequently in academic writing. Examples of separable transitive phrasal verbs that occur with high frequency are *get back/bring back* (=return), *pick up*, *put on*, *look up* (=consult), *make up*, *take off*, *take on*, *turn off*, *turn down* (=refuse), *leave out* (=omit), *pass out* (=distribute), etc.

(2) Inseparable phrasal verbs '11 Choice

A small group of transitive phrasal verbs do not permit the particle to move over the direct object even if it is a pronoun, as (2) and (3) illustrate. **Particle movement** is not possible with these *inseparable phrasal verbs*.

(2) a. Don't pick on my brother.

b. Don't pick on him.

c. *Don't pick him on.

(3) a. Look after my sister, will you?

b. Look after her, will you?

c. *Look her after, will you?

As with separable transitive phrasal verbs, the meanings of inseparable transitive phrasal verbs usually cannot be deduced from the sum of their parts. For example, the meaning "annoy, pester" is not obvious from the verb + particle combination *pick on* in (2). This small group of verbs includes *come by* ("acquire"), *look into* ("investigate"), *run into* ("encounter"), *bump into* ("encounter"), *come across* ("discover"), *come upon* ("encounter"), *get over* ("recover from"), *go over* ("review"), *fall for* ("become attracted to"), *hit on* ("make romantic overtures to"), *level with* ("tell the truth to"), *look after* ("care for someone"), *pick on* ("mistreat"), *run across* ("discover"), *stand by* ("support"), etc.

(3) Permanently separated phrasal verbs

A very small group of transitive phrasal verbs require that the direct object occur between the verb and the particle. These verbs are therefore referred to as ***permanently separated transitive phrasal verbs***. The particle cannot appear directly after the verb, as (4) and (5) illustrate.

(4) a. That job is getting Janice down.

　　b. That job is getting her down.

　　c. *That job is getting down Janice.

(5) a. The judge let the thief off with a light sentence.

　　b. The judge let him off with a light sentence.

　　c. *The judge let off the thief with a light sentence.

In addition to ***get*** (someone) ***down*** and ***let*** (someone) ***off***, this group of verbs includes ***ask*** (someone) ***out*** ("invite"), ***do*** (something) ***over*** ("redo"), ***see*** (something) ***through*** ("complete"), ***narrow*** (something) ***down*** ("reduce"), ***put*** (someone) ***on*** ("fool"), and ***string*** (someone) ***along*** ("delude").

13 Dative Alternation

1 Subcategorization of English Verbs that Take Indirect Objects

Many common English verbs can take indirect objects in two different syntactic configurations:

① <u>postverbal</u> position (V NP NP)

　　John gave ***Mary*** the book.

② <u>postprepositional</u> position (V NP Prep NP)

　　John gave the book to ***Mary***.

Other verbs that behave like *give* are *hand*, *tell*, *pass*, *sell*, *send*, *get*, *show*, *throw*, *lend*, *teach*, *offer*, *fax*, and *wire*, among others.

Many verbs can take indirect objects only in the postprepositional position:

*I explained Mary the problem.
I explained the problem to Mary.

Other verbs that behave like *explain* are *donate*, *announce*, *recommend*, *reveal*, *confess*, *introduce*, *narrate*, *describe*, *transmit*, *refuse*, *deny*, and so on.

Finally, a small number of verbs take only the immediate postverbal position and allow no indirect object in postprepositional position:

The book cost me $10.
*The book cost $10 to me.

A few other verbs that seem to behave like *cost* are *bill* and (*over*)*charge*.

Therefore, verbs taking indirect objects need to be marked in the lexicon according to which syntactic configuration(s) they may or may not occur in. In general, monosyllabic verbs — which are generally of Germanic origin — take indirect objects in immediate postverbal position more readily than do multisyllabic verbs, which tend to be of Latinate origin and which tend not to allow indirect objects in postverbal position.

2 Semantics Governing Postverbal Position for Indirect Objects

Postverbal position for indirect objects is limited semantically to cases where the indirect object is "animate" and is a "projected possessor" of the direct object. Thus we can explain the acceptable and unacceptable alternations in the following sets:

(1) a. Joe sent a letter to Sue.
    b. Joe sent Sue a letter.
    c. Joe sent a letter to Cincinnati.
    d. *Joe sent Cincinnati a letter.

(2) a. I opened a beer for Sam.

b. I opened Sam a beer.

c. I opened the door for Sam.

d. *I opened Sam the door.

In 1b **Sue** is the animate, projected possessor of the letter, whereas in 1d, **Cincinnati** is merely the location of the letter. In 2b, **Sam** is the animate, projected possessor of a beer, whereas in 2d, **Sam**, while animate, is not the projected possessor of the door.

3 The Ambiguity of *For* Phrases

One related point to consider is that sentences with prepositional objects preceded by *for*, such as the following, may be ambiguous:

John bought the book for me.

There are two possible interpretations of this sentence:

Proxy: John bought it for me (i.e. he acted on my behalf) because I didn't have time to buy it myself.

Benefactive: John bought it for me because my birthday was coming up and he wanted to give me a gift.

However, if the indirect object occurs directly after the verb in the above sentence (i.e., **John bought me the book**), only the benefactive interpretation seems to be possible.

This double meaning of *for* helps explain why the indirect object can come immediately after the verb *open* in the first sentence below (where *for* is benefactive) but not the second:

Benefactive: Open me a beer, please.

(The addressee will presumably open a can/bottle of beer and give it to the speaker.)

Proxy: Open the door for me, please.

*Open me the door.

(The addressee does not give the door to the speaker, but merely opens the door on his/her behalf.)

4 Conditions on Indirect Object Alternation

Information Structure and Word Order (Three discourse principles)	
Information Flow Principle (Given-Before-New Principle)	The old, predictable information comes first, and new, unpredictable information last in a sentence. (Susumo Kuno, 1978)
End-Focus Principle	A clause normally has at least one point of focus, which typically falls upon the end of the clause.
End-Weight Principle	Put "heavier" (= longer) elements at the end of the sentence.

※ Information flow principle and end-focus/weight principle normally agree with each other.

(1) End-focus principle '12 Essay

The notion of dominance helps us understand why certain conditions such as the following are placed on indirect object alternation:

For many, though not all dialects of English, the indirect object cannot be postverbal if the direct object is a pronoun (especially *it*) and the indirect object is a noun.

  We sent it to John.   *We sent John it.

On the other hand, when the indirect object is a pronoun and the direct object is a noun (especially an indefinite one), the alternate pattern is likely to be selected.

  We sent him a package.

These observations can be explained by noting that pronouns are, as a rule, less dominant than nouns. Since pronouns usually have an anaphoric referent or a referent in the immediate physical environment, it is unlikely that a speaker would need to direct attention to them — their meaning is already clear from the text or context. This is not to say that an indirect object that is a pronoun would never occupy the dominant position, but when this does occur, a different interpretation would be necessary — for example, a contrastive one.

> We sent a package to him. (not her)

(2) End-weight principle
If the direct object is a long complex phrase or clause (i.e., dominant), a postverbal indirect object is necessary to avoid awkwardness:

> ?/* I told that John would be coming to his girlfriend.
> I told John's girlfriend that he would be coming.

Clauses are always more dominant than NPs, and so the clausal direct object moves to the dominant position. On the other hand, if the indirect object is heavily modified, postverbal position is less likely:

> I bought a present for my new little niece, the first daughter of my eldest brother.
> ?/* I bought my new little niece, the first daughter of my eldest brother, a present.

The speaker who elaborates either the direct or indirect object has already given it dominance. Such objects, therefore, move to the dominant final position if the verb permits the preferred order.

(3) Verbs that Are Restricted to One Pattern
The main verb must belong to the class of verbs permitting both postverbal and postprepositional position for indirect objects. Verbs like *give*, *send*, *ask*, *sell*, *pay*, *tell*, *hand*, *lend*, *show*, *offer*, and *teach* all readily accept the above conventions; however, *explain*, *reveal*, and *announce*, for example, do not.

> Explain the answer to me.
> *Explain me the answer.

All verbs that take indirect objects have to be marked in the lexicon according to whether or not they occur in postverbal position, postprepositional position, or both.

+ alternation	+ postprepositional position only	+ postverbal position only
give	announce	cost
send	explain	charge
lend	describe	bill
teach	mention	.
tell	say	.
.	.	.
.	.	

They mentioned the new restaurant on Putney Road <u>to me</u>.

They mentioned <u>to me</u> the new restaurant on Putney Road.

*They mentioned me the new restaurant on Putney Road.

14 Constructions

1 Cleft and Pseudo-cleft Sentences

(1) Structure '06

(1) a. You need a good rest most.
　　b. ***It's*** a good rest ***that*** you need most. [Cleft]
　　c. ***What you need most*** is a good rest. [Pseudo-cleft]

Unlike the cleft sentence, the pseudo-cleft sentence rather freely permits marked focus to fall on the predication:

(2) What he's done is ***(to) spoil the whole thing***.

Here are the structures of cleft and pseudo-cleft sentences:

(3) It + be + focus position + that [who] …
　　　　　　　new information　old information

(4) What + ... + be + focus position.
　　　⎵⎵⎵⎵⎵⎵　⎵⎵⎵⎵⎵⎵⎵⎵
　　　old information　new information

(2) Clefting is a presupposition trigger

Both cleft and pseudo-cleft sentences are **presupposition triggers**. Hence, the sentences (1b) and (1c) presuppose the following proposition.

(5) You need something most.

(3) Ambiguity

We need to remember that an example like the following is **ambiguous** between a cleft sentence and an SVC where C is postmodified noun phrase.

It is the dog that scared me.

In the relative-clause version, the S could be replaced by another pronoun (such as *this*) and *that* could be replaced by *which*. In cleft sentences, such alternatives are not generally acceptable.

Except for the presence of contrastive stress in cleft sentences, they resemble relative clauses. For example, note the **ambiguity** of the following sentence:

(6) It's the woman that [who] cleans the house.
　　(answer to "Who's that?" = relative clause)
　　(answer to "Who cleans the house — the man or the woman?" = *it*-cleft)

When spoken, however, the sentence would have different stress patterns since the *it*-cleft reading would give special stress to *woman* and the relative clause reading would not.

< More examples >

An *it*-cleft is superficially similar to a clause in which it is an ordinary referential pronoun and the relative clause is a modifier within the structure of the NP containing the antecedent, as in *It's something I've been wanting for a long time*. There may indeed be **ambiguity** between an *it*-cleft and a clause of this latter type. Compare:

(7) a. A: I hear they sacked the secretary.

   B: No, it's the director who was sacked.

b. A: Who's that talking to the police?

   B: It's the director who was sacked.

In (7a) the underlined clause is interpreted as an *it*-cleft: "the one they sacked is the director"; the non-cleft counterpart is **The director was sacked**. In (7b), by contrast, *it* refers to the person talking to the police and the relative clause **who was sacked** is part of the NP **the director who was sacked**, which functions as complement of *be*.

◆ **Differences**

① stress pattern

   In (7a) the focal stress will fall on ***director***, whereas in (7b) the default place for it is on ***sacked***.

② constituency

   A major distinguishing feature of the *it*-cleft construction is thus that the relative clause does not form a constituent with its antecedent. This correlates with the fact that the range of antecedents in an *it*-cleft is considerably greater than in the construction of (7b). Note, for example, that ***It's Kim who was sacked*** could be substituted for B's response in (7a) but not in (7b): it is admissible as an *it*-cleft version of ***Kim was sacked***, but ***Kim who was sacked***, with an integrated relative clause, could not occur as the complement of *be* in (7b).

2 Existential Sentences

◆ **Pragmatic constraints on Existential Sentences** '09 Choice, '12 Essay, '17

The existential construction is characteristically used to introduce addressee-new entities into the discourse, and for this reason the displaced subject NP is usually indefinite. In many cases, the presence of an indefinite NP makes the existential pragmatically obligatory in that the corresponding non-existential is infelicitous:

(1) a. There is a serious flaw in your own argument.
   b. *A serious flaw is in your own argument.

Conversely, replacing an indefinite NP in an existential with a corresponding definite often results in infelicity:

(2) a. There is a more serious flaw, however, in your own argument.
   b. *There is the more serious flaw, however, in your own argument.

(1) Indefinite NPs: preference for the existential over the non-existential

With indefinite NPs, there is in general a preference for the existential. In many cases, the non-existential is infelicitous. Compare (3) and (4), where the non-existentials are felicitous in the former but not the latter:

(3) a. A furniture van was in the drive.   b. There was a furniture van in the drive.
   a. *Sincerity was in her voice.   b. There was sincerity in her voice.
   a. *Peace was in the region.   b. There was peace in the region.

When the indefinite NP denotes **a physical entity**, as in (3), both constructions are felicitous, but when it denotes **an abstract entity**, as in (4), the existential is generally required.

(2) Displaced definite NPs

There is a strong tendency, we have noted, for the displaced NP to be indefinite. It must be emphasized, however, that definite NPs are certainly not excluded from the existential construction: they are admissible provided they represent addressee-new information.

▲ Addressee-old entities newly instantiating a variable

(5) A: What can I get Mary for her birthday?
   B: There's the new book on birdwatching we were talking about yesterday.

The definite article in this example is felicitous because the NP is addressee-old: I assume you know which book I am referring to. But at the same time the NP serves to instantiate, i.e. to specify the value of, the variable in an open proposition that represents discourse-old information. In (5) the open proposition is "A can get Mary *x* for her birthday", which is a presupposition of A's question, and again the underlined NP provides a new value for *x*. If the definite NP doesn't provide a new value for a variable in this way, the existential will be infelicitous. Compare, for example:

(6) a. A: Who was at the party last night?
   B: [There was Mary, Sue, Fred, Matt and Sam.]
   b. I had a really great time last night. [#There was Mary, Sue, Fred, Matt, and Sam at this party I went to.]

In (6b), the relevant open proposition is not salient in the context, and the utterance is correspondingly infelicitous. This variable-instantiating use of the existential often involves a list, as in (6a): we are given a list of values for the variable in the open proposition "*x* was at the party last night".

◆ Summary: Pragmatic Constraints on Existential Sentences

Both indefinite and definite NPs are possible.	existential vs. non-existential sentence

There + be + indefinite NP (new information)
 There + be + definite NP (new information)
 The presence of **an indefinite NP** makes the existential pragmatically obligatory.
 However, a definite NP can appear as a logical subject if it carries new information.
	indefinite NP (a physical entity):
	    Both constructions are felicitous.
	 indefinite NP (an abstract entity):
	    The existential is required.

◆ Nonreferential *There* with Verbs Other Than *Be* '17

Although nonreferential *there* is usually followed by a form of copula *be*, there are cases in which it is followed by other verbs, as shown in (7).

(7) a. In 1963, ***there occurred*** a tragic event in the history of the United States.
   b. Deep within his breast ***there smoldered*** an unquenchable desire.
   c. ***There comes*** a time in everyone's life when you need to take a stand.

Verbs other than *be* that occur in sentences with nonreferential *there* include
① verbs that describe existence or position (***exist, live [dwell], remain, stand ↔ lie***)

There *exist* several alternatives.

At the edge of the forest there *dwelt* a troll.

② verbs of motion or direction (***come*** ↔ ***go***, ***walk***, ***run*** [***gallop***], ***fly***, ***approach***) and

There *came* three suspicious-looking men down the street.

Along the river there *walked* an old woman.

③ verbs of happening or materializing (***seem***, ***appear*** [***emerge***, ***arise***], ***happen*** [***occur***, ***ensue***], ***begin*** [***develop***]).

There *arose* a conflict.

There *ensued* a dispute.

▲ Ergative verbs are not allowed.

A number of **ergative verbs** like ***break***, ***change***, ***decrease***, ***die***, ***disappear***, and ***increase*** do not appear in nonreferential ***there*** sentences, as (8) illustrates.

(8) a. *Over the past 10 years, there have died a number of famous authors.

b. *Soon afterward, there broke a large stained glass window in the cathedral.

c. *One day there disappeared a workman in the stockyard '09 Choice

3 Tough Movement '05, '10, '12 Essay

(1) Object-to-Subject Raising (Tough Movement)

(1) ***To teach Elizabeth*** is a pleasure [easy].

~It is a pleasure [easy] ***to teach Elizabeth***.   [It-extraposition]

~***Elizabeth***$_i$ is a pleasure [easy] to teach [t_i].   [Tough Movement]

O-to-S Raising (Tough Movement)

(2) It's impossible to deal with **Bill**.

~**Bill** is impossible to deal with.

(3) It's easy/difficult to beat **them**.

~**They**'re easy/difficult to beat.

(4) It's fun (for us) to be with **Margaret**.

~**Margaret** is fun (for us) to be with.

The tough construction must have ease/difficulty adjectives: **easy**, **hard**, **challenging**, **difficult**, **annoying**, **important**, **impossible**, **safe**, **dangerous**, **nice**, **boring**, **interesting**, and **fun**:

It's easy to please my friend John. = My friend John is easy to please.

It's fun to play this game. = This game is fun to play.

It's impossible to solve the problem. = The problem is impossible to solve.

It's not safe to eat those mushrooms. = Those mushrooms are not safe to eat.

While the above movements are from direct object position, they may occur from a prepositional object position as well when the verb phrase of the main clause includes a PP, as for example,

to work on *a computer* → Computers are fun to work on.

to deal with *a problem* → This problem is hard to deal with.

to play with *a toy* → That toy is dangerous to play with.

to run around *a track* → The track is easy to run around.

(2) Subject-to-Subject Raising

There is a similar construction with **be sure**, **be certain**, **seem**, **appear**, **be said**, **be known**, etc., except that in these cases the corresponding construction with anticipatory *it* requires a ***that***-clause and it is the **subject** of the extraposed clause that is fronted.

(5) It seems that **you**'ve made a mistake.

~**You**$_i$ seem [t_i] to have made a mistake.

S-to-S Raising

(6) It's certain that *we'll* forget the address.

　~*We*'re certain to forget the address.

(7) It is known that *he's* a coward.

　~*He*'s known to be a coward.

Semantics & Pragmatics 01-02 mind map

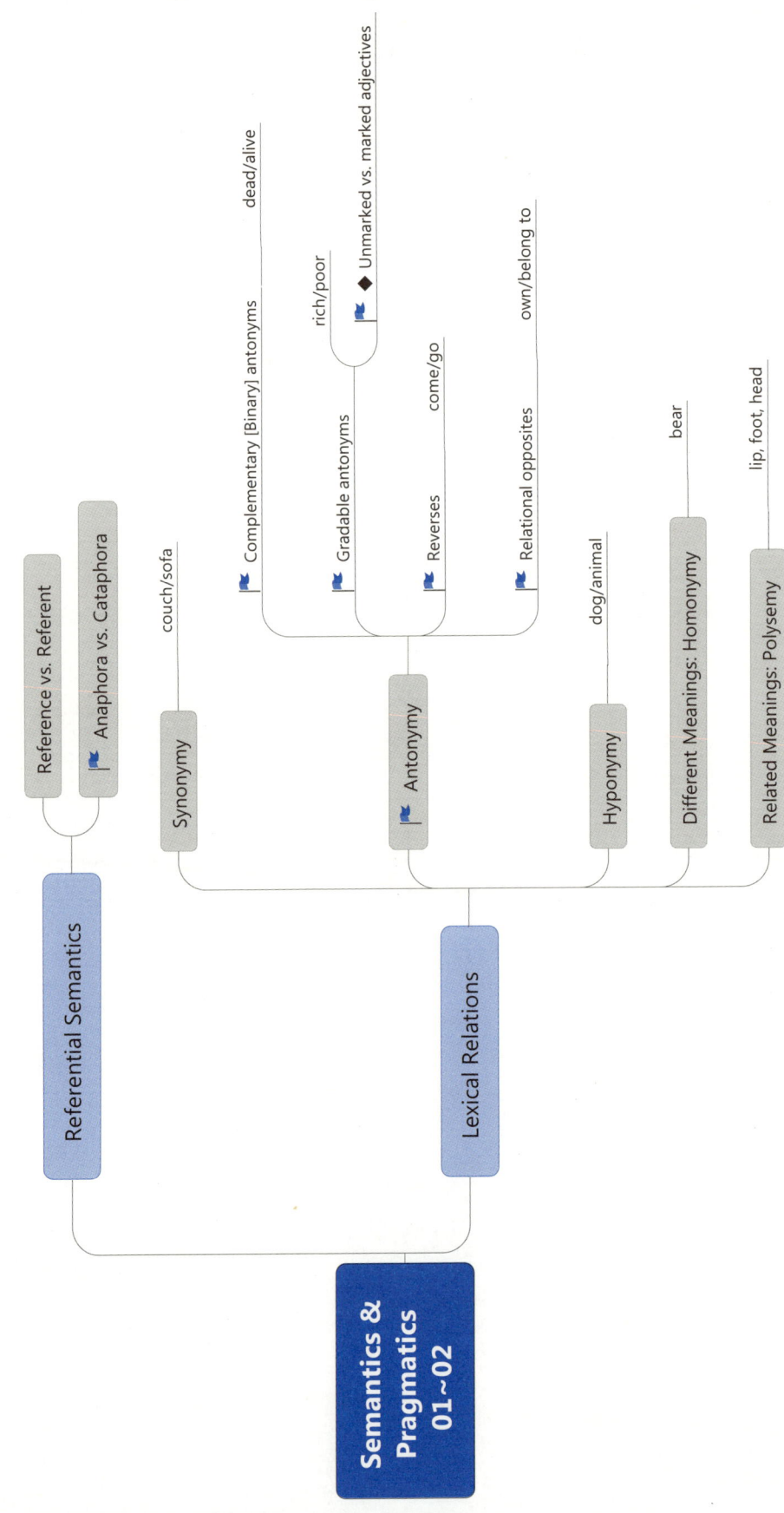

Semantics & Pragmatics 03 mind map

Sentence Relations

Entailment
- whenever the first sentence is true the second one is also true
  - The park wardens killed the bear.
  - The bear is dead.

Presupposition
- He's *stopped* turning into a werewolf every full moon.
- He used to turn into a werewolf every full moon.
- "Constancy Under Negation" Test
  - The mayor of Liverpool is in town.
  - There is a mayor of Liverpool.

Presupposition Triggers
- Wh-question
  - When will you take out that trash?
  - You will take out that trash.
- Factive predicates vs. Non-factive predicates
  - Brown's presentation *demonstrates* that the new system is superior.
  - Brown's presentation *suggests* that the new system is superior.

Factive Predicates vs. Non-factive Predicates
- Factive Predicates: comprehend, regret, be significant, be odd, …
- Nonfactive Predicates: believe, claim, maintain, …

Implicative Verbs
- Positive implicative: manage, succeed, remember
- Negative implicative: fail, neglect, forget

Semantics & Pragmatics 03

Semantics & Pragmatics 04-05 mind map

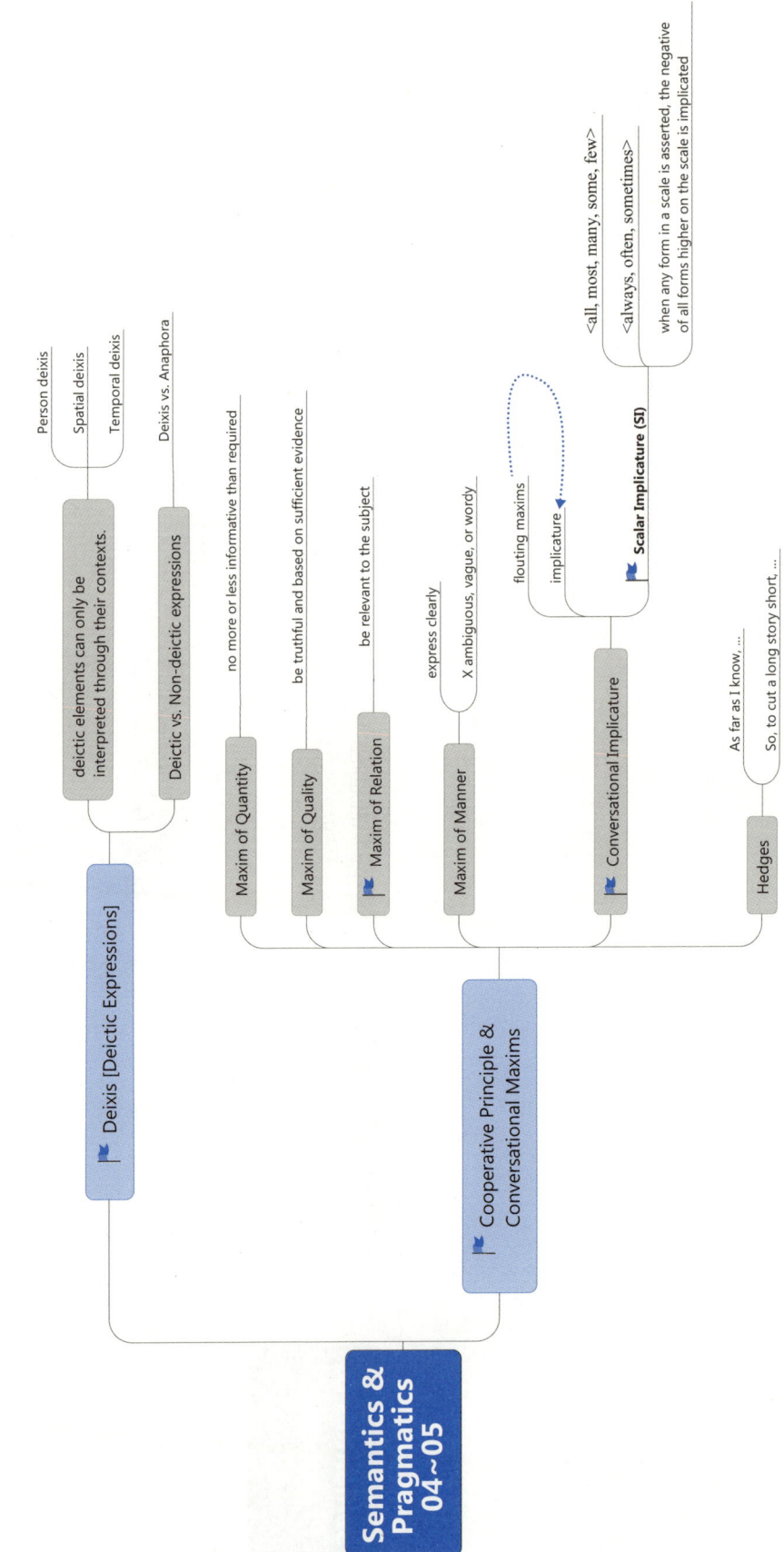

Semantics & Pragmatics 06 mind map

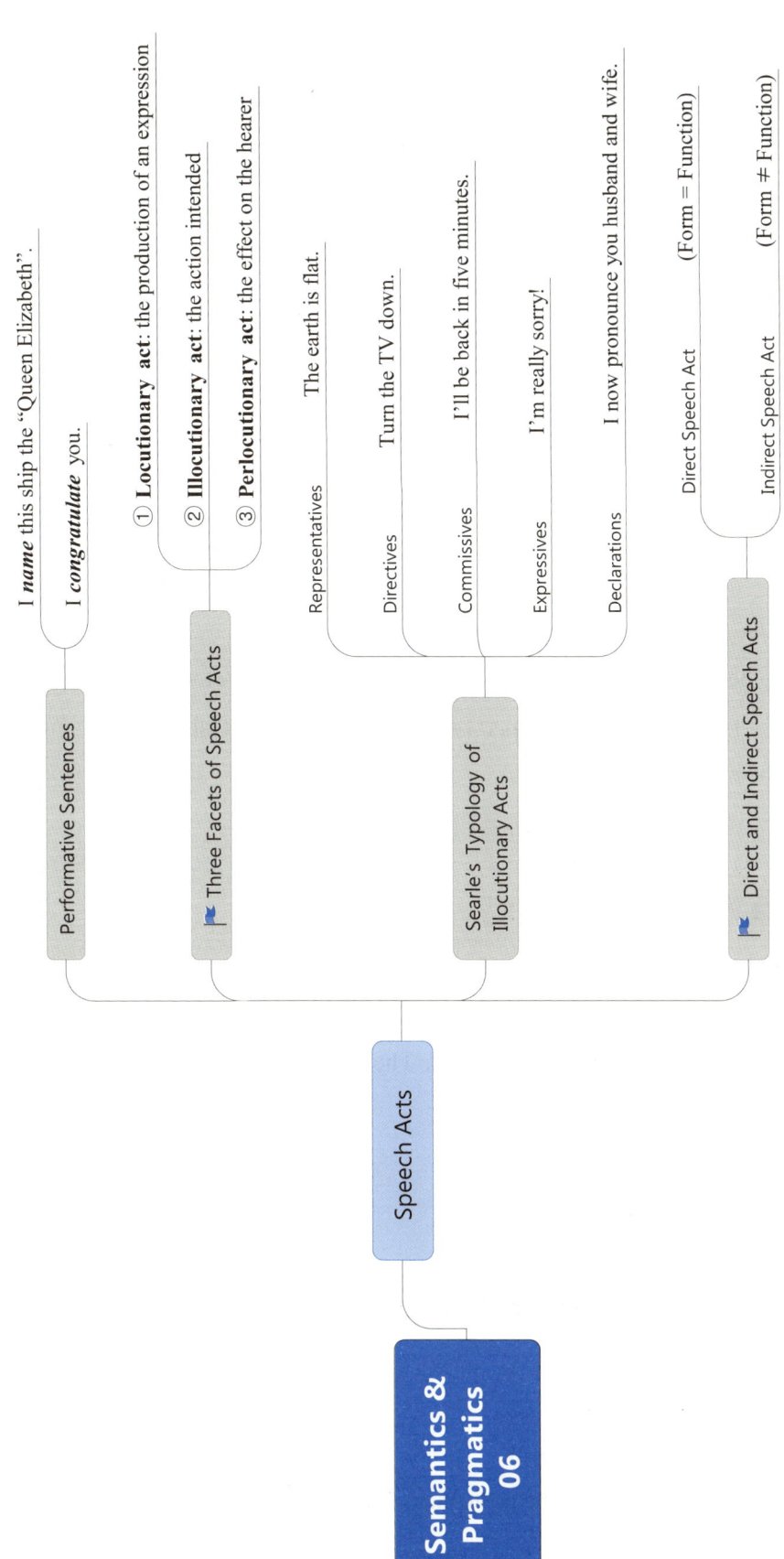

Chapter 05 Semantics & Pragmatics

01 Referential Semantics

1 Reference vs. Referent '00

- **reference**: relationship between piece of language and the things in the world.
- **referent**: A referent is concrete object (a person or thing) that is designated by a word or expression.

The referent of *the capital of Korea* is Seoul.

The relationship between *the capital of Korea* and Seoul is called reference.

The referent of *a toad* in *I've just stepped on a toad* would be the unfortunate animal on the bottom of my shoe.

2 Anaphora vs. Cataphora '20

Anaphora (/əˈnæfərə/) is the use of an expression which depends specifically upon an antecedent expression, and thus is contrasted with cataphora, which is the use of an expression which depends upon a postcedent expression. The anaphoric (referring) term is called an **anaphor**.

Sally arrived, but nobody saw her.
antecedent   anaphor
(The pronoun *her* is an anaphor, referring back to the antecedent *Sally*.)

Before her arrival, nobody saw Sally.
     cataphor   antecedent
(The pronoun *her* refers forward to the postcedent *Sally*, so *her* is now a cataphor.)

02 Lexical Relations

1 Synonymy

Synonyms are different phonological words which have the same or very similar meanings. Some examples might be the pairs below:

(1) couch/sofa　　　　lawyer/attorney　　　toilet/lavatory　　　large/big
　　police officer/cop　　conceal/hide　　　　stubborn/obstinate

2 Antonymy [11]

(1) Complementary [Binary] antonyms

This is a relation between words such that <u>the negative of one implies the positive of the other</u>. The pairs are also sometimes called **complementary pairs** or **binary pairs**. In effect, the words form a two-term classification. Examples would include:

(2) dead/alive (of e.g. animals)
　　pass/fail (a test)
　　hit/miss (a target)

So, using these words literally, *dead* implies *not alive*, etc.

(2) Gradable antonyms

This is a relationship between <u>opposites where the negative of one term does not necessarily imply the positive of the other</u>, e.g.

(3) rich/poor　　fast/slow　　young/old　　beautiful/ugly

This relation is typically associated with adjectives and has two major identifying characteristics: firstly, <u>there are usually intermediate terms</u> so that between the gradable antonyms *hot* and *cold* we can find:

(4) hot (warm tepid cool) cold

This means, of course, that something may be neither hot nor cold. Secondly, the terms are usually relative, so *a thick pencil* is likely to be thinner than *a thin girl*, and *a late dinosaur fossil* is earlier than *an early Elvis record*. A third characteristic is that in some pairs one term is more basic and common, so for example of the pair **long**/**short**, it is more natural to ask of something **How long is it?** than **How short is it?**

Other examples of gradable antonyms are:

(5) tall/short   clever/stupid   far/near   interesting/boring

◆ **Unmarked vs. marked adjectives** '99, '07

Also, observe that in the case of gradable antonyms the two terms are not equal: one member of the pair is **marked** and the other **unmarked**. The unmarked member is the one that is normally expected. Compare:

(6) *Unmarked*   *Marked*

　　How big is your house?   vs. How small is your house?
　　How well do you play the guitar?   vs. How badly do you play the guitar?

Where the unmarked member of the pair is used, the speaker is not prejudging anything. But where the marked member is used, the speaker presupposes that the house is small or that you play the guitar badly.

◆ **Gradable antonyms**

Unmarked Adjectives	Usually used in *how*-questions & answers e.g. How old is John?	No presupposition
Marked Adjectives	Sometimes used in *how*-questions & answers e.g. How young is John?	Presupposition (John is young.)

(3) Reverses

The characteristic **reverse** relation is between terms describing movement, where one term describes movement in one direction, →, and the other the same movement in the opposite direction, ←; for example, the terms **push** and **pull** on a swing door, which tell you in which direction to apply force. Other such pairs are

(7) come/go   go/return   ascend/descend
     inflate/deflate expand/contract   fill/empty

(4) Converses [Relational opposites]

Converse antonyms or **relational opposites** are terms which describe a relation between two entities from alternate viewpoints, as in the pairs:

(8) own/belong to   above/below   employer/employee

Thus, if we are told *Alan owns this book* then we know automatically *This book belongs to Alan*. Or from *Helen is David's employer* we know *David is Helen's employee*. Again, these relations are part of a speaker's semantic knowledge and explain why the two sentences below are **paraphrases**:

(9) My office is above the library.
     The library is below my office.

◆ Summary: Antonymy (four types)

Complementary	Gradable	Reverses	Converses
dead/alive	long/short	come/go	teacher/student
male/female	fat/thin	inflate/deflate	parent/child
pass/fail	thick/thin	enter/exit	defeat/lose to
asleep/awake	tall/short	pack/unpack	wife/husband
true/false	rich/poor	tie/untie	above/below
single/married	high/low	wrap/unwrap	in front of/behind
	hot/cold	dress/undress	buy/sell
	fast/slow	get on/get off	lend/borrow
	old/young		give/receive

3 Hyponymy

Hyponymy is a relation of inclusion. A hyponym includes the meaning of a more general word, e.g.

(10) *dog* and *cat* are hyponyms of *animal*
 sister and *mother* are hyponyms of *woman*

The more general term is called the **superordinate** or **hypernym**. Much of the vocabulary is linked by such systems of inclusion, and the resulting semantic networks form the hierarchical taxonomies mentioned above.

(11)
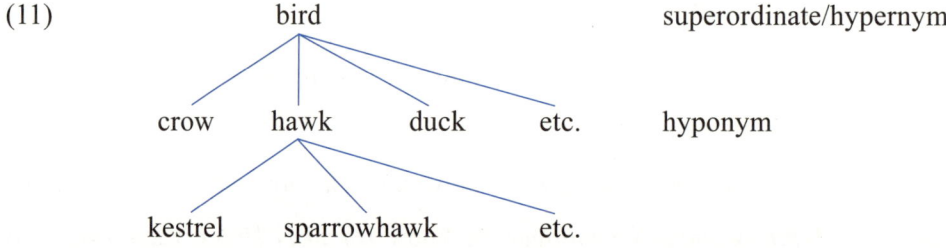

Here *kestrel* is a hyponym of *hawk*, and *hawk* a hyponym of *bird*.

A **hyponym** is a word that contains the meaning of a more general word, known as the **superordinate**. For example, *oak* contains the meaning of *tree*; therefore, *oak* is a hyponym of the superordinate *tree*.

4 Different Meanings: Homonymy

Words that sound the same but have different (unrelated) meanings are called **homonyms** (Greek *homeos* 'same', *onoma* 'name'). The verb *bear* can mean 'to have children' or 'to tolerate'. So, ***She can't bear children*** is ambiguous because *bear* is a homonym. **Homophones** do not necessarily share the same spelling (*sole/soul*, *gorilla/guerilla*, *to/too/two*), but they sound the same; **homographs** have different meanings, the same spelling, but different pronunciations (the *bow* of a ship versus a *bow* and arrow).

(12) homonyms (sound the same, same spelling): bear, saw

homophones (sound the same, different spelling): sole/soul, gorilla/guerilla

homographs (same spelling, sound different): bow, wind, wound

5 Related Meanings: Polysemy

Words that are **polysemous** have two or more related meanings (Greek *poly* 'many', *semy* 'meanings'). For example, *lip* is polysemous because we can use it not only to refer to a part of one's mouth but also in phrases such as *lip of the cliff* or the *lip of a cup*, and we also have the expression *don't give me any lip*. We call a furry, burrowing animal a *mole*, and *mole* can also refer to a spy who pretends to be a legitimate member of the group on which he or she is spying. *Foot* is polysemous as well: in addition to meaning 'the lowest part of the body' (with the top being the *head*), we have *foot/head of the bed*, as well as *foot of the stairs* and *foot of the mountain*. Body parts are often polysemous; we use *leg* to refer to the leg of a chair and the leg of a table, *arm* to refer to the arm of a chair, and *eye* to refer to the eye of a storm. Most polysemy makes use of figurative, or nonliteral, meanings.

03 Sentential Relations

1 Entailment [10]

If you know that the sentence *Jack swims beautifully* is true, then you also know that the sentence *Jack swims* is true. This meaning relation is called **entailment**. We say that *Jack swims beautifully* entails *Jack swims*. More generally, one sentence entails another if whenever the first sentence is true the second one is also true in all conceivable circumstances.

Generally, entailment goes only in one direction. So while the sentence *Jack swims beautifully* entails *Jack swims*, the reverse is not true. Knowing merely that *Jack swims* is true does not necessitate the truth of *Jack swims beautifully*. Jack could be a poor swimmer.

(1) Entailment defined by truth:

A sentence **p** entails a sentence **q** when the truth of the first (**p**) guarantees the truth of the second (**q**), and the falsity of the second (**q**) guarantees the falsity of the first (**p**).

The notion of entailment can be used to reveal knowledge that we have about other meaning relations. For example, two sentences are **synonymous** (or **paraphrases**) if they are both true or both false with respect to the same situations. Sentences like ***Jack put off the meeting*** and ***Jack postponed the meeting*** are synonymous, because when one is true the other must be true; and when one is false the other must also be false. We can describe this pattern in a more concise way by using the notion of entailment:

Two sentences are synonymous if they entail each other.

< More examples >

When the truth of one sentence guarantees the truth of another sentence, we say there is a relation of **entailment**.

(2) a. The park wardens killed the bear.
b. The bear is dead.

(3) a. Robin is a man.
b. Robin is human.

The (a) sentences in (2) and (3) entail the (b) sentences.

2 Presupposition

A **presupposition** is a proposition (expressed in a sentence) that must be ***assumed*** to be true in order to judge the truth or falsity of another sentence. In the following examples, the a sentence is said to presuppose the b sentence:

(1) a. He's <u>stopped</u> turning into a werewolf every full moon.
b. He used to turn into a werewolf every full moon.

(2) a. Her husband is a fool.
b. She has a husband.

(3) a. I don't <u>regret</u> leaving London.
    b. I left London.

(4) a. The Prime Minister of Malaysia is in Dublin this week.
    b. Malaysia has a prime minister.

(5) a. I do <u>regret</u> leaving London.
    b. I left London.

(1) "Constancy Under Negation" Test

(6) Truth table for presupposition

p		q
T	→	T
F	→	T
T/F	←	T

The truth table like (6) allows us to capture an important difference between **entailment** and **presupposition**. <u>If we negate an entailing sentence, then the entailment fails; but negating a presupposing sentence allows the presupposition to survive.</u> Take for example the entailment pair in (7):

(7) a. I saw my father today.
    b. I saw someone today.

If we negate (7a) to form (8a), then it no longer entails (7b), repeated as (8b):

(8) a. I didn't see my father today.
    b. I saw someone today.

Now (8b) no longer automatically follows from the preceding sentence: again it might be true, we just don't know. Compare this with the presupposition pair:

(9) a. The mayor of Liverpool is in town.
    b. There is a mayor of Liverpool.

If we negate (9a) to form (10a), the resulting sentence still has the presupposition, shown as (10b):

(10) a. The mayor of Liverpool isn't in town today.
　　b. There is a mayor of Liverpool.

So negating the presupposing sentence does not affect the presupposition, whereas, as we saw, negating an entailing sentence destroys the entailment. So it seems that viewing presupposition as a truth relation allows us to capture one interesting difference between the behavior of presupposition and entailment under negation.

◆ **Entailment vs. Presupposition**

	Entailment	Presupposition
Test	p　　q T → T F ← F	p　　q T → T F → T
Example	a. Jack swims beautifully. b. Jack swims. (a) entails (b).	a. I <u>don't regret</u> leaving London. b. I left London. (a) presupposes (b).
difference	"Constancy Under Negation" Test → If we negate an entailing sentence, then the entailment **fails**; but negating a presupposing sentence allows the presupposition to **survive**.	

3 Presupposition Triggers

(1) *Wh*-question

　　Presupposition triggers are either structures or words that assume, or presuppose, the truth of the proposition expressed in a sentence or the speaker's attitude about it. One structure that serves as a presupposition trigger is a ***wh*-question**. Consider, for example, (1a–c).

(1) a. When will you take out that trash?
　　b. Will you take out that trash?

c. If you take out that trash, put it by the curb.

Sentence (1a) is a *wh*-question and presupposes the truth of the proposition it expresses, 'You will take out that trash.' On the other hand, (1b) is a *yes-no* question and does not presuppose the truth of the proposition. Sentence (1c), containing an *if*-clause, likewise does not presuppose the truth of the proposition 'You will take out that trash.'

(2) Factive predicates vs. Non-factive predicates

There are entire classes of words that serve as presupposition triggers. One such class includes **factive verbs**. Consider, for example, (2a) and (2b).

(2) a. Brown's presentation *demonstrates* that the new system is superior.
b. Brown's presentation *suggests* that the new system is superior.

Sentence (2a) contains the factive verb *demonstrates* and presupposes the truth of the proposition in the subordinate clause. On the other hand, (2b) contains the **nonfactive verb** *suggests* and does not presuppose the truth of the proposition in the subordinate clause; it does not assume that 'the new system is superior.'

4 Factive Predicates vs. Non-factive Predicates '06

(1) Factive Predicates

Kiparsky and Kiparsky distinguished verbs and adjectival predicates according to whether they carry **presuppositions**, or inherent assumptions, regarding the factual status of their complements. Some examples are listed below:

Factive	*Non-factive*
comprehend	believe
regret	claim
bear in mind	maintain
be significant	seem

be odd　　　　　　　be likely

be clear　　　　　　be possible

A factive complement clause is a clause that is true regardless of whether the higher clause is affirmative, negative, or interrogative:

John regrets that he committed the crime.

John does not regret that he committed the crime.

Does John regret that he committed the crime?

In all three examples, it remains a presumed truth that John committed the crime. In a courtroom trial, the defense attorney would likely object if the question above were posed directly to the defendant as "Do you regret that you committed the crime?" Whether the question is answered "yes" or "no," the response amounts to an admission of guilt. The same quality holds with the other words and expressions on the above list of factives: Whether the sentence *It is odd that our friend disappeared* is negated, questioned, or left in the affirmative, it remains true that *our friend disappeared*.

(2) Non-factive Predicates

Compare now a nonfactive complement, which yields different results:

The police maintain that John committed the crime.

The police do not maintain that John committed the crime.

Do the police maintain that John committed the crime?

In these sentences, there is no presumption about whether John did or did not commit the crime, regardless of whether the police have strong beliefs about John's guilt or innocence. In a similar way, to say *It is likely that the Yankees won the game* does not presume that the Yankees won or did not win; nor is this presumed if the sentence is made negative or cast as a question.

◆ Summary: Factive Predicates are presupposition triggers.

Factive Predicates	Nonfactive Predicates
know [be aware] bear in mind [remember] ↔ forget regret, resent be odd be surprising [remarkable] be clear [make clear] be significant acknowledge demonstrate [show, prove] comprehend [grasp] note, take into consideration [account]	allege [claim, maintain, assert], charge assume, believe, conclude, conjecture, fancy think [suppose, figure] suggest

5 Implicative Verbs '06

Karttunen identified a further distinction among verbs in which the factuality or nonfactuality of the complement depends both on the verb itself and on whether the main clause asserts or denies the complement. These verbs can be "positive implicatives" or "negative implicatives" as follows:

Positive implicative	*Negative implicative*
manage	neglect
succeed	fail
remember	forget

If we say, **Mary managed to finish her work**, we assume that Mary did in fact finish it. If we say, **Mary failed to finish her work**, we assume that she did not. The same holds for the other verbs on the list. When implicatives are negated, however, the situation reverses:

Mary did not manage to finish her work. (She did not finish it.)

Mary did not fail to finish her work. (She finished it.)

In the first use (a negated positive implicative) Mary did not finish her work, while in the second (a negated negative implicative) she did.

(1) a. You *failed* to enclose your check.
b. You *forgot* to enclose your check.
c. You *did not* enclose your check.

All three of these express the proposition 'You did not enclose your check.' However, the implicative verbs *fail* and *forget* in (1a) and (1b) further imply an unmet obligation: 'You were supposed to enclose a check but you didn't.'

04 Deixis [Deictic Expressions] '10

The most primitive way of referring to something is to point to it. Of course, this kind of reference can only be accomplished with people and concrete things in one's immediate environment. On a less primitive level, every language has **deictic words** which 'point' to 'things' in the physical-social context of the speaker and addressee(s) and whose referents can only be determined by knowing the context in which they are used. For example, if we should encounter a message like the following, on paper or on an electronic recording

(1) I was disappointed that you didn't come this afternoon.
I hope you'll join us tomorrow.

we wouldn't be able to identify the referents of *I*, *you*, *us*, *this afternoon* or *tomorrow* though we understand how the first three and the last two are related to one another. The meaning of any lexeme depends to some extent on the context in which it occurs, but deictic elements can only be interpreted through their contexts.

English examples of deictic words include (1) pronouns *I, you* and *we*, which 'point' to the participants in any speech act; *he, she, it* and *they*, when they are used to refer to others in the environment; (2) locative expressions *here* and *there*, which designate space close to the speaker or farther away; *this/these* and *that/those*, which respectively indicate entities close to or removed from the speaker; and (3) temporal expressions: *now*, *then*, *yesterday*, *today*, *tomorrow*, *last week*, *next month* and so on. These last are all relative to the time when they are used.

Person deixis	Place [spatial] deixis	Time [temporal] deixis
I, you, she/her, he/his/him *this* person *that* man *these* women *those* children (→ Demonstratives indicate *proximity* of certain items distinct from others.)	here, there *this* place *these* parks *that* place *those* towers over there *yonder* mountains **<directional deixis>** before/behind left/right front/back **<motion verbs>** come/go bring/take	now, then yesterday, today, tomorrow *this* morning *this* time, *that* time seven days ago two weeks from now last week next April

1 Deictic vs. Non-deictic expressions

Words which can be deictic are not always so. **Today** and ***tomorrow*** are deictic in "We can't go today, but tomorrow will be fine." They are not deictic in "Today's costly apartment buildings may be tomorrow's slums." Yet the relation between the two words is analogous. Similarly, ***here*** and ***there*** are deictic in "James hasn't been here yet. Is he there with you?" They are not deictic in "The children were running here and there." The pronoun ***you*** is not deictic when used with the meaning 'one; any person or persons,' as in "You can lead a horse to water but you can't make him drink." Similarly, ***they*** has a generalized, non-deictic reference to people in general (**generic use**), especially those in charge of some endeavor or other, as in "They say that an ounce of prevention is worth a pound of cure," "They don't make good cider the way they used to."

(1) Deixis vs. Anaphora

Note that deixis can intersect with anaphora. Consider, for example, the sentence

Members of Congress believe they deserve a raise. The expression ***they*** can refer either to the expression ***members of Congress*** or to some other plural entity in the context of the utterance. When, as in the first case, a pronoun refers to another linguistic expression, it is used anaphorically; when, as in the second case, it refers to some entity in the extralinguistic context, it is used deictically.

05 Cooperative Principle & Conversational Maxims '01, '09

Grice proposes that conversations are governed by what he calls the **Cooperative Principle**: the assumption that participants in a conversation are cooperating with each other. This Cooperative Principle, in turn, consists of four **conversational maxims**: **Quantity** — a participant's contribution should be informative; **Quality** — a participant's contribution should be true; **Relation** — a participant's contribution should be relevant; and **Manner** — a participant's contribution should be clear.

Grice's claim, however, is not that we strictly adhere to these maxims when we converse; rather, he claims that we interpret what we hear *as if* it conforms to these maxims. That is, when a maxim is violated, we draw an inference (i.e., an **implicature**) which makes the utterance conform to these maxims. Grice used the term **flouting** to describe the *intentional* violation of a maxim for the purpose of conveying an unstated proposition. This, then, would constitute a theory of how implicatures arise. Let's now consider how this theory of conversational implicature applies in some hypothetical cases.

1 Maxim of Quantity

This maxim states that each participant's contribution to a conversation should be no more or less informative than required. Suppose Kenny and Tom are college roommates. Kenny walks into the living room of their apartment, where Tom is reading a book. Kenny asks Tom, ***What are you reading?*** Tom responds with ***A book***, which raises an implicature. Kenny reasons (unconsciously) as follows: I asked Tom what he was reading, and my question required him to tell me either the title of his book or at least its subject matter. Instead, he told me what I could already see for myself. He appears to be flouting the Maxim of Quantity. There must be a reason that he gave less information than the situation requires. The inference (i.e., the implicature) that I draw is that he does not want to be disturbed, and thus is trying to end the conversation.

2 Maxim of Quality

This maxim states that each participant's contribution should be truthful and based on sufficient evidence. Suppose an undergraduate in a geography class says, in response to question from the instructor, **Reno's the capital of Nevada**. The instructor, Mr. Barbados, then says, **Yeah, and London's the capital of New Jersey**. The instructor's utterance raises an implicature. The student reasons (unconsciously) as follows: Mr. Barbados said that London is the capital of New Jersey; he knows that is not true. He appears to be flouting the Maxim of Quality; there must be a reason for him saying something patently false. The inference (i.e., the implicature) that I draw is that my answer is false (i.e. Reno is not the capital of Nevada).

3 Maxim of Relation

This maxim states that each participant's contribution should be relevant to the subject of the conversation. Suppose a man wakes up in the morning and asks his wife, **What time is it?** She responds with **Well, the paper's already come**. Her statement raises an implicature. The husband reasons (unconsciously) as follows: I asked about the time, and she mentioned something seemingly unrelated — the arrival of the newspaper. She appears to be flouting the Maxim of Relation; there must be some reason for her seemingly irrelevant comment. The inference (i.e., the implicature) I draw is that she doesn't know the exact time, but the arrival of the newspaper has something to do with the time, namely that it is now past the time of day that the newspaper usually comes (i.e., 7:00 A.M.)

4 Maxim of Manner

This maxim states that each participant's contribution should be expressed in a reasonably clear fashion; that is, it should not be vague, ambiguous, or excessively wordy. Suppose Mr. and Mrs. Jones are out for a Sunday drive with their two preschool children. Mr. Jones says to

Mrs. Jones, ***Let's stop and get something to eat***. Mrs. Jones responds with ***Okay, but not M-c-D-o-n-a-l-d-s***. Mrs. Jones's statement raises an implicature. Mr. Jones reasons (unconsciously) as follows: She spelled out the word ***McDonald's***, which is certainly not the clearest way of saying it. She appears to be flouting the Maxim of Manner; there must be a reason for her lack of clarity. Since the kids cannot spell, the inference (i.e., the implicature) I draw is that she does not want the children to understand that part of her statement.

> **Conversational Implicature**
>
> In summary, an implicature is a proposition implied by an utterance, but neither part of nor a logical consequence of that utterance. An implicature arises in the mind of a hearer when the speaker **flouts** (i.e., intentionally violates) one of the maxims of Quantity, Quality, Relation, or Manner.

5 Conversational Implicature '03, '04

(**Conversational**) **implicatures** are inferences that are not made strictly on the basis of the content expressed in the discourse. Rather, they are made in accordance with the conversational maxims, taking into account both the linguistic meaning of the utterance as well as the particular circumstances in which the utterance is made.

Here are a few examples of conversational implicatures:

(1) Sue: Does Mary have a boyfriend?
    Bill: She's been driving to Santa Barbara every weekend.

(2) John: Do you know how to change a tire?
    Jane: I know how to call a tow truck.

(3) Dana: Do these slacks make my butt look big?
    Jamie: You look great in chartreuse.

In (1), Bill asserts that Mary has been driving to Santa Barbara every weekend. But he ***implicates*** that Mary has a boyfriend (and that the boyfriend lives in Santa Barbara). In (2),

Jane asserts that she knows how to call a tow truck. But she *implicates* that she doesn't know how to change a tire. In (3), well, you figure it out.

◆ **Summary**

Implicatures are the inferences that may be drawn from an utterance in context when one or another of the maxims is violated (either purposefully or naively). When Mary says *It's cold in here*, one of many possible implicatures may be "Mary wants the heat turned up." Implicatures are like entailments in that their truth follows from sentences of the discourse, but unlike **entailments**, which are necessarily true, implicatures may be cancelled by information added later. Mary might wave you away from the thermostat and ask you to hand her a sweater. **Presuppositions** are situations that must be true for utterances to be appropriate, so that *Take some more tea* has the presupposition "already had some tea."

Entailment	Presupposition	Implicature
One sentence entails another if whenever the first sentence is true the second one is also true.	A proposition that must be true for another utterance to be true.	inferences made when a maxim is violated.
Jack swims beautifully. ‖- Jack swims.	e.g. Take some more tea. >> The addressee already had some tea.	e.g. It's cold in here. +> Turn up the heat.
Always true (regardless of any context)	**defeasible (cancellable)** e.g. A: Take some more tea. 　　B: What? I haven't drunk any tea, yet.	**defeasible (cancellable)** e.g. A: It's cold in here. 　　B: I'll turn up the heat. 　　A: No, please shut the window.

(1) Scalar Implicature (SI) '13 Choice

Certain information is always communicated by choosing a word which expresses one value from a scale of values. This is particularly obvious in terms for expressing quantity, as shown in the scales in in (1), where terms are listed from the highest to the lowest value.

(1) <all, most, many, some, few>
　　<always, often, sometimes>

When producing an utterance, a speaker selects the word from the scale which is the most informative and truthful (quantity and quality) in the circumstances, as in (2).

(2) I'm studying linguistics and I've completed some of the required courses.

By choosing 'some' in (2), the speaker creates an implicature (+> not all). This is one scalar implicature of uttering (2). The basis of **scalar implicature** is that, when any form in a scale is asserted, the negative of all forms higher on the scale is implicated. The first scale in (1) had 'all', 'most', and 'many', higher than 'some'. Given the definition of scalar implicature, it should follow that, in saying 'some of the required courses', the speaker also creates other implicatures (for example, +> not most, +> not many).

If the speaker goes on to describe those linguistics courses as in (3), then we can identify some more scalar implicatures.

(3) They're sometimes really interesting.

By using 'sometimes' in (3), the speaker communicates, via implicature, the negative of forms higher on the scale of frequency (+> not always, +> not often).

There are many scalar implicatures produced by the use of expressions that we may not immediately consider to be part of any scale. For example, the utterance of (4a) will be interpreted as implicating '+> not certain' as a higher value on the scale of 'likelihood' and (4b) '+> not must' on on a scale of 'obligation' and '+> not frozen' on a scale of 'coldness'.

(4) a. It's possible that they were delayed.
    b. This should be stored in a cool place.

One noticeable feature of scalar implicatures is that when speakers correct themselves on some detail, as in (5), they typically cancel one of the scalar implicatures.

(5) I got some of this jewelry in Hong Kong — um actually I think I got most of it there.

In (5), the speaker initially implicates '+> not most' by saying 'some', but then corrects herself by actually asserting 'most'. That final assertion is still likely to be interpreted, however, with a scalar implicature (+> not all).

6 Hedges

The importance of the maxim of **quality** for cooperative interaction in English may be best measured by the number of expressions we use to indicate that what we're saying may not be totally accurate. The initial phrases in (1a-c) and the final phrase in (1d) are notes to the listener regarding the accuracy of the main statement.

(1) a. <u>As far as I know</u>, they're married.
   b. <u>I may be mistaken</u>, but I thought I saw a wedding ring on her finger.
   c. <u>I'm not sure if this is right</u>, but I heard it was a secret ceremony in Hawaii.
   d. He couldn't live without her, <u>I guess</u>.

The conversational context for the examples in (1) might be a recent rumor involving a couple known to the speakers. **Cautious notes**, or **hedges**, of this type can also be used to show that the speaker is conscious of the **quantity** maxim, as in the initial phrases in (2a-c), produced in the course of a speaker's account of her recent vacation.

(2) a. <u>As you probably know,</u> I am terrified of bugs.
   b. So, <u>to cut a long story short</u>, we grabbed our stuff and ran.
   c. <u>I won't bore you with all the details</u>, but it was an exciting trip.

Markers tied to the expectation of relevance (from the maxim of **relation**) can be found in the middle of speakers' talk when they say things like 'Oh, by the way' and go on to mention some potentially unconnected information during a conversation. Speakers also seem to use expressions like 'anyway', or 'well, anyway', to indicate that they may have drifted into a discussion of some possibly non-relevant material and want to stop. Some expressions which may act as hedges on the expectation of relevance are shown as the initial phrases in (3a-c), from an office meeting.

(3) a. <u>I don't know if this is important</u>, but some of the files are missing.
   b. <u>This may sound like a dumb question</u>, but whose handwriting is this?
   c. <u>Not to change the subject</u>, but is this related to the budget?

The awareness of the expectations of **manner** may also lead speakers to produce hedges of the type shown in the initial phrases in (4a-c), heard during an account of a crash.

(4) a. <u>This may be a bit confused</u>, but I remember being in a car.
 b. <u>I'm not sure if this makes sense</u>, but the car had no lights.
 c. <u>I don't know if this is clear at all</u>, but I think the other car was reversing.

All of these examples of hedges are good indications that the speakers are not only aware of the maxims, but that they want to show that they are trying to observe them. Perhaps such forms also communicate the speakers' concern that their listeners judge them to be cooperative conversational partners.

Exercise 1   Flouting Maxims & Conversational Implicature

An implicature can result through the **flouting** of one of the maxims by the speaker (B), in which the hearer (A) can infer something not explicitly said if the speaker (B) disregards one of the maxims (whether intentionally or not), though the hearer (A) assumes that the speaker is not doing so. Give an implicature of B's utterance in each of the following situations, and then identify the maxim(s) (i.e. relevance, informativeness, or clarity) that has/have been flouted (and thus which led the hearer to this implicature).

(1) A: Professor, will you write a letter of recommendation for me?
 B: Certainly. I will say that you were always neatly dressed, punctual, and are unfailingly polite.
Implicature of B's utterance: _____
Maxim(s) flouted: _____

(2) A: I'm not feeling very well today.
 B: There's a hospital across the street.
Implicature of B's utterance: _____
Maxim(s) flouted: _____

(3) A: (by an obviously immobilized car) My car's broken down.
 B: There is a garage round the corner.
Implicature of B's utterance: _____
Maxim(s) flouted: _____

(4) A: Do you like my new sofa?
   B: Well, its colour is lovely.
Implicature of B's utterance: _____
Maxim(s) flouted: _____

(5) A: What did you think of that new movie?
   B: Well, the costumes were authentic.
Implicature of B's utterance: _____
Maxim(s) flouted: _____

(6) A: Do you like ice-cream?
   B: Is the Pope Catholic?
Implicature of B's utterance: _____
Maxim(s) flouted: _____

(7) A: How's the weather?
   B: It's 86.7 degrees Fahrenheit. The air is humid, muggy, and the pavement is so hot I can feel it through my shoes.
Implicature of B's utterance: _____
Maxim(s) flouted: _____

(8) A: What's your recipe for a birthday cake?
   B: It should have icing. Use unbleached flour and sugar in the cake and bake it for an hour. Preheat the oven to 325 degrees and beat in three fresh eggs.
Implicature of B's utterance: _____
Maxim(s) flouted: _____

(9) A: How do you like my new suit?
   B: Well, your shoes look nice.
Implicature of B's utterance: _____
Maxim(s) flouted: _____

(10) A: Have you done your homework and taken out the garbage?
    B: I've taken out the garbage.
Implicature of B's utterance: _____
Maxim(s) flouted: _____

(11) A: I may win the lottery for $83 million.
    B: There may be people on Mars, too.
Implicature of B's utterance: _____
Maxim(s) flouted: _____

(12) A: Whoa! Has your boss gone crazy?
    B: Let's go get some coffee.
Implicature of B's utterance: _____
Maxim(s) flouted: _____

(13) A: Is Betsy in?
    B: Her light is on.
Implicature of B's utterance: _____
Maxim(s) flouted: _____

Answers

1. Implicature of B's utterance: A is not good enough for the professor to write a recommendation letter for him/her.
   Maxim(s) flouted: relevance

2. Implicature of B's utterance: You can go to the hospital across the street to get some kind of treatment.
   Maxim(s) flouted: relevance

3. Implicature of B's utterance: The garage probably has a mechanic who can repair A's car.
   Maxim(s) flouted: relevance

4. Implicature of B's utterance: B doesn't like the sofa.
   Maxim(s) flouted: quantity, relevance

5. Implicature of B's utterance: B didn't like the movie. (Or there was nothing good

except the costumes.)

Maxim(s) flouted: quantity (not enough information is given), relevance (B's response is not as relevant as it normally required by A's question.)

6. Implicature of B's utterance: The answer to the question is "Obviously, yes!"
    Maxim(s) flouted: relevance

7. Implicature of B's utterance: It's very hot today.
    Maxim(s) flouted: manner (Be brief), quantity

8. Implicature of B's utterance: B does not want to let A know the recipe.
    Maxim(s) flouted: manner (Be orderly)

9. Implicature of B's utterance: B does not like A's suit.
    Maxim(s) flouted: relevance (shoes are not related to suit)

10. Implicature of B's utterance: B has not done the homework.
    Maxim(s) flouted: quantity

11. Implicature of B's utterance: It's almost impossible that A wins that amount of money.
    Maxim(s) flouted: relevance

12. Implicature of B's utterance: B cannot answer the question at the current place.
    Maxim(s) flouted: relevance

13. Implicature of B's utterance: Betsy's light being on is usually a sign of whether she is in or not.
    Maxim(s) flouted: relevance

06 Speech Acts

1 Performative Sentences

Austin observes that — contrary to the position of logicians — not all utterances have "truth value". He thus makes a fundamental distinction between **constatives**, which are assertions which are either true or false, and **performatives**, which cannot be characterized as either true or false, but are, in Austin's terms, "felicitous" (happy) or "infelicitous" (unhappy). These are utterances by which the speaker carries out an action, hence the term *speech act*. Examples of performatives are utterances such as the following:

I *name* this ship the "Queen Elizabeth". I *promise*.
I *refuse* to answer that question. I *congratulate* you.
I will *pay* you tomorrow. I *bet* you a quarter.
We *authorize* the payment. I *swear* it's true.

Simply by uttering each of these statements, the speaker performs an action, such as naming, congratulating, promising, and betting. These actions require no further action other than the linguistic action in order to be what they are. As in the examples given, speech acts may contain an explicit **performative verb**, which is normally first person and simple present tense (i.e., *I name*, *I congratulate*, *I promise*, *I bet*, and so on). Performatives can occur with "hereby". Austin says that there are 1,000 such verbs in English. Searle rejects Austin's distinction between constative and performative, interpreting all utterances as performatives, even those which we might understand as representing a state of affairs and hence true or false, for example, *It is raining*. He categorizes such a speech act as a **Representative**. Before looking at his categorization, however, we will consider how he analyzes speech acts and the bases he uses for his taxonomy.

constatives	performatives
describe or report something	do not describe or report
are true or false	are not true or false (rather, are felicitous or infelicitous)
uttering a constative is "just" saying something	uttering a performative is not "just" saying something (it is *doing* something)

2 Three Facets of Speech Acts '04, '07

Austin claimed that all utterances, in addition to meaning whatever they mean, perform specific acts via the specific communicative force of an utterance. Furthermore, he introduced a threefold distinction among the acts one simultaneously performs when saying something.

(1) Three facets of a speech act
  ① **Locutionary act**: the production of a meaningful linguistic expression.
  ② **Illocutionary act**: the action intended to be performed by a speaker in uttering a linguistic expression.
  ③ **Perlocutionary act**: the bringing about of consequences or effects on the audience through the uttering of a linguistic expression.

In every speech act, we can distinguish three components, following Austin (1962). A **locutionary act** or **locution** is what is said, the utterance.

When we say something, we usually say it with some purpose in mind. This is the illocutionary act or illocution. In other words, an **illocutionary act** or **illocution** refers to the type of function the speaker intends to fulfil or the type of action the speaker intends to accomplish in the course of producing an utterance. It is an act defined within a system of social conventions. In short, it is an act accomplished in speaking. Examples of illocutionary acts include accusing, apologizing, blaming, congratulating, giving permission, joking, nagging, naming, promising, ordering, refusing, swearing, and thanking. The functions or actions that have been just mentioned are also commonly referred to as the **illocutionary force** of the utterance. … Indeed, the term 'speech act' in its narrow sense is often taken to refer specifically to illocutionary acts.

Finally, a **perlocutionary act** or **perlocution** concerns the effect an utterance may have on the addressee. Put slightly more technically, a perlocutionary act is the one by which the performance of an illocutionary act produces a certain effect in or exerts a certain influence on the addressee. Still another way to put it is that a perlocutionary act represents a consequence or by-product of speaking, whether intentional or not. It is therefore an act performed by speaking. For example, in an armed bank robbery, a robber may utter (2) to get cashier to open the safe. This effect of the act performed by speaking is also generally known as the **perlocutionary effect**.

(2) My gun is loaded.

Components of Speech Acts

Austin argues that every utterance can be understood as consisting of three parts:

1. a **locutionary act**, including both an utterance act and a propositional act; a locutionary act is the recognizable grammatical utterance (its form and meaning);

2. an **illocutionary act**, such as stating, promising, or commanding; an illocutionary act is the communicative purpose of an utterance, the use to which language is being put, or what the speaker is trying to do with his locutionary act, and

3. a **perlocutionary act**, such as persuading, annoying, consoling, or alarming; the perlocutionary act is the intended or actual effects of a locutionary act, the consequences these acts have on hearers' attitudes, beliefs, or behavior. The effects of a speech act are not conventional but depend upon the context.

---

3 Seearle's Typology of Illocutionary Acts

Under Searle's taxonomy, speech acts are universally grouped into five types:

(1) Representatives

Representatives are those kinds of speech acts that state what the speaker believes to be the case or not, and thus carry a truth-value. Paradigmatic cases include asserting, claiming, concluding, reporting, and stating. Representatives are illustrated in (3).

(3) a. The earth is flat.

   b. It was a warm sunny day.

   c. The soldiers are struggling on through the snow.

(2) Directives

Directives are those kinds of speech acts that the speaker use <u>to get the addressee to do something</u>. They express the speaker's desire/wish for the addressee to do something. Paradigmatic cases include advice, commands, orders, questions, and requests. Directives are exemplified in (4).

(4) a. Turn the TV down.

   b. Please don't use my electric shaver.

   c. Could you please get that lid off for me?

(3) Commissives

Commissives are those kinds of speech acts <u>that commit the speaker to some future course of action</u>. They express the speaker's intention to do something. Paradigmatic cases include offers, pledges, promises, refusals and threats. Examples of commissives are presented in (5).

(5) a. I'll be back in five minutes.

   b. We'll be launching a new policing unit to fight cyber crime on the internet soon.

   c. I'll never buy you another computer game.

(4) Expressives

Expressives are those kinds of speech acts <u>that express what the speaker feels</u> such as joy, sorrow, and likes/dislikes. Paradigmatic cases include apologizing, blaming, congratulating, praising, and thanking.

(6) a. I'm really sorry!

   b. Congratulations!

   c. Wow, great!

(5) Declarations

Declarations are those kinds of speech acts <u>that effect immediate changes in some current state of affairs</u>. Because they tend to rely on elaborate extralinguistic institutions for their successful performance, they may be called '**institutionalized performatives**'. Paradigmatic cases include bidding in bridge, declaring war, excommunicating, firing from employment, and nominating a candidate.

    (7) a. Priest: I now pronounce you husband and wife.
         b. Referee: You're out!
         c. Jury Foreman: We find the defendant guilty.

In using a declaration, the speaker changes the world via words.

4 Direct and Indirect Speech Acts '03, '04, '08, '12

    A different approach to distinguishing types of speech acts can be made on the basis of structure. A fairly simple structural distinction between three general types of speech acts is provided, in English, by the three basic sentence types. As shown in (8), there is an easily recognized relationship between the three structural forms (declarative, interrogative, imperative) and the three general communicative functions (statement, question, command/request).

    (8) a. You wear a seat belt.   (declarative)
         b. Do you wear a seat belt?   (interrogative)
         c. Wear a seat belt!   (imperative)

Whenever there is a direct relationship between a structure and a function, we have a **direct speech act**. Whenever there is an indirect relationship between a structure and a function, we have an **indirect speech act**. Thus, a declarative used to make a statement is a direct speech act, but a declarative used to make a request is an indirect speech act. As illustrated in (9), the utterance in (9a) is a declarative. When it is used to make a statement, as paraphrase in (9b), it is functioning as a direct speech act. When it is used to make a command/request, as paraphrased in (9c), it is functioning as an indirect speech act.

(9) a. It's cold outside.
  b. I hereby tell you about the weather.
  c. I hereby request of you that you close the door.

Different structures can be used to accomplish the same basic function, as in (10), where the speaker wants the addressee not to stand in front of the TV. The basic function of all the utterances in (10) is a command/request, but only the imperative structure in (10a) represents a direct speech act. The interrogative structure in (10b) is not being used only as a question, hence it is an indirect speech act. The declarative structures in (10c) and (10d) are also indirect requests.

(10) a. Move out of the way!
  b. Do you have to stand in front of the TV?
  c. You're standing in front of the TV.
  d. You'd make a better door than a window.

One of the most common types of indirect speech act in English, as shown in (11), has the form of an interrogative, but is not typically used to ask a question (i.e. we don't expect only an answer, we expect action). The examples in (11) are normally understood as requests.

(11) a. Could you pass the salt?
  b. Would you open this?

Indeed, there is a typical pattern in English whereby asking a question about the hearer's assumed ability ('Can you?', 'Could you?') or future likelihood with regard to doing something ('Will you', 'Would you?') normally counts as a request to actually do that something.

◆ Direct vs. Indirect Speech Act

Direct Illocutionary [Speech] Act (Form = Function)	**Indirect Illocutionary [Speech] Act** (Form ≠ Function)
Syntactic Form = Illocutionary Act ① Imperative = Directive ② Interrogative = Question ③ Exclamatory = Expressive ④ Declarative = Representative ⑤ Declarative = Commissive ⑥ Declarative = Declaration	**Syntactic Form ≠ Illocutionary Act** Interrogative ≠ Directive Declarative ≠ Directive … …

MEMO

MEMO

MEMO

MEMO

MEMO

최진호 영어학 Intemediate

ISBN 979-11-90700-83-2

- 발행일 · 2020년 12月 10日   초판 1쇄
- 발행인 · 이용중
- 저   자 · 최진호
- 발행처 · 도서출판 배움
- 주   소 · 서울시 영등포구 영등포로 400 신성빌딩 2층 (신길동)
- 주문 및 배본처 | Tel · 02) 813-5334 | Fax · 02) 814-5334

저자와의
협의하에
인지생략

본서의 無斷轉載 · 複製를 禁함. 본서의 무단 전재 · 복제행위는 저작권법 제136조에 의거 5년 이하의 징역 또는 5,000만 원 이하의 벌금에 처하거나 이를 병과할 수 있습니다. 파본은 구입처에서 교환하시기 바랍니다.

정가 21,000원